PRAISE FOR PREVIOUS EDITIONS OF
EXPLORER'S GUIDE NAPA & SONOMA

"Some of the best advice on where to go and what to do in Wine Country."
—*New York Times*

"This marvelous book, splendidly researched, packed with terrific advice and considerable insider information, is essential reading for any visitor."'
—Robert Parker, *Wine Advocate*

"A carefully designed, well-researched, and entertainingly written baedeker to the Napa and Sonoma wine trails."
—*Los Angeles Times*

PRAISE FOR
THE EXPLORER'S GUIDE SERIES

"Consistently rated the best guides to the regions covered ... Readable, tasteful, appealingly designed. Strong on dining, lodging, and history."
—*National Geographic Traveler*

D1051592

EXPLORER'S GUIDE

NAPA & SONOMA

EXPLORER'S GUIDE

NAPA & SONOMA

ELEVENTH EDITION

PEG MELNIK WITH TIM FISH

THE COUNTRYMAN PRESS
A division of W. W. Norton & Company
Independent Publishers Since 1923

Manufacturing by Versa Press
Series book design by Chris Welch

For information about permission to reproduce selections from this book, write to
Permissions, The Countryman Press, 500 Fifth Avenue, New York, NY 10110

For information about special discounts for bulk purchases, please contact
W. W. Norton Special Sales at specialsales@wwnorton.com or 800-233-4830

Library of Congress Cataloging-in-Publication Data

Names: Melnik, Peg, author. | Fish, Timothy, 1959– author.
Title: Explorer's guide Napa & Sonoma / Peg Melnik with Tim Fish.
Other titles: Explorer's guide Napa and Sonoma
Description: Eleventh edition. | New York : The Countryman Press, a division
of W. W. Norton & Company, [2019] | Series: Explorer's guide | Includes
bibliographical references and index.
Identifiers: LCCN 2018056855 | ISBN 9781682682302 (pbk. : alk. paper)
Subjects: LCSH: Napa County (Calif.)—Guidebooks. | Sonoma County
(Calif.)—Guidebooks.
Classification: LCC F868.N2 M46 2019 | DDC 917.94/1904—dc23
LC record available at https://lccn.loc.gov/2018056855

The Countryman Press
www.countrymanpress.com

A division of W. W. Norton & Company, Inc.
500 Fifth Avenue, New York, NY 10110
www.wwnorton.com

10 9 8 7 6 5 4 3 2 1

We dedicate this book to our beloved, adventuresome children, Sophie and Tucker. Watching you grow up in this amazing place called Wine Country has been a delight.

EXPLORE WITH US!

This edition of *Explorer's Guide Napa & Sonoma* orients you in the region with our smart feature *What's Trending*, offering tasty eats and drinks and everything in-between. Next, we set you up with logistics in our segment *What's Where in Napa Valley & Sonoma County.* In it you'll find all the information to make your trip to Wine Country as seamless as possible, including tips on transportation to and around the region, climate considerations, and a list of helpful resources to guide your travel plans. What follows logistics is a primer of sorts called *How to Travel Like a Wine-Savvy Insider*, covering everything you'll need to be in the know. For instance, you'll learn about the explosive growth in the city of Napa and why it has the appeal to attract droves of tourists. You'll also learn what's behind the family-oriented resort approach at the Francis Ford Coppola Winery in Geyserville. After we share insider information, we give you the opportunity to bone up on your wine knowledge with this irresistible offer: *Take Our Crash Course in Wine Tasting.* We've included our step-by-step tasting advice, and, if you're interested in taking your wine education to the next level, you'll find information about wine classes in the Napa and Sonoma area. Next, we appeal to history buffs with *A Brief History of Napa & Sonoma*. It provides a historical overview, where you'll learn how and why wine became the organizing principle of the region. Finally, we delve into the major cities of Wine Country, providing detailed listings for *To See & Do, Wineries, Lodgings, Where to Eat, Entertainment, Selected Shopping*, and *Special Events*. Our segment on wineries has a detailed list of winery entries to give you a feel for our rich wine culture.

Pay close attention to our Top Overall Picks for each city. Here travelers will find our top recommendations for restaurants, bars, hotels, markets, and other attractions. It was tough to narrow our list, but we managed by focusing on the crème de la crème. These picks will come in handy if your time is limited.

The suggested outings will suit a range of interests: foodies, romantics, outdoor enthusiasts, art lovers, and others will find recommendations tailored to their personal obsessions. See also regional highlights in our Best Day in San Francisco, Best Day in Napa Valley, and Best Day in Sonoma County.

A note on the lodging and dining listings: We use price codes to convey a general understanding of cost (because specific prices are likely to change). Here are the corresponding rates for the price codes you will find throughout.

LODGING PRICE CODES

$ (Inexpensive):	Up to $175
$$ (Moderate):	$175 to $275
$$$ (Expensive):	$275 to $375
$$$$ (Very Expensive):	$375 and up

DINING PRICE CODES

$ (Inexpensive):	Up to $30
$$ (Moderate):	$30 to $35
$$$ (Expensive):	$45 to $65
$$$$ (Very Expensive):	$65 and up

Dining price codes reflect the cost of a single meal, including appetizer, entrée, and dessert, but not including cocktails, wine, tax, or tip.

Please send any comments or corrections to:

Explorer's Guide Editor
The Countryman Press
A division of W. W. Norton & Company
500 Fifth Avenue
New York, NY 10110

KEY TO SYMBOLS

- ✪ **Authors' favorites.** These are the places we think have the most to offer in each region, whether that means great food, outstanding rooms, beautiful scenery, or overall appeal.
- ⚭ **Weddings.** The wedding rings symbol appears beside facilities that frequently serve as venues for weddings and civil unions.
- ✋ **Special value.** The special-value symbol appears next to lodgings and restaurants that combine high quality and moderate prices.
- ✎ **Child-friendly.** The kids-alert symbol appears next to lodgings, restaurants, activities, and shops of special appeal to youngsters.
- ✿ **Pets.** The dog-paw symbol appears next to lodgings that accept pets (usually with a reservation and deposit) as of press time.

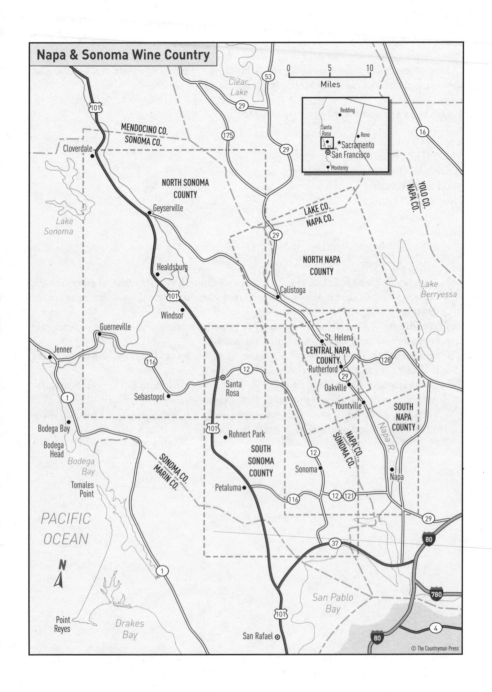

Napa & Sonoma Wine Country

CONTENTS

MAPS

ACKNOWLEDGMENTS

Many people made this book possible. We want to thank all the wineries, restaurants, inns, and other businesses that put up with our phone calls, e-mail inquiries, and spontaneous visits. Numerous organizations proved to be great resources.

We would also like to acknowledge the smart and devoted team at The Countryman Press, particularly Róisín Cameron and Michael Tizzano. Closer to home, we'd like to thank those who contributed, and the brilliant trio of Jean Doppenberg, Sarah Stierch, and Carey Sweet. We'd also like to thank two publications that are dear to us: the Pulitzer Prize–winning *Santa Rosa Press Democrat* and *Wine Spectator*. While this book is produced independently of both publications, we are grateful to them for providing us gainful employment while we pursue this project in our off hours.

Finally, we want to thank our children, Sophie and Tucker, for their patience with us over the years. Sophie was born the week of our very first deadline in 1991 and has grown up with this book. Tucker followed eight years later, and as long as we bribed him with ice cream, he tagged along willingly as we traveled the trails of Napa and Sonoma.

Now we would like to hear from you. What do you like about this book, and how do you think it might be improved? Also, let us know about your experiences in Wine Country—both good and bad. We hope the inns, restaurants, wineries, and other businesses that are mentioned here live up to our recommendations. If they don't, let us know. Contact Peg Melnik directly at pegmelnik@gmail.com.

—Peg Melnik and Tim Fish

INTRODUCTION

Welcome to the eleventh edition of *Explorer's Guide Napa & Sonoma*, the definitive guide to this lovely area and all the things to see and do in it. The guide has been endorsed by the esteemed wine critics Harvey Steiman, who praised its lack of "stuffiness or pomposity," and Robert Parker Jr., who called it "essential reading for any visitor."

This thoroughly revised and updated edition, personally researched by the authors, has a number of new features, with the most compelling being our *What's Trending* section. As always, you can trust your tour guides: Tim Fish is senior editor of the international magazine *Wine Spectator*. Peg Melnik is a veteran columnist, wine blogger, and tasting coordinator for the *Santa Rosa Press Democrat*, the premier daily newspaper in Wine Country.

If you follow our lead, you'll sidestep tourist traps to experience the region at its most authentic.

Get ready to tour Napa and Sonoma like a genuine insider. See you in Wine Country!

WORKERS HARVEST CABERNET SAUVIGNON IN THE EARLY MORNING AT JOSEPH PHELPS VINEYARDS JOSEPH PHELPS

WHAT'S TRENDING

We begin with the hip standouts in each city, a select group of places that are turning heads. They may be iconic, spirited, or edgy, or a combination of the three. Whatever the case, they have great appeal for adventuresome travelers. A caveat: We've included the town of Petaluma here because even though it's on the outskirts of Wine County, it has become an irresistible playground for those nearby.

What's Trending in Napa

CARNEROS RESORT AND SPA This modern resort has farmhouse chic bungalows dotting the landscape. Carneros offers farm-to-table California cuisine at its two on-site restaurants. It also has a spa and pool, as well as complimentary bicycles that allow guests to tour the surrounding wineries and vineyards (www.thecarnerosinn.com, 707-299-4900, 888-400-9000, 4048 Sonoma Highway, Napa, CA 94559; $$$$).

DI ROSA This is a must visit for those seeking a splash of contemporary art with their pinot noir. di Rosa is an art museum surrounded by vineyards, showcasing works by Northern California artists, including pieces by Mark di Suvero and Bruce Conner (www.dirosaart.org, 707-226-5991, 5200 Sonoma Highway, Napa, CA 94559).

NAPA VALLEY WINE TRAIN One of the most unique ways to experience Napa Valley, the Wine Train offers scenic views with exclusive winery visits, multi-course farm-to-table gourmet cuisine, and fine wine, all in the comfort of vintage, beautifully restored train cars (www.winetrain.com, 707-253-2111, 800-427-4124, 1275 McKinstry Street, Napa, CA 94559).

OXBOW PUBLIC MARKET Locals and visitors alike flock to this foodie mecca, located in downtown Napa, for its locally sourced butcher shops, artisan food stands, cheese and wine bar, fresh local oysters, and in-house brewery (www.oxbowpublicmarket.com, 707-226-6529, 610 & 644 First Street, Napa, CA 94559).

CADET WINE BAR The hip and happening set gather nightly at Cadet, where vintage vinyl records provide the soundtrack, fresh prepared cheese and charcuterie fill bellies, and carefully curated, small-production wine and beers are sipped (www.cadetbeerandwinebar.com, 707-224-4400, 930 Franklin Street, Napa, CA 94559).

SILO'S WINE BAR & JAZZ CLUB A local's hangout for live music in downtown Napa, Silo's is an intimate venue for nightly jazz from local and regional musicians paired with craft cocktails and Napa Valley wines (www.silosnapa.com, 707-251-5833, 530 Main Street, Napa, CA 94559).

COMPLINE WINE BAR, RESTAURANT & MERCHANT Two sommeliers teamed up to open Compline, a charming yet elegant wine bar in downtown Napa serving up cool wines from around the world, a seasonal menu, and weekly wine education classes (www.complinewine.com, 707-492-8150, 1300 First Street #312, Napa, CA 94559).

HERITAGE EATS Global flavors abound at Heritage Eats, a self-described "fast fine restaurant" that dishes up sandwiches, salads, wraps, rice bowls, and tacos, inspired by exotic spots from Vietnam to Jamaica. You can count on sustainable local ingredients here (www.heritageeats.com, 707-226-3287, 3824 Bel Aire Plaza, Napa, CA 94558; $$).

KENZO NAPA Break out of the Wine Country cuisine mode and experience Kenzo, a Michelin-starred Japanese restaurant with a handful of

THIS HAPPY PUP IS ON DISPLAY AT THE DI ROSA PRESERVE IN NAPA VALLEY DI ROSA PRESERVE

AT THE OXBOW MARKET, WHO CAN RESIST EXPLORING THE DECADENT SAUCES AT ANETTE'S CHOCOLATES?

reservations-required seats that provide a personalized multicourse dining experience. Kenzo blends nouveau cuisine with Japanese tradition (www.kenzonapa.com, 707-294-2049, 1339 Pearl Street, Napa, CA 94559, Reservations required; $$$$).

ASHES & DIAMONDS Inspired by old school Napa Valley, this spot has a new school mentality. Ashes & Diamonds blends mid-century modern aesthetics with cellar-worthy cabernet sauvignons, which it pours on sunny patios with options for in-house, chef-prepared seasonal food pairings (www.ashes diamonds.com, 707-666-4777, 4130 Howard Lane, Napa, CA 94558).

What's Trending in Yountville & Stags Leap District

KOLLAR CHOCOLATES Artisan chocolatier Chris Kollar has made a name for himself with his European-inspired chocolate creations, which include delectable, colorful truffles made with organic ingredients. They include locally grown lavender, honey, and of course, wine (www.kollarchocolates.com, V Marketplace, 6525 Washington Street, Yountville, CA 94599).

ATELIER BY JCB Picnic provisions and artisan food abound at the Atelier, which offers a selection of world-class charcuterie and cheese (including free tastes!), gourmet foods, imported French bread, caviar, truffles, and a coffee bar for a much-needed boost of energy after wine tasting (www.atelierfinefoods.com, 707-967-7600 ext. 2, 6505 Washington Street, Yountville, CA 94599).

SOUTHSIDE CAFE Southside Cafe is a modern eatery serving all-day breakfast and lunch, inspired by California's diverse food scene (from avocado toast to carne asada tortas), and craft coffee. It's a cool place to grab a bite while making the rounds at tasting rooms in Yountville (www.southsidenapa.com, 707-238-4632, 6752 Washington Street, Yountville, CA 94599; $$–$$$).

PROTEA Serving Caribbean cuisine in a colorful setting, Protea is a refreshing addition to downtown Yountville, offering patio dining and flavorful empanadas, tacos, and sandwiches that change daily (www.proteayv.com, 707-415-5035, 6488 Washington Street, Yountville, CA 94599; $–$$).

KELLY'S FILLING STATION & WINE SHOP Fill up your rental car at Kelly's, which offers the only gas in Yountville, as well as an impressive selection of fine wine, craft beverages, Napa-centric gifts, and artisan coffee, the latter crafted to order (707-944-8165, 6795 Washington Street, Yountville, CA 94599).

JCB TASTING SALON Bubbly and French-crafted Burgundian wines flow at the eccentric yet elegant JCB Tasting Salon. Here one can sip sparkling wine on leopard-print couches, peruse Baccarat crystal collectibles, and explore the unique world of vintner Jean-Charles Boisset (www.jcbwines.com, 707-934-8237, 6505 Washington Street, Yountville, CA 94599).

AT THE JCB TASTING SALON, BUBBLY AND BURGUNDIAN WINES ARE UNCORKED IN THIS EXOTIC LOUNGE

CLIFF LEDE VINEYARDS Located on 60 acres in the Stags Leap District, Cliff Lede offers a blend of Bordeaux-style old world wines made with innovative technologies. The winery impresses with gardens, vineyard views, contemporary art, and tastings inspired by owner Cliff Lede's love for rock 'n' roll music (www .cliffledevineyards.com, 707-944-8642, 1473 Yountville Cross Road, Yountville, CA 94599).

STEWART CELLARS A small, family-owned winery producing small production cabernet sauvignon, Stewart Cellars offers casual tastings in its downtown Yountville tasting room, cabernet flights in its cozy Nomad Heritage Library, and a cozy Bohemian indoor-outdoor living room that will make you feel like you're at home (Reservations suggested, www .stewartcellars.com, 707-963-9160, 6752 Washington Street, Yountville, CA 94599).

STAGS' LEAP WINERY This winery is the epitome of Wine Country romance because tastings of its iconic Bordeaux-style wine take place on the elegant patio of the castle-like historic Manor Home built in 1893 (Reservations required, www.stagsleap.com, 707-257-5790, 6150 Silverado Trail, Napa, CA 94558).

ODETTE ESTATE Bold and elegant is the theme at Odette, where wine aficionados of organic chardonnay and cabernet flock to the chic tasting room that is co-owned by politico Gavin Newsom (Reservations required, www.odette estate.com, 707-224-7533, 5998 Silverado Trail, Napa, CA 94558).

BOUCHON If you're a Francophile, you won't be able to resist this French bistro that makes you feel like you're in Paris. This is the late-night stop for many who work in Wine Country, and the menu doesn't disappoint. Specialties include an incredible *steak frites* (French for "steak with fries"); equally delectable is the roasted chicken with Savoy cabbage, roasted parsnips, and bacon lardons (www.thomaskeller.com, 707-944-8037, 6534 Washington Street, Yountville, CA 94599; $$$; cuisine: French).

FRENCH LAUNDRY GARDEN Across the street from **The French Laundry** (6640 Washington Street) is the

THE FRENCH LAUNDRY'S 2½-ACRE GARDEN ACROSS THE STREET IS FARM-TO-TABLE AT ITS BEST

restaurant's two-and-a-half-acre garden. Here you'll see a map detailing the crops, which might include edible blossoms, tomatoes, greens, and squash, among other items destined for the dinner table. The people in charge are friendly and willing to chat. Oh, and you'll more than likely come across their chickens on the property.

What's Trending in Oakville & Rutherford

OAKVILLE GROCERY The oldest continually operated grocery store in California, Oakville Grocery is a perfect place to grab sandwiches, fresh salads, local fruit, and artisan snacks for a picture-perfect wine picnic. (www .oakvillegrocery.com, 707-944-8802, 7856 St. Helena Highway, Oakville, CA 94562)

AUBERGE DU SOLEIL Named one of the best resorts in the world by *Forbes*, Auberge du Soleil impresses with its

mountainside million-dollar views of Napa Valley, an award-winning spa, and a Michelin-starred restaurant. For the uninitiated, Auberge du Soleil means "sun inn" in French. (aubergedusoleil .aubergeresorts.com, 800-348-5406, 180 Rutherford Hill Road, Rutherford, CA 95473; $$$$)

THE RESTAURANT AT AUBERGE
Gorgeous views are guaranteed at this Michelin-starred mountaintop restaurant, which pampers guests with Maine lobster omelets paired with champagne at brunch. For dinner, try the truffle tortellini and pair it with one of 15,000 bottles of wine it has in its cellar. (auberge dusoleil.aubergeresorts.com, 707-967-3111, 180 Rutherford Hill Road, Rutherford, CA 95473; $$$$)

RUTHERFORD GRILL Serving up modern American comfort food, Rutherford Grill is a tasty stop for locals and visitors alike in Napa Valley. Customers settle into leather booths or opt for the giant bar when they want to converse with like-minded comfort food enthusiasts

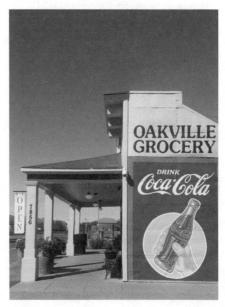
PREP FOR A WINE COUNTRY PICNIC AT OAKVILLE GROCERY

AUBERGE DU SOLEIL HAS SPECTACULAR VIEWS, ESPECIALLY WHEN YOU'RE POOLSIDE

(www.rutherfordgrill.com, 1180 Rutherford Road, Rutherford, CA 94573; $$–$$$).

MUMM NAPA Founded by famed champagne producer G.H. Mumm in the 1970s, Mumm Napa pours handcrafted sparklers on umbrella-filled patios overlooking vast vineyards. Don't miss the art gallery inside, featuring original works by Ansel Adams and other photographers (www.mummnapa.com, 707-967-7700, 800-686-6272, 8445 Silverado Trail, Rutherford, CA 94573).

ST. SUPÉRY ESTATE VINEYARDS & WINERY Owned by the fashion house Chanel, this is a stylish yet unpretentious winery where you can sip sustainably grown sauvignon blanc next to your dog, because your four-legged pet is welcome. Here you'll partake in casual and unique tastings, including vegetarian small bites paired with St. Supéry wines (reservations required, www.stsupery.com, 707-963-4507, 8440 St. Helena Highway, Rutherford, CA 94573).

ROUND POND ESTATE Sip highly collectible cabernet sauvignon amid vineyards, elegant gardens, and 2,000 olive trees at Round Pond. The estate offers food and wine pairings, as well as hands-on olive oil-making experiences (reservations required, www.roundpond .com, 888-302-2575, 875 Rutherford Road, Rutherford, CA 94573).

B CELLARS A tour at B Cellars offers a taste of all things Wine Country, with a visit to the winery's culinary gardens, production facility, and wine caves. The visit is followed by a multicourse food and wine pairing created by the winery's chef de cuisine (reservations required, www.bcellars.com, 707-709-8787, 703 Oakville Cross Road, Oakville, CA 95462).

BEAULIEU VINEYARD A visit to Napa Valley isn't complete without a visit to Beaulieu Vineyard, one of the most historic wineries in the country. Here, guests can sip the winery's coveted Georges de Latour Private Reserve Cabernet Sauvignon (one of the first cult cabernets in California) and take in the history, with winery walls more than 100 years old (www.bvwines.com, 800-373-5896, 1960 St. Helena Highway, Rutherford, CA 94573).

FROG'S LEAP A breath of fresh air in Napa Valley, Frog's Leap offers on its porch patio unpretentious wine tastings of the award-winning organic sauvignon blanc, zinfandel, and cabernet sauvignon it has been producing since 1981 (reservations required, www.frogsleap.com, 707-963-4704, 8815 Conn Creek Road, Rutherford, CA 94573).

What's Trending in St. Helena

WYDOWN HOTEL Fans of Scandinavian design will find themselves at home at the 12-room boutique Wydown Hotel, located in downtown St. Helena. It offers luxury rooms with plush king beds, a locally sourced complimentary breakfast, and personalized concierge services to make the most of your visit (www.wydownhotel.com, 707-963-5100, 1424 Main Street, St. Helena, CA 94574; $$).

ACACIA HOUSE BY CHRIS COSENTINO The first Wine Country outpost of celebrity chef Chris Cosentino (*Top Chef*), Acacia House offers thoughtfully prepared California cuisine, using sustainable ingredients, in a casual farmhouse setting (www.lasalcobasnapavalley.com, 707-963-9004, 1915 Main Street, St. Helena, CA 94574; $$$).

GOOSE & GANDER Locals and visitors alike flock to Goose & Gander to sip craft cocktails on the lush patio and to enjoy a menu that changes with the seasons. Items include locally sourced vegetable and mushroom dishes, as well as rich chicken, duck, and steak entrées (www.goosegander.com, 707-967-8779, 1245 Spring Street, St. Helena, CA 94574; $$$).

CLIF FAMILY BRUSCHETERRIA The Clif family (of CLIF protein bar fame) has gained a cult following for its food truck, which serves up seasonal "farm-to-truck" small bites with a focus on bruschetta. It's all served at the Clif family's bicycle friendly wine-tasting room (www.cliffamilywiney.com, 707-301-7188, 709 Main Street, St. Helena, CA 94574; $).

TWO BIRDS ONE STONE *Top Chef* winners Douglas Keane and Sang Yoon team

THE FAMILY OF CLIF BAR FAME SELLS ITS NAMESAKE LABEL AT ITS POPULAR TASTING ROOM

up to offer California-inspired Japanese cuisine, serving aesthetically pleasing lunch and dinner offerings including kimchee fries and mouth-watering Wagyu beef, primed for pairing with their wide selection of Japanese whiskeys (www.twobirdsonestonenapa.com, 707-302-3777, 3020 St. Helena Highway N., St. Helena, CA 94574; $$–$$$).

BALE GRIST MILL STATE HISTORIC PARK Enjoy some fresh air coupled with a touch of St. Helena history at this state park. It features a working water-powered grist mill dating from 1846, the first church in Napa Valley, a pioneer cemetery, and lush hiking trails (www.napavalleystateparks.org, 707-942-4575, 3369 St. Helena Highway N., St. Helena, CA 94574).

RAYMOND VINEYARDS Offering a wine experience unlike any other in Napa Valley, Raymond offers bold red wines poured in an equally bold setting. The vineyard resembles a colorful nightclub, with hands-on experiences, such as having guests wear white lab coats and learn how to blend their own wine, taking home their own handcrafted bottle (www.raymondvineyards.com, 707-963-3141, 849 Zinfandel Lane, St. Helena, CA 94574).

CHARLES KRUG Sip fine wine and nibble on delicious artisanal cheese at Charles Krug, the oldest winery in Napa Valley. It offers handpicked charcuterie and wood-fired pizza at its Salumeria, which celebrates the Italian heritage of winery matriarch Rosa Mondavi (www.charleskrug.com, 707-967-2229, 2800 Main Street, St. Helena, CA 94574).

EHLERS ESTATE Estate-grown wines are paired with a chic Bohemian-inspired setting at Ehlers Estate, where tastings of its sauvignon blanc and cabernet sauvignon are offered daily. FYI: The winery has a one-of-a-kind "early bird" tasting with a vineyard walk and wines paired with Bouchon Bakery pastries (www.ehlersestate.com, 707-963-5972, 3222 Ehlers Lane, St. Helena, CA 94574).

HALL WINES Hall Wines offers a world-class wine tasting experience with its cabernet sauvignon, merlot, and sauvignon blanc. Its modern winery also offers an up-close-and-personal, modern art experience, making the winery museum-like (www.hallwines.com, 707-967-2657, 800-688-4255, 401 St. Helena Highway S., St. Helena, CA 94574).

THIS MASSIVE STONE BUILDING HOUSES THE CHARLES KRUG TASTING ROOM

What's Trending in Calistoga

INDIAN SPRINGS RESORT & SPA Since 1861, Indian Springs has welcomed spa enthusiasts, families, and celebrities to bathe in its healing hot springs located in a 17-acre resort. It offers a modern summer-camp feel, with historic bungalows for couples or groups, hot spring–fed pools, and a spa offering mud baths, as well as manicured gardens, outdoor games, and an on-site restaurant (www .indianspringscalistoga.com, 707-709-8139, 844-378-3635, 1712 Lincoln Avenue, Calistoga, CA 94515; $$$–$$$$).

CALISTOGA MOTOR LODGE & SPA A renovated 1940s roadside motel, the Calistoga Motor Lodge & Spa offers a vintage experience reminiscent of the great American road trip, with no shortage of things to keep you busy, including dog-friendly rooms, three pools, a bocce court, games, and a spa (www.calistoga motorlodgeandspa.com, 707-942-0991, 1880 Lincoln Avenue, Calistoga, CA 94515; $$–$$$).

SOLAGE A Forbes five-star resort, Solage is an expansive property with 89 rooms, including six suites, decorated in relaxed, modern furnishings that evoke relaxation. Its luxurious amenities include a world-class spa, fitness center, and two pools, alongside a Michelin-starred on-site restaurant (solage .aubergeresorts.com, 707-266-7531, 866-942-7442, 755 Silverado Trail N., Calistoga, CA 94515; $$$$).

PETRIFIED FOREST Over 3.4 million years ago, a volcano erupted at Mt. St. Helena, and as a result the local redwood trees were covered with ash, which eventually preserved them so they could be discovered on this site. Now this spot is a privately owned park offering easily walkable trails with spectacular up-close

A GLIMPSE OF THE PATIO AT SAM'S SOCIAL CLUB JUST IN TIME FOR A ROUND OF CRAFT COCKTAILS

views of giant petrified redwoods (www .petrifiedforest.org, 707-942-6667, 4100 Petrified Forest Road, Calistoga, CA 94515).

SOLBAR Consistently earning a Michelin star year after year, Solbar offers locally sourced, sustainable, and seasonal California cuisine that includes everything from foie gras to mussels to guinea hen, with an award-winning wine list to boot. The modern Solbar is a relaxed setting for a laid-back meal (www.solage.aubergersorts.com, 707-226-0850, 755 Silverado Trail N., Calistoga, CA 94515; $$$$).

SAM'S SOCIAL CLUB Named after Samuel Brannan, California's first millionaire, who helped put Calistoga on the map, Sam's Social Club attracts both locals and visitors with its great

TANK GARAGE WINERY IS LOCATED IN A 1930S GAS STATION WITH OFF-BEAT BOTTLINGS LIKE "RATTLE & ROLL"

patio-side happy hour, craft cocktails, and changing daily menu, which includes plentiful options for vegans, vegetarians, and carnivores alike (www.samssocialclub.com, 707-942-4969, 1712 Lincoln Avenue, Calistoga, CA 94515).

VERAISON Veraison offers colorful, locally sourced cuisine using French techniques as presented by chef James Richmond, in a casual French bistro setting. It also has an expansive international wine list and a rotating selection of local craft beers on tap (www.veraisoncalistoga.com/, 707-942-5938, 1457 Lincoln Avenue, Calistoga, CA 94515; $$$–$$$$).

DAVIS ESTATES Mike and Sandy Davis purchased a century-old winery in 2011, transforming it into a world-class facility designed by acclaimed architect Howard Backen. Today the winery offers Bordeaux varietals overlooking panoramic views of Napa Valley, complete with food and wine pairings and great service (reservations required, www.davisestates.com, 707-942-0700, 4060 Silverado Trail, Calistoga, CA 94515).

TANK GARAGE WINERY Located in downtown Calistoga in a renovated 1930s gas station, Tank Garage Winery pours easy-to-drink white and reds with colorful names like "Post Disco," "Nothing Corporate," and "Rattle & Roll," and they have equally colorful wine labels (www.tankgaragewinery.com, 707-942-8265, 1020 Foothill Boulevard, Calistoga, CA 94515).

PICAYUNE CELLARS Offering handcrafted, small-lot wines by French-born winemaker Claire Weinkauf, Picayune offers a variety of wines, including rosé, sauvignon blanc, and pinot noir. Wines are poured in a charming, small tasting room in downtown Calistoga that also sells artisan housewares (www.picayunecellars.com, 707-888-9885, 1458 Lincoln Avenue, Suite 9, Calistoga, CA 94515).

What's Trending in Healdsburg

JOURNEYMAN MEAT CO. You get the idea that this artisanal meat shop is

THE SIDURI TASTING ROOM IS A HOUSE OF PINOT, WITH BOTTLINGS FROM A BROAD GEOGRAPHIC REACH

Leo Steen Wines (www.leosteenwines .com), Medlock Ames (www.medlockames .com), Rafanelli Winery (www.rafanelli winery.com), Ramey Wine Cellars (www .rameywine.com), and Siduri (www.siduri.com).

DIAVOLA PIZZERIA & SALUMERIA
Located just north of Healdsburg in the quirky historic town of Geyserville, Diavola serves carefully crafted hand-made pastas and pizzas and other locally sourced creations prepared in a wood-burning oven, and the restaurant makes its own in-house sausage that it sells by the pound (www.diavola pizzeria.com, 707-814-0111, 21021 Geyserville Avenue, Geyserville, CA 95441; $–$$).

HARMON GUEST HOUSE
Located just off the historic Healdsburg Plaza, Harmon Guest House has 39 chic and airy rooms with balconies. It offers a complimentary breakfast, a private on-site park, a pool, and a rooftop terrace with nightly cocktails (www.harmonguest house.com, 707-431-8221, 227 Healdsburg Avenue, Healdsburg, CA 95448; $$–$$$$).

VALETTE RESTAURANT
The creation of two brothers, one a chef and one a

irreverent fun from the minute you see the doorknob is a meat cleaver. The meat is cut, cured, and crafted just 20 miles away, and here, in what feels like Little Italy, you'll find a curated butcher counter. There's a good lineup of brews and wine, including its namesake label Journeyman. Foodies will love the Pizza Bianco made in the wood-fired oven (www.journeymanmeat.com, 404 Center Street, 707-395-MEAT, Healdsburg, CA 95448).

BOUTIQUE WINEMAKING
This short list highlights some of the best boutique winemaking in Healdsburg, along with the labels mentioned in other hip entries. The vintners and winemakers at these wineries truly are crafting nectar of the gods: Arista (www.aristawinery.com), Banshee Wines (www.bansheewines .com), Davis Family Vineyards (www .davisfamilyvineyards.com), Jesse Katz of Devil Proof Vineyards and Aperture brands (www.devilproofvineyards.com)

VALETTE CATERS TO THE CARNIVORE

restaurant manager, Valette is Wine Country at its best with its signature "Trust Me" Chef's Menu. The restaurant offers hearty California cuisine, utilizing hyperlocal food sources and carefully selected wines (reservations recommended, www.valettehealdsburg.com, 707-473-0946, 344 Center Street, Healdsburg, CA 95448; $$$$).

SINGLETHREAD FARM SingleThread has earned two Michelin stars for its 11-course customized tasting menu that emphasizes farm and foraged food sourcing, as well as presentations so beautiful the dishes could be considered works of art (reservations required; www.single threadfarms.com, 707-723-4646, 131 North Street, Healdsburg, CA 95448; $$$$).

MOUSTACHE BAKED GOODS Sweet treats abound at Moustache Baked Goods, where small-batch cupcakes, cookies, brownies, French macarons, and ice cream sandwiches are crafted. This delectable fare is made from chocolate, coffee, fruit, and other ingredients from purveyors throughout Sonoma County (www.moustachebakedgoods.com, 707-395-4111, 381 Healdsburg Avenue, Healdsburg, CA 95448).

DUKE'S SPIRITED COCKTAILS Cultivated craft cocktails with local ingredients put Duke's on the map; here, friendly mixologists make colorful drinks to order, including unique carbonated cocktails served on tap, topped with colorful flowers and herbs from local gardens (www.drinkatdukes.com, 707-431-1060, 111 Plaza Street, Healdsburg, CA 95448).

PRESTON FARM & WINERY The Preston family has farmed this land for 45 years, and today, it also makes organic and biodynamic wines it offers in a fun farmhouse setting. This is a favorite for locals, who picnic on-site, sipping organic jug wine, while playing bocce, playing with the winery cats, or petting the sheep that reside there (www.preston farmand winery.com, 707-433-3372, 9282 W. Dry Creek Road, Healdsburg, CA 95448).

REEVE WINES The concept of "less is more" rings true at Reeve Wines, where winemaker Noah Dorrance crafts a super-small production of pinot noirs from unique vineyard sites; they're poured exclusively at Reeve Wines' rustic tasting room in Dry Creek Valley. Here, hip wine drinkers sip rosé or pinot noir with cheese plates on the sunny patio (www.reevewines.com, 707-235-6345, 4551 Dry Creek Road, Healdsburg, CA 95448, by appointment only).

GARY FARRELL VINEYARDS & WINERY
A visit to Russian River Valley isn't complete without a visit to Gary Farrell, where, in an elegant tasting room and on a shady patio overlooking rolling hills, single-vineyard chardonnay and pinot noir are poured, paired with a selection of cheeses (www.garyfarrellwinery.com, 707-473-2909, 10701 Westside Road, Healdsburg, CA 95448, by appointment only).

What's Trending in Sonoma

SONOMA PLAZA A walk around the Sonoma Plaza is a walk through history. There are six historic properties nearby, including the California Mission, the Lachryma Montis, and the historic home of General Vallejo, which offers visitors insight into how California became a state (www.parks.ca.gov, 707-938-9560, Sonoma, CA 95476).

SIGH This bar caters to bubble fanatics—people who are crazy about sparkling wine and champagne. The decor is playful, done up in pinks and creams, but the wine list is serious. Here you'll find producers from across the pond like Dom Perignon and local favorites like Iron Horse Vineyards and Gloria Ferrer (www.sighsonoma.com, 707-996-2444, 120 W. Napa Street, Sonoma, CA 95476; tastings daily).

SCRIBE WINERY This hot winery has a cult following, including celebrities like Amy Schumer. The vintners built their popularity by tapping into the chef circuit, hence drawing an endless supply of foodies. The winery's historic hacienda lures day-trippers who sip rosé and estate pinot noir, two striking wines that built Scribe's reputation for quality (www.scribewinery.com, 707-939-1858, 2100 Denmark Street, Sonoma, CA 95476).

HARE & HATTER SAUSAGE EMPORIUM Head down the rabbit hole for a leisurely bite at the small but mighty Hare & Hatter, which serves locally made sausages in sandwiches and pizzas, as well as local wines, beers, and fair trade coffee (www.harehatter.com, 707-235-1127, 414 First Street E., Sonoma, CA 95476).

EL MOLINO CENTRAL It has been named the best Mexican restaurant in the Bay Area by the *San Francisco Chronicle,* and for good reason. El Molino produces seasonal menus comprising traditional Mexican food with a California touch, including tamales, tacos, pozole, and mole, served with in-house ground organic tortillas. This scrumptious food has locals coming back every week (www.elmolinocentral.com, 707-939-1010, 11 Central Avenue, Sonoma, CA 95476; $).

OSO SONOMA Located on the Sonoma Plaza, OSO is the creation of award-winning chef David Bush, who creates an ever-changing menu of shareable plates that emphasize both fresh food and comfort food. Dishes include local oysters, Dungeness crab, deviled eggs, salads, and steak in a cool industrial setting (www.ososonoma.com, 707-931-6926, 9 E. Napa Street, Sonoma, CA 95476; $$–$$$).

SONOMA'S BEST From breakfast burritos to made-to-order sandwiches, Sonoma's Best is a prime spot to stock up on picnic provisions for a day out, including

SIGH IS A BUBBLE-CENTRIC TASTING ROOM, FOCUSING ON SPARKLING WINE AND CHAMPAGNE

salads, cheeses, and wine, as well as handpicked Sonoma-centric house-wares (www.sonomas-best.com, 707-996-7600, 1190 E. Napa Street, Sonoma, CA 95476; $).

STARLING BAR SONOMA Locals flock to the Starling to relax in the vintage furniture or at the bar, sipping craft cocktails that emphasize regionally made spirits and house-made touches such as tonic and bitters, all while listening to live, independent local and regional music (www.starlingsonoma .com, 707-938-7442, 19380 Highway 12, Sonoma, CA 96576).

CORNER 103 This swanky spot offers an elegant wine-tasting experience that pairs seven of its small-production wines with six locally sourced small bites. Guests learn about the wine growing and winemaking process, as well as how to pour, serve, taste, and pair wine (reservations required, www.corner103.com, 707-931-6141, 103 W. Napa Street, Sonoma, CA 95476).

THREE STICKS WINES Located just off the Sonoma Plaza, Three Sticks Wines offers intimate tasting experiences at the Vallejo-Casteñada Adobe, built in 1842. The lineup includes its chardonnay and pinot noir, all of which are sourced from the most sought-after vineyards in Sonoma County (reservations required, www.threestickwines.com, 707-996-3328, 143 W. Spain Street, Sonoma, CA 95476).

PASSAGGIO WINES After more than 20 years in law enforcement, Cynthia Cosco decided to move from Virginia to the Bay Area to pursue her dream of making wine, and today she does just that. Cosco crafts small-lot wines from a diverse array of varietals, with an emphasis on elegant white wines that she offers in her relaxed, dog-friendly downtown tasting room (www .passaggiowines.com, 707-934-8941, 25 E. Napa Street, Suite C, Sonoma, CA 95476).

WINERY SIXTEEN 600 Stop by Winery Sixteen 600's Tasting House, a recently renovated 120-year-old-farmhouse, replete with Grateful Dead memorabilia and fine art. Here you can taste organically grown grenache, syrah, and zinfandel from small vineyards in Sonoma Valley, some as small as one acre (www .winerysixteen600.com, 707-721-1805, 589 First Street W., Sonoma, CA 95476).

FARMHOUSE INN & SPA This is one of the most stylish inns in Wine Country, thanks to its class-act restaurant and its savvy owners. It keeps winning impressive accolades, including high marks from *Conde Nast Traveler*. The Shaker-style dining room is where a rich breakfast feast is spread, and here's the best part: the owners have a dessert first policy on their breakfast menu. They take decadence seriously here. Perhaps that's why this inn has become such a popular spot for weddings and conferences. It has the luxurious amenities of a hotel and the charm of a bed & breakfast (www .farmhouseinn.com, 707-887-3300, 800-464-6642, 7871 River Road, Forestville, CA 95436; $$$–$$$$).

What's Trending in Bodega Bay & West County

BODEGA BAY LODGE Nestled right in Bodega Bay, the lodge offers wildlife viewings and sunsets galore, whether from one of its elegant private decks, from the communal fire pit, or from the heated coastal-side pool. You can also spy the great outdoors while dining at the on-site Drakes Sonoma Coast Kitchen, which serves locally caught seafood nightly (www.bodegabaylodge.com, 707-875-3525, 103 Coast Highway 1, Bodega Bay, CA 94923).

TIMBER COVE RESORT This cliffside resort features mid-century modern touches, including kitchenettes and in-room record players, in a beautiful lodge-like setting that boasts endless ocean views. It also has an award-winning restaurant and bar and an "Outdoor Living Room" that provides a pool table, a ping-pong table, and fireside drinks (www.timbercoveresort.com, 707-847-3231, 21780 Coast Highway 1, Jenner, CA 95405; $$–$$$).

THE BARLOW A self-described "open-air marketspace," The Barlow comprises unique boutiques, cafes, restaurants, wineries, and breweries, all located in a 12.5-acre walkable area of downtown Sebastopol. It's a remarkable spot, trendy and spirited. With so many artists, chefs, and winemakers in close proximity, it makes you wonder if there's a muse right on the premises (www.thebarlow.net, 707-824-5600, 6770 McKinley Street, Sebastopol, CA 95472).

FORT ROSS STATE HISTORIC PARK Explore the role of Russian fur trappers in early California who resided at this coastal fort from 1812 to 1841. Here you can tour a museum and a preserved Russian settlement or take a scenic hike that may earn you a whale sighting (www.fortross.org, 707-847-3437, 19005 Coast Highway 1, Jenner, CA 95450).

BOON EAT + DRINK Located right in the middle of Main Street in downtown Guerneville, Boon Eat + Drink is a modern California bistro that serves unpretentious comfort food. It uses artisan cheeses, local meats, and vegetables from its estate garden less than a mile away (www.eatatboon.com, 707-869-0780, 16248 Main Street, Guerneville, CA 95446; $–$$).

FISHETARIAN FISH MARKET A fisherman-owned, fun, and funky seaside fish market and restaurant, the

BARLOW IS A MARKETPLACE WITH UNIQUE GALLERIES, CAFES, AND RESTAURANTS

Fishetarian serves award-winning clam chowder. It serves clams, fish and chips, sandwiches, tacos, fresh oysters, and salads, and it includes vegetarian and gluten-free options (www.fishetarian fishmarket.com, 707-875-9092, 599 Coast Highway 1, Bodega Bay, CA 94923; $–$$).

EL BARRIO A modern Mexican cocktail lounge in downtown Guerneville, El Barrio offers a wide range of tequilas, mezcals, and bourbons, along with shareable snacks. Some include the house-made tortilla chips and salsa, queso made with local goat cheese, and tacos (www .elbarriobar.com, 707-604-7601, 16230 Main Street, Guerneville, CA 95446).

HORSE & PLOW Visit the tasting barn at Horse & Plow for a truly West County experience: organic, vegan, non-GMO crafted wine and cider are poured in a rustic setting that is dog- and kid-friendly and surrounded by two acres of gardens and orchards (www.horse andplow.com, 707-827-3486, 1272 Gravenstein Highway N., Sebastopol, CA 95472).

RUSSIAN RIVER VINEYARDS Russian River Vineyards serves up gewurztraminer and pinot noir in a cool, farm-like setting overlooking rolling hills and estate organic produce gardens. Here guests can play bocce ball, lounge the afternoon away with music, and enjoy lunch or dinner at its on-site, award-winning restaurant (www.russianriver vineyards.com, 707-887-3344, 5700 Highway 116, Forestville, CA 95436).

RED CAR WINE CO. Elegant chardonnay, pinot noir, and syrah from coastal vineyards mere miles from the ocean can be tasted at Red Car's tasting room, where guests can play vinyl records while sipping rosé on a shaded patio (www.redcarwine.com, 707-829-8500, 8400 Graton Road, Sebastopol, CA 95472).

What's Trending in Santa Rosa

RUSSIAN RIVER BREWING COMPANY Beer mania is now a spring rite of passage. This pub draws incredibly long lines every February when it releases its sought-after, world-renowned Pliny the Younger Triple IPA. It's no wonder. Brewmaster Vinnie Cilurzo is something of an inventor, experimenting by aging beer in wine barrels to make his brews more complex (www.russianriverbrewing.com, 707-545-BEER, 725 Fourth Street, Santa Rosa, CA 95404).

BENOVIA Crafting some of the best bottlings in Wine Country, winemaker Mike Sullivan never misses. He makes striking pinot noir, chardonnay, zinfandel and now, sparklers. The entire lineup is impressive, but it appears he's

particularly gifted with pinot noir and sparkling wine. Savvy vintners Joe Anderson and Mary Dewane are generous in giving Sullivan what he needs to go the distance (www.benoviawinery .com, 707-526-4441, 3339 Hartman Road, Santa Rosa, CA 95401; tastings by appointment).

THE ASTRO A former blighted 1960s motel, The Astro is a renovated mid-century modern gem with 34 rooms decorated in vintage art and locally crafted furnishings. The lounge offers beer and coffee, and The Astro has a bicycle garage, so guests can tour Wine Country on two wheels. Best of all, if you like the furnishings, the owners will help you buy the pieces online (www.theastro.com, 707-200-4655, 323 Santa Rosa Avenue, Santa Rosa, CA 95404; $$).

PERCH & PLOW An intimate restaurant and bar that overlooks the historic Courthouse Square, Perch & Plow offers a select but impressive menu of small plates, salads, seafood, and larger comfort food dishes. It also has a stellar cocktail program that has earned the praise of spirits enthusiasts (www .perchandplow.com, 707-541-6896, 90 Old Courthouse Square, Santa Rosa, CA 95404; $$–$$$).

CRIMINAL BAKERY CO. & NOSHERY This popular brunch spot serves up granola, waffles, quiche, frittatas, sandwiches, and house-made baked goods to hungry visitors of the SOFA arts neighborhood, making it a perfect spot to begin an afternoon of gallery exploring (www.criminalbaking.com, 707-888-3546, 463 Sebastopol Avenue, Santa Rosa, CA 95404; $).

BIRD & THE BOTTLE From the minds of James Beard–nominated restauranteurs Mark and Terri Stark, Bird & the Bottle incorporates international flavors to create a diverse selection of shareable plates that offer something for everyone

AT RUSSIAN RIVER BREWING COMPANY, PATIENCE IS A VIRTUE WHEN IT RELEASES ITS PLINY THE YOUNGER BREW EVERY SPRING

in a cool, tavern-like setting (www .birdandthebottle.com, 707-568-4000, 1055 Fourth Street, Santa Rosa, CA 95404; $$–$$$).

THE SPINSTER SISTERS The flagship restaurant of the up-and-coming SOFA neighborhood, the Spinster Sisters is a modern bistro serving breakfast, lunch, and dinner with a locavore spin that has

BIRD IN THE BOTTLE MAKES A CLASS-ACT, ASIAN-STYLED MATZOH BALL SOUP

earned it the title Best Restaurant in Sonoma County at the *Bohemian* (www .thespinstersisters.com, 707-528-7100, 401 S. A Street, Santa Rosa, CA 95401; $$$$).

SAFARI WEST The African Safari meets Wine Country at Safari West, a wildlife sanctuary that serves as a home for giraffes, rhinos, cheetahs, and other animals. Guests can visit on a safari-like tour, with the option to "glamp" over-night in its well-equipped luxury safari tents, with dinner included (www.safari west.com, 707-579-2551, 800-616-2695, 3115 Porter Creek Road, Santa Rosa, CA 95404).

LUTHER BURBANK HOME & GARDENS The final home of Luther Bur-bank, world-renowned horticulturalist, this facility offers daily tours of his his-toric house and experimental gardens. It's home to the original russet potato and shasta daisy, as well as rose and herb gardens (www.lutherburbank.org, 707-524-5445, 204 Santa Rosa Avenue, Santa Rosa, CA 95404).

DONELAN FAMILY WINES The Donelan family serves highly coveted syrah, pinot noir, chardonnay, and other fine wines in its Santa Rosa tasting room, where guests can taste current release and reserve flights in a private setting nestled within the family's working winery (www.donelanwines.com, 707-591-0782, 3352-D Coffey Lane, Santa Rosa, CA 95403; tastings by appointment only).

HENHOUSE BREWING COMPANY A visit to Santa Rosa isn't complete without beer, and HenHouse serves up Saisons, IPAs, stouts, and whatever else the brewmasters feel like making, with an emphasis on small-batch and unique ingredients. At its brewery and taproom, it also offers wood-fired pizza on the weekends (www.henhousebrewing.com, 707-978-4577, 322 Bellevue Avenue, Santa Rosa, CA 95407).

COOPERAGE BREWING COMPANY Focusing on hoppy and Belgian-style ales, the Cooperage rotates its drafts frequently to ensure fresh and innovative offerings. They are available weekly, especially for its growing legion of fans, who visit its brewery for a no-thrills but delicious experience, bringing their own food and playing shuffleboard amid sips (www.cooperagebrewing.com, 707-293-9787, 981 Airway Court, Suite G, Santa Rosa, CA 95403).

What's Trending in Petaluma

METRO HOTEL & CAFE The charm of Paris meets the eccentricity of Petaluma at the Metro, an intimate boutique hotel with a handful of rooms simply decorated with a nod to France. The vintage Airstream suites are complete with AstroTurf lawns and pink flamingos, and there's a complimentary breakfast in the on-site cafe (www.metrolodging.com, 707-773-4900, 508 Petaluma Boulevard S., Petaluma, CA 94952; $–$$).

HOTEL PETALUMA Originally built in 1923, Hotel Petaluma recently underwent impressive renovations that lent a modern and elegant style to this downtown hotel. It offers pet-friendly rooms, and features an on-site oyster bar, wine tasting room, and a boutique lifestyle goods store (www.hotelpetaluma.com, 707-559-3393, 205 Kentucky Street, Petaluma, CA 94952; $–$$).

PETALUMA ARTS CENTER The creative hub of this artistic city, Petaluma Arts Center features rotating exhibitions featuring works from local, regional, and national artists touching on an array of timely and relevant subjects. It also offers art classes, poetry readings, and film screenings (www.petalumaartscenter.org, 707-762-5600, 230 Lakeville Street, Petaluma, CA 94952).

McEVOY RANCH A producer of world-class organic olive oil, McEvoy Ranch offers guests a chance to taste olive oil, sample its olive oil–based goods, and try its wines, amid a bucolic setting that makes people think they're in Italy, not Petaluma (www.mcevoyranch.com, 707-769-4100, 5935 Red Hill Road, Petaluma, CA 94952; reservations required).

THISTLE MEATS This modern-day butcher shop specializes in locally sourced meats and house-made charcuterie, which is popular with locals and chefs alike. Thistle Meats' lunch offers fresh meat pies, salads, sandwiches, soups, and more for take-out or dine-in (www.thistlemeats.com, 707-772-5442, 160 Petaluma Boulevard, Petaluma, CA 94952).

GRIFFO DISTILLERY A local distillery specializing in handcrafted, small-batch spirits, Griffo offers tastings of its gold medal–winning gin and barrel-aged whiskey, both of which are standards at bars throughout Sonoma County. Griffo also offers tours at its distillery (www .griffodistillery.com, 707-879-8755, 1320 Scott Street, Suite A, Petaluma, CA 94954).

WISHBONE Grab a sustainable bite to eat at Wishbone, where ingredients come from local farms and gardens, including Wishbone's own Tilted Ranch. Cocktails are crafted using locally made spirits from Sonoma County, which include Bloody Marys (www.wishbonepetaluma .com, 707-763-2663, 841 Petaluma Boule-vard, Petaluma, CA, 94952; $).

CROCODILE An intimate, casual bis-tro, Crocodile serves French country food, including classics like escargot and croque madame. The restaurant's wine list focuses on French varietal wines grown in California from small producers and includes natural wines. Best of all, the Crocodile has a setting

that's delightfully unstuffy (www .crocodilepetaluma.com, 707-981-8159, 140 Second Street, Suite 100, Petaluma, CA 94952; $–$$).

THE BIG EASY Serving up live music six days a week, the Big Easy is an under-ground restaurant and music venue in downtown Petaluma. It features local, regional, and national acts playing everything from big band and traditional jazz to blues and folk, rounded out with a full dinner menu (www.bigeasypetaluma .com, 707-776-7163, 128 American Alley, Petaluma, CA 94952).

MARIO & JOHN'S A neighborhood hangout, Mario & John's is a drinking establishment with the largest spirits menu in town and it specializes in whis-key. Here bartenders celebrate the art of the cocktail amid a slightly cleaned up, but hip scene, with pool and shuffleboard (707-981-7661, 428 E. D Street, Petaluma, CA 94952).

WHAT'S WHERE IN NAPA VALLEY & SONOMA COUNTY

Getting Here & Getting Around

Gridlock is not the rarity it used to be in Wine Country, so it pays to know your way around. Highways 101 and 29, the main thoroughfares through Napa and Sonoma counties, are always hectic, especially on weekends. In addition, the terrain conspires against smooth travel—any approach requires a minor mountain expedition.

Perhaps that's why, in the late 1700s, the earliest explorers came by water. The Sonoma coast was the area's first highway marker, and as sailing ships from around the globe made for the New World, the Napa and Petaluma rivers, which connect with San Pablo Bay, allowed early settlers a fast way inland.

By the mid-1800s, trails from the Central Valley took travelers along Clear Lake to Bodega Bay as well as south and east along the bay to Benicia. Carts and stagecoaches brought folks along

VINEYARDS ARE THE BACKDROP OF WINE COUNTRY TIM FISH

primitive roads, stirring up dust in the summer and churning up mud in the winter. By the 1860s, steamships were chugging up and down the Napa and Petaluma rivers, but soon railroads steamed onto the scene, with names like Southern Pacific and San Francisco North Pacific, connecting the towns of the two budding counties to the East Bay.

The automobile changed everything, for better and for worse. Sonoma County remained somewhat innocently isolated from San Francisco—it's a long loop around that bay—until the big day in May 1937 when the Golden Gate Bridge opened a speedier route north, and Napa and Sonoma counties became travel destinations for San Francisco and for the rest of the world. Today, in fact, 50 percent of the people who visit Wine Country each year start their getaway in San Francisco.

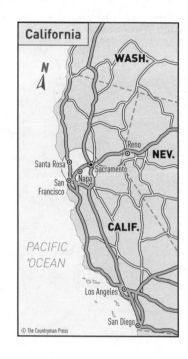

BY AIR Air travelers bound for Wine Country can arrive at and depart from one of three major airports handling numerous domestic and international airlines, and there's also a regional airport serving the area.

San Francisco International (SFO), Oakland International (OAK), and Sacramento International (SMF) are all within easy driving distance of Napa and Sonoma counties. Charles M. Schulz–Sonoma County Airport (STS) is a regional airport located just a few miles northwest of Santa Rosa: 707-565-7240. It's home to Alaska Airlines, which operates daily service to LAX in Los Angeles, Orange County, and flights to San Diego, Phoenix, Portland, and Seattle/Tacoma. United also operates a shuttle to and from SFO. The regional airport is named after the famed cartoonist of the *Peanuts* comic strip, who lived and worked in Santa Rosa for more than 40 years.

BY CAR Although planes and trains will bring you to the threshold of Wine Country, a car is a necessity in Wine Country proper. Public transportation is limited,

and the landscape is so vast that you'll need your own wheels. Traffic is common on Saturday and Sunday and during peak summer months, so an ambitious itinerary can be cut short by the weekend tourist crush.

RENTING A CAR Because a car is almost a requirement in Wine Country, visitors arriving by air inevitably rent a vehicle. Most major rental companies, of course, work out of the metro airports, and they're typically helpful in plotting routes and will often supply drivers with basic maps to reach their destinations. Just in case, here are a few directions:

San Francisco International Airport: To find your way to Wine Country from the Bay Area's largest airport, take Highway 101 north into San Francisco. The highway empties onto the streets, so watch the signs carefully. Continue through the city across the Golden Gate Bridge, and you'll soon find yourself in central Sonoma County. To reach the town of Sonoma or the Napa Valley, take Highway 37 in Novato and connect with Highway 121.

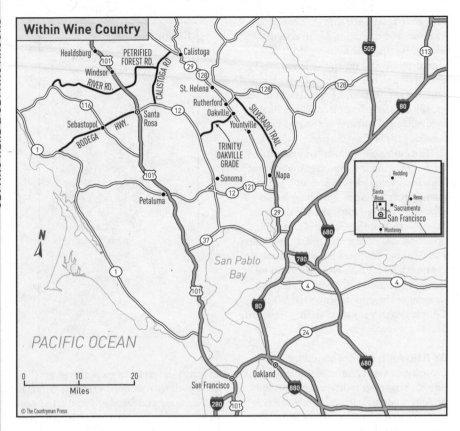

Within Wine Country

Healdsburg • | PETRIFIED FOREST RD. | Calistoga •
Windsor •
Santa Rosa
Sebastopol •
St. Helena •
Rutherford •
Oakville •
Yountville •
TRINITY/ OAKVILLE GRADE
SILVERADO TRAIL
Sonoma •
Napa •
Petaluma •
San Pablo Bay
PACIFIC OCEAN
Oakland
San Francisco

Redding
Santa Rosa
Reno
★ Sacramento
San Francisco
Monterey

0   10   20
Miles
© The Countryman Press

Miles: 72 to central Sonoma County; 82 to Napa Valley.

Time: 90 minutes.

Oakland International Airport: To reach Napa County and the city of Sonoma, take I-80 north through Oakland and connect with Highway 29 North. For Napa, stay on Highway 29, and for the city of Sonoma, take Highway 12/121. To reach central Sonoma County, take I-80 North through Oakland, exit on I-580, and then connect with Highway 101 North, which takes you into the heart of Sonoma County.

Miles: 82 to central Sonoma County; 46 to Napa Valley.

Time: 1 hour to Sonoma; 45 minutes to Napa.

Sacramento International Airport: Take I-5 South and connect with the I-80 West bypass. Follow the signs to San Francisco. Take Highway 12 to Napa, continuing west to the cities of Sonoma and Santa Rosa.

Miles: 61 to Napa; 97 to central Sonoma County.

Time: 90 minutes to Napa; 2 to 2.5 hours to central Sonoma County.

You can also rent a car after arriving in Napa and Sonoma counties. Local information and reservation numbers are listed below. Reservations up to a week in advance are recommended.

NAPA COUNTY

Avis (707-258-8564 or 800-331-1212)
Enterprise Rent-A-Car (707-253-8000 or 800-261-7331)
Hertz (707-265-7575 or 800-654-3131)

SONOMA COUNTY

Avis (707-571-0465 or 800-331-1212)

Budget Rent-A-Car (707-528-2195 or 800-527-0700)

Enterprise Rent-A-Car (707-570-3600 or 800-261-7331)

Hertz (707-528-0834 or 800-654-3131)

National (707-570-3600 or 877-222-9058)

AIRPORT SHUTTLE Here's an alternative to renting a car at the airport: reasonably priced express shuttle buses and vans operate to and from the San Francisco, Oakland, and Sacramento airports. These comfortable vehicles operate 16 to 20 hours a day, seven days a week. Shuttles depart from airports roughly every one to two hours, depending on the operator, and deliver passengers to selected drop-off points in Wine Country.

One-way fares (cash only) range from $28 to $40, depending on the operator, the drop-off point, and any excess luggage requirements. Reservations are not usually required, but on weekends and in peak seasons buses fill up, and you may be forced to stand in the aisle. Schedules fluctuate, so it's smart to reserve shuttle services in advance.

Airport Express, SFO and OAK (Oakland) to Santa Rosa (707-837-8700, 800-327-2024)

California Wine Tours, SFO and OAK to the city of Napa (800-294-6386)

Evans Airport Service, SFO and OAK to Napa (707-255-1559, 707-944-2025, 800-294-6386)

BY BUS Greyhound bus service to Sonoma and Napa counties is very limited. It's also possible to ride Greyhound to San Francisco and then make connections on Golden Gate Transit to reach Wine Country. A travel agent will have the most up-to-date information on Greyhound schedules and connections.

Greyhound in San Francisco (800-231-2222)

Golden Gate Transit (415-923-2000, 415-455-2000 or 707-541-2000) For travel between San Francisco and Sonoma County; one-way fare from San Francisco to Santa Rosa is $13 for adults and $6.50 for seniors, disabled, and youth.

Once inside Wine Country, public bus service is available through Sonoma County Transit and Napa Valley Transit (The VINE). This method of travel could be indispensable for the Wine Country visitor on a tight budget. One drawback

MANY HOTELS LIKE THIS ONE CATER TO THE WINE COUNTRY TRAVELER WITH VINEYARD VIEWS

is that bus stops, which can be few and far between, are usually not close to wineries and other tourist attractions.

One-way fares average between $1.50 and $3.90, and weekend service is limited. If buses will be your primary form of transportation, it may be essential to gather the most current timetables and route maps, which are updated frequently. The cities of Santa Rosa, Napa, Healdsburg, and Petaluma also offer bus service within their city boundaries.

NAPA COUNTY

The VINE (800-696-6443, 707-251-2800) The Napa city bus travels mainly along Highway 29 between Calistoga and Vallejo, with bus and ferry connections to and from San Francisco.

SONOMA COUNTY

Sonoma County Transit (707-576-7433, 800-345-7433) For travel within Sonoma County.
Santa Rosa Transit (707-543-3333) City bus.
Petaluma Transit (707-778-4460) City bus.
Healdsburg Shuttle Route 67 (707-576-7433) City bus.

BY TRAIN Amtrak's westbound *California Zephyr* and north-to-south *Coastal Starlight* trains drop off Napa County–bound passengers in the city of Martinez, about 40 miles south of Napa. Amtrak has continuing ground transportation that delivers passengers directly to Napa but not Sonoma.

For Amtrak information and reservations, call 800-872-7245 (or 800-USA-RAIL) or check the website at www.amtrak.com. It's advisable to consult a travel agent for assistance in booking Amtrak.

Just for the record, the Napa Valley Wine Train is actually a gourmet restaurant on rails and not a true form of transportation. (See page 57 for listing.)

BY LIMOUSINE The ultimate in personal transportation is the limousine, and for many visitors to Wine Country, chauffeured travel goes hand in hand with wine tasting. For others, the pricey, three-hour ride to the Sonoma coast can be a romantic and unforgettable luxury.

Both Napa Valley and Sonoma County have an abundance of professional limousine services that will map out wine-tasting itineraries for the novice or deliver connoisseurs to wineries of their choosing. Most also offer daylong, fixed-rate touring packages with extras, such as gourmet picnic lunches or evening dining, included in the price. Per-hour rates range from $65 to $165, depending on the limo and the tour. That doesn't include taxes, driver gratuities, parking fees, or bridge tolls. A three- or four-hour minimum is standard, and complimentary champagne is often served. Reservations are required at least two or three days in advance and as much as a week in advance during peak vacationing months. Some recommend booking at least a month ahead of time.

For your added safety, the limousine service you engage should be both licensed and insured. Ask your hotel concierge to recommend a service or talk to your travel agent. Listed below are some of Wine Country's most popular limousine services. Companies may be based in one county, but they frequently take passengers all over Wine Country and beyond.

NAPA COUNTY

Antique Tours and Classic Convertible Wine Tours (707-226-9227)
Evans Inc. (707-255-1559)

SONOMA COUNTY

California Wine Tours (800-294-6386)
Ultimate Limousine Service (707-766-8500)
Pure Luxury Limousine Service (707-775-2920, 800-626-5466)

BY TAXI When buses are too inconvenient and limousines too expensive, call for an old standby: a taxicab. The cab companies below are on duty 24 hours a day, seven days a week. Per-mile fares average $3.

NAPA COUNTY

Black Tie Taxi (707-259-1000)
Yellow Cab Napa (707-226-3731)

SONOMA COUNTY

Bill's Taxi Service (707-869-2177)
Vern's Taxi Service (707-938-8885)
George's Yellow and Checker Taxi (707-544-4444)
Santa Rosa Taxi (707-579-1212 or 707-206-2006)

Tip: You can contact Bay Area 511 by dialing 511 from your cell or landline to get direct access to traffic info, public transportation, freeway aid, Clipper, Rideshare, bicycling, and FasTrak information. You may also go to 511.org for updated transportation information and advisories.

General Information & Resources

NAPA COUNTY

Calistoga Chamber of Commerce (www.visitcalistoga.com, 707-942-6333, 1133 Washington Street, Calistoga, CA 94515)
Visit Napa Valley Welcome Center (www.visitnapavalley.com, 707-251-5895, 600 Main Street, Napa, CA 94559)
St. Helena Chamber of Commerce (www.sthelena.com, 707-963-4456 and 800-799-6456, 657 Main Street, St. Helena, CA 94574)
Yountville Chamber of Commerce (www.yountville.com, 707-944-0904, 6484-F Washington Street, Yountville, CA 94599)

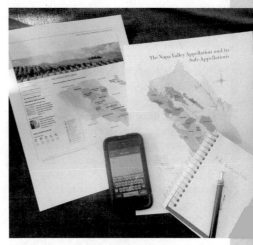

PLAN AHEAD BY MAKING RESERVATIONS TIM FISH

SONOMA COUNTY

Bodega Bay Chamber (www.bodegabayca.com, 707-347-9645, 850 Highway 1, Bodega Bay, CA, 94923)
Healdsburg Chamber of Commerce and Visitors Bureau (www.healdsburg.com, info@healdsburg.com, 707-433-6935, 217 Healdsburg Avenue, Healdsburg, CA 95448)
Petaluma Area Chamber of Commerce (www.petalumachamber.com, pacc@petalumachamber.com, 707-762-2785, 6 Petaluma Boulevard North, Suite A2, Petaluma, CA 94952)
Russian River Chamber of Commerce and Visitor Center (www.russianriver.com, ed@russianriver.com, 707-869-9000 and 877-644-9000, 16209 First Street, Guerneville, CA 95446)
Korbel Visitor Center (www.russianriver.com, ed@russianriver.com, 707-869-9000 and 877-644-9001, 13250 River Road, in the railroad station, Guerneville, CA 95446)
Santa Rosa Metro Chamber of Commerce (www.santarosametrochamber.com, info@santarosametrochamber.com, 707-545-1414, 50 Old Courthouse Square, Ste. 110, Santa Rosa, CA 95401)
Sebastopol Chamber of Commerce & Visitor Center (www.sebastopol.org,

info@sebastopol.org, 707-823-3032, 265 S. Main Street, Sebastopol, CA 95472)

Sonoma Coast Visitor Center (www .sonomacounty.com/chamberscvbs/ sonoma-coast-visitors-center, 707-875-3866, 850 Highway 1, Bodega Bay, CA 94923)

Sonoma County Tourism (www.sonoma county.com, info@sonomacounty.com, 707-522-5800 and 800-576-6662, 400 Aviation Boulevard, Ste. 500, Santa Rosa, CA 95403)

Sonoma Valley Visitors Bureau (www.sonomavalley.com, info@ sonomavalley.com, 707-996-1090 and 866-966-1090, 453 First Street E., Sonoma, CA 95476. A second office is located at Cornerstone Sonoma, 707-966-1090, 23570 Arnold Drive [Highway 121], Sonoma, CA 95476)

IN EARLY SUMMER, THE COVER CROPS BETWEEN ROWS ARE NOT ONLY BEAUTIFUL BUT ALSO NUTRITIOUS TO THE SOIL TIM FISH

Visit Santa Rosa (www.visitsantarosa .com, 707-577-8674 and 800-404-7673, 9 Fourth Street, Santa Rosa, CA 95401)

CLIMATE The late Luther Burbank, known as the plant wizard, called Napa and Sonoma counties "the chosen spot of all the earth as far as nature is concerned." The moderate weather is a blessing for those who have suffered midwestern and northeastern blizzards. In Napa and Sonoma, the winter is cool, with temperatures dipping down to the 40s. The rainy season begins in late December and lingers until April. Of course, the droughts in recent years have made the season somewhat unpredictable, and the locals count raindrops with good cheer. Rain makes for a lush countryside and hillsides ribbed with green vineyards.

AVERAGE TEMPERATURES

	Napa	Sonoma
October	62.0	62.2
January	47.6	47.2
April	56.6	56.6
July	67.4	70.0

Average Annual Total Precipitation

	Napa	Sonoma
Rain	24.64	29.94
Snow	0	0

WEATHER REPORTS

Napa County (www.wunderground.com /weather-forecast /US/CA/Napa.html)

Sonoma County (www.wunderground/ weather-forecast/US/CA/Santa_Rosa .html)

GUIDED TOURS Looking for some packaged fun? Consult the tour companies listed here. A wide range of options are available, from bicycle rambles to helicopter tours of Wine Country.

    Getaway Adventures (www.getaway adventures.com, 707-568-3040 and 800-499-2453, 2228 Northpoint Parkway, Santa Rosa, CA 95407). Day trips priced at $149 per person have bikers pedaling

A COLORFUL DISPLAY OF BOTTLES AND TASTY TREATS FOR FOODIES AT CLIF FAMILY WINERY TASTING ROOM

with lunch, and a tour of Napa for those departing from San Francisco.

Wine & Dine Tours (www.wineand dinetour.com, 707-963-8930, 800-946-3868, P.O. Box 204, St. Helena, CA 94574). This tour operator is for the discriminating traveler who would like to stop in at small boutique wineries in Napa Valley and Sonoma Valley. Most of the wineries are private or by appointment only.

LATE NIGHT FOOD AND FUEL Insomnia after too much gourmet food or wine? Or perhaps you're just a weary traveler looking for a place to gas up. Whatever the case, here are some options for night birds.

NAPA COUNTY

Chevron/Extra Mile (707-252-7141, 2008 Redwood Road, Napa, CA 94558)
Lucky Supermarkets (707-255-7767, 1312 Trancas Street, Napa, CA 94558; 707-256-3407, 2355 California Boulevard, Napa, CA 94558)

SONOMA COUNTY

Flamingo Shell (707-542-4456, 2799 Fourth Street, Santa Rosa, CA 95405)
Safeway (707-528-3062, 1799 Marlow Road, Santa Rosa, CA 95401)
Safeway (707-522-1455, 2751 Fourth Street, Santa Rosa, CA 95405)
Safeway (707-996-0633, 477 W. Napa Street, Sonoma, CA 95476)

MEDICAL CARE **Healdsburg District Hospital** (707-431-6500, 1375 University Avenue, Healdsburg)
Petaluma Valley Hospital (707-778-1111, 400 N. McDowell Boulevard, Petaluma)
Queen of the Valley Hospital (707-252-4411, emergency room: 707-257-4038, 1000 Trancas Street, Napa)
Santa Rosa Memorial Hospital (707-546-3210 and 707-525-5300, 1165 Montgomery Drive, Santa Rosa)

to three or four wineries, with a gourmet lunch to boot. The company also books weekend and four- to six-day bike and multisport trips (biking, hiking, kayaking). Adventurers will find the Pedal 'N Paddle Tour invigorating. It features a half-day of kayaking and a half-day of bicycling. Rentals are available.

Viviani Destination Specialists (www .viviani.com, 707-265-1940, P.O. Box 280, Sonoma, CA 95476). This is highbrow travel at its best. Viviani specializes in corporate, incentive, and exclusive events in California's Wine Country, offering private, customized tours that bestow special access. You'll meet winemakers, hike in private vineyards, and learn the art of *méthode champenoise* that monks perfected so long ago in Champagne. Among its many offerings are half-day winery tours, full-day tours

Sonoma Valley Hospital (707-935-5000, emergency room: 707-935-5100, 347 Andrieux Street, Sonoma).

St. Helena Hospital (707-963-3611, emergency room: 707-963-6425, 10 Woodland Road, St. Helena)

Sutter Medical Center of Santa Rosa (707-576-4000, emergency room: 707-576-4040, 30 Mark West Springs Road, Santa Rosa)

RADIO STATIONS **KRCB 90.9 FM** (707-584-2000, Rohnert Park), National Public Radio and classical and eclectic music.
KFGY 92.9 (707-543-0100, Santa Rosa), Country.
KJZY 93.7 FM (707-528-9393, Santa Rosa), Light jazz.
KRSH 95.5 and **95.9 FM** (707-588-0707, Santa Rosa), Adult alternative.
KNOB 96.7 FM (707-284-9967, Santa Rosa), Adult alternative.
KVRV 97.7 FM (707-543-0100, Santa Rosa), Classic rock.
KXTS 98.7 FM (707-588-0707, Santa Rosa), Hispanic.
KVYN 99.3 FM (707-258-1111, Napa), Adult contemporary.
KSXY 100.9 (707-588-0707, Middletown/ Santa Rosa), Top 40.

KZST 100.1 FM (707-528-4434, Santa Rosa), Adult contemporary.
KHTH 101.7 FM (707-543-0100, Santa Rosa), Top 40.
KMHX 104.9 FM (707-543-0100, Santa Rosa), Today's mix.
KSRO 1350 AM (707-543-0100, Santa Rosa), News and talk.
KVON 1440 AM (707-258-1111, Napa), News, talk, sports.

ROAD SERVICES Puncture your tire on a broken bottle of 1995 Rafanelli zinfandel? Stranger things have happened. For emergency road service from AAA anywhere in Napa or Sonoma counties, call 800-222-4357. Listed below are other 24-hour emergency road services.

NAPA COUNTY

Calistoga Towing (707-942-4445)
Vine Towing (707-226-3780)

SONOMA COUNTY

ABC Towing (707-433-1700, Healdsburg)
Sebastopol Tow (707-823-1061)
Santa Rosa Towing (707-542-1600)

HOW TO TRAVEL LIKE A WINE-SAVVY INSIDER

W hat's the advantage of being an insider in Wine Country? You get the authentic Napa and Sonoma experience and can take full advantage of all this beautiful area has to offer. But first you have to be in the know.

✳ Acquaint Yourself with the Latest Developments

THE RISE OF THE PALATE TRAVELER Cosmopolitan travelers are giving rise to a paradigm shift in Wine Country vacations known as "Palate Travel." What's behind this trend are sophisticated millennials, who range roughly in age between 22 and 37. For them, the palate is their compass; their likes and dislikes dictate their itinerary. This research reveals that the palate traveler is determined to taste wine where the grapes are groomed. A 2015 national survey by Dr. Liz Thach of Sonoma State University found 30 percent of millennials said they had traveled to wineries to taste wine, compared to 18 percent of Gen-Xers and 17 percent of Boomers. For palate travelers, those who fancy pinot noir want to explore the Russian River Valley and the Sonoma Coast, both in Sonoma County, and the Carneros, a sprawling region at the base of both Sonoma County and Napa Valley. Cabernet fanatics, meanwhile, want to venture into to Napa Valley's Stags Leap District, Oakville and Rutherford, and Sonoma County's Alexander Valley. Palate travelers meander through Napa Valley and Sonoma County seamlessly, sometimes in nanoseconds. For those who argue with you, you'll want this example up your sleeve. Pride Mountain Vineyards, perched 2,100 feet atop the Mayacamas Mountains, has its crush pad running along the county line so people can stand with one foot in Sonoma County and one foot in Napa Valley. Palate travelers, it appears, never opt for Napa Valley over Sonoma County or vice versa. For them, taste always trumps geography.

THE CROSSOVER EFFECT—WINE, SPIRITS & BREWS Wine Country has become a place for the eclectic connoisseur, one who appreciates cult cab, rye whiskey, and pale ale in equal measure. The number of distilleries in Sonoma County, for example, grew roughly 200 percent between 2013 and 2015. Meanwhile, there's been an outpouring of new breweries opening up, with 20-plus craft brewers in Sonoma County. Here people are quite fussy about their wine *and* their beer, don't you know. Vinnie Cilurzo of Russian River Brewing Company in Santa Rosa is among the region's serious brewmasters. This being Wine Country, Cilurzo is, in fact, experimenting with beer aged in used wine barrels, imparting complex and distinctive flavors to it. Producers of wine, spirits, and brews say the impetus for the crossover is the ever-curious millennials who want to explore drink in all its incarnations.

EXPLOSIVE GROWTH IN NAPA Napa is evolving faster than any other city in Wine Country, and with the development of the riverfront at the south end of downtown and the First Street Napa development, it now has the sex appeal to attract tourists in droves. Getting everyone's attention are the Japanese restaurant Kenzo, Charlie Palmer Steaks, Cadet Wine Bar, and Carpe Diem, among other hot spots. Anchored by the trendy Archer Hotel Napa, First Street Napa is a thriving mecca for restaurant-goers and shoppers. What's more, there are 20-plus tasting rooms within walking distance of downtown Napa. (See pages 57–62 for details.)

"Wine Country" refers to the California wine-growing region north of San Francisco, most famously Napa Valley and Sonoma County. Napa Valley includes the cities of Napa and Yountville and the Stags Leap District, Oakville and Rutherford, St. Helena, and Calistoga. Sonoma County is home to Healdsburg, Bodega Bay and West County (short for West Sonoma County), the city of Sonoma, and Santa Rosa. Sonoma Valley is a subset of Sonoma County, and its base is the city of Sonoma.

THE MILLENNIALS HAVE ARRIVED This generation of wine drinkers, the offspring of the baby boomers, range in age from 22 to 37. If you are in this age group, expect to be courted in Wine Country. Vintners are well aware of marketing studies that reveal millennials have plenty of disposable income to tour and shop.

COPPOLA'S SAVVY APPROACH The Francis Ford Coppola Winery in Geyserville takes a family-oriented resort approach, with a pool near the tasting room, bocce courts, a movie gallery, and more. Coppola, the Academy Award–winning director best known for *The Godfather* trilogy and *Apocalypse Now*, envisions it as "a wine wonderland . . . where people of all ages can enjoy the best things in life—food, wine, music, dancing, games, swimming, and performances . . ."

THE "TRUE WINE" MOVEMENT Wine Country is part of the "true wine" movement. The "natural," or true wine, trend that started in Italy and took hold in France

INSIDE THE WINE CAVES AT JARVIS IN NAPA VALLEY COURTESY JARVIS WINERY

AFTER THE WILDFIRES

In Northern California, the 2017 wildfires managed to sidestep, for the most part, what we regard as Wine Country. The wineries, the tasting rooms, the restaurants, the shops, and the vineyards largely went unscathed. For example, 99.8 percent of the region's vineyards were not affected by the fires. As for the wineries in Napa Valley and Sonoma County, just a handful of them suffered major structural damage. For example, Paradise Ridge Winery's tasting room and event center in Santa Rosa and Signorello Vineyards' tasting room and business office in Napa burned to the ground. The wineries are rebuilding, and Paradise Ridge is going a step further. It's creating a memorial to chronicle the fire by putting together charred artifacts, videos, and timelines. We encourage you to come and witness the robust rebirth of this unique region beloved by so many; plant scientist Luther Burbank, for one, coined Santa Rosa, one of Wine Country's major cities, "the chosen spot."

in recent years has reached California, where a growing number of wineries are using plants instead of chemicals to keep pests at bay. Some wineries even boast they're vegan. Wineries that follow the movement's precepts might also eschew the practice of adding sugar or acid to aid fermentation and to fix a wine's flavor balance during the process. Some reject filtering their wine, believing that true wine is truly a product of the place it was grown and pressed—conveying *terroir*, or the unique qualities derived from geology, geography, and climate. True wine is clearly a growing trend in Wine Country. Check out the doings of industry leader Benziger Family Winery in Glen Ellen (page 159).

Take Our Crash Course in Wine Tasting

There's nothing snooty to it—simply swirl and sniff; sip and swish; and spit. And in the end, trust your palate. Whether you're an experienced wine taster or a novice, it's all about what *you* like.

1. SWIRL AND SNIFF When you swirl the wine in your glass (gently, in small circles, for 10 seconds or so), you release the molecules that produce the aromas. *Insider tip:* To get the full effect of the aromas released, put one hand over the glass while swirling it with the other.

Did you know that 75 percent of taste comes from one's sense of smell? Jot down the aromas you detect—fruit, herbs, spices, etc.

2. SIP AND SWISH The tongue plays a major role in wine tasting because it holds the taste buds that recognize sour, sweet, and salty. Let the wine make an impression on you. Is the wine rich or light? Is it harsh or smooth? Does it have an aftertaste? Is it dry? Sour? Sweet? Salty? Jot down what you taste.

3. SPIT In tasting rooms you'll see a spit bucket on the counter. Use it, especially if you're touring by automobile and don't have a designated driver. Visiting tasting room after tasting room, your wine intake can quickly catch up with you if you consume every sample.

That's all there is to it! Now that you know the ropes, maybe you'd like to take your wine knowledge to the next level. There are plenty of learning opportunities out there.

THE AROMA WHEEL

The Aroma Wheel was created by Ann Noble, professor emeritus of viticulture and enology at the University of California at Davis, as a guide to help people describe aromas they detect in wine. To learn more, visit her website at www.winearomawheel .com. Noble has also filmed a presentation available on YouTube: www.youtube.com/watch?v=2skRwwR5Nbk.

Further Your Wine Education

For those who consider learning an adventure, a great wine education can be had at the Culinary Institute of America (CIA), the West Coast campus at Greystone in St. Helena. Programs range from two-hour Wine Exploration courses for the traveler, offered on Saturdays, to two- to five-day continuing-education courses, a one-month Wine Immersion course, and an Advanced Wine and Beverage program.

CIA Greystone's faculty is the best and the brightest in Wine Country. Its director is Karen MacNeil, author of *The Wine Bible,* and among the many noted faculty members is celebrity chef John Ash, an award-winning cookbook author.

In addition to choice instructors, the program has a state-of-the-art facility at the Rudd Center. Once the distillery of the old Christian Brothers winery, the remodeled center has two tasting theaters, an air-filtration system, spit sinks at each tasting area, and inset lighting. Each seat is also equipped with a computer that can quickly tally votes in blind tastings. Wine education has gone high-tech! (To find out

THE TRUE WINE MOVEMENT TAKES ROOT AT BENZIGER FAMILY WINERY WITH ITS BIODYNAMIC FARMING BENZIGER FAMILY WINERY

more about class offerings, visit www.ciaprochef.com/winestudies or call 800-888-7850.)

KNOW THE BACK STORY: THE PARIS TASTING OF 1976 California and French wine lovers have a longstanding love-hate relationship—California loves French wine and France hates California's. We exaggerate—but only somewhat. California winemakers have always aspired to the quality and reputation of Bordeaux and Burgundy wines, while French enthusiasts ignored the wines of California. That is, until May 24, 1976.

It began with British wine merchant Steven Spurrier, who had a taste for California wine but had a difficult time convincing his English and European customers of its quality. Spurrier hit on the idea of staging a blind tasting of California and French wines, using the nine greatest palates of France. It was unheard of. California had beaten French wines in past tastings, but the judges were always American, and what did they know?

The French judges were aware that they were sampling both French and American wines, although the identities of the individual wines were concealed. As the tasting progressed, the tasters began pointing out the wines they believed were from California, and their comments about them grew increasingly patronizing. When the bottles were unmasked, however, the judges were mortified: the wines they thought were classic Bordeaux or Burgundy were in reality from California. Six of the 11 highest-rated wines were, in fact, from California—almost entirely from Napa. The 1973 Stag's Leap Wine Cellars cabernet sauvignon beat 1970 vintages of Château Mouton-Rothschild and Château Haut-Brion, and a 1973 Chateau Montelena chardonnay bested Burgundy's finest whites. France contested the findings, of course, but it was too late. California, particularly Napa, had earned its place on the international wine map.

BROADEN YOUR ENOLOGICAL VOCABULARY A quick rundown of the top wine varietals . . .

CABERNET FRANC (cab-ehr-NAY FRAHN): Red wine of Bordeaux, similar to cabernet sauvignon, but lighter in color and body. Often used in blends.

CABERNET SAUVIGNON (cab-ehr-NAY so-vihn-YOHN): Red, fragrant, and full-bodied wine of Bordeaux. Dry and usually tannic. Can age in the bottle five to 10 years. Also referred to simply as "cabernet" or "cab."

CHARDONNAY (shar-doe-NAY): California's most popular white grape, famed in France as the essence of white burgundy. Produces wine that's fruity, with hints of citrus or butter.

CHENIN BLANC (SHEH-nin BLAHNK): A white grape that produces a wine that's more delicate and less complex than chardonnay. Slightly sweet.

FUMÉ BLANC (FOO-may BLAHNK): Same as sauvignon blanc. The name has traditionally been used to describe a dry-style sauvignon blanc.

GEWÜRZTRAMINER (geh-VURZ-trah-MEE-ner): A white grape that yields a medium-bodied, semisweet, and lightly spicy wine.

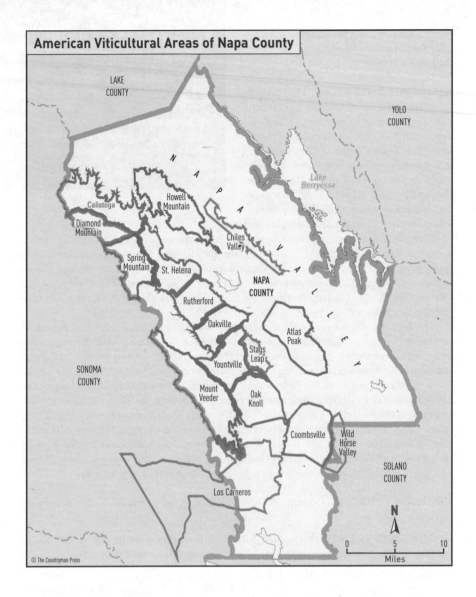

American Viticultural Areas of Napa County

LAKE COUNTY

YOLO COUNTY

Lake Berryessa

Calistoga

Howell Mountain

Diamond Mountain

Chiles Valley

N A P A   V A L L E Y

Spring Mountain

St. Helena

NAPA COUNTY

Rutherford

Oakville

Atlas Peak

SONOMA COUNTY

Stags Leap

Yountville

Mount Veeder

Oak Knoll

Coombsville

Wild Horse Valley

SOLANO COUNTY

Los Carneros

© The Countryman Press

N

0   5   10
Miles

MERLOT (mehr-LOW): Increasingly popular red grape from Bordeaux. Similar to cabernet sauvignon, but softer and more opulent.

PETITE SIRAH (peh-TEET ser-AH): Dark, rich, intense red wine.

PINOT BLANC (PEA-no BLAHNK): In America, it's best known as a less complex version of chardonnay. In France's Alsace region, the grape is used to make dry, crisp white wines.

PINOT NOIR (PEA-no NWAHR): Silky, fruity, dry red grape that is also used to produce French Burgundy.

RIESLING (REEZ-ling): A white grape that produces a delicate wine, medium-bodied and semisweet, with a melony fruit taste. Many of the best hail from Germany.

One of the most stunning (and undiscovered) drives in Wine Country is the stretch from Occidental to Bodega Bay on Coleman Valley Road. (The locals would prefer to keep this hush-hush, so don't tell them we sent you.) This route is the most scenic approach to the bay; you'll see sheep, cows, and the occasional llama. (Take Coleman Valley Road from Occidental to Bodega Bay.)

SANGIOVESE (san-joh-VEY-zeh): The sturdy and often spicy red grape used in Chianti.

SAUVIGNON BLANC (SOH-vihn-yohn BLAHNK): A crisp, light white wine with hints of grass and apples.

SÉMILLON (say-mee-YAWN): A cousin to sauvignon blanc; the two are often blended together.

SYRAH (ser-AH): Ruby-colored grape of the Rhone region in France. Smooth, yet with rich and massive fruit.

VIOGNIER (vee-oh-NYAY): This highly perfumed white wine is surprisingly dry on the palate. Native to the Rhone area of France, it's increasingly chic in California.

ZINFANDEL (ZIN-fan-dell): A spicy and jam-like red wine. A California specialty. Used also to make a blush wine called white zinfandel.

A WINE GLOSSARY No one expects you to be an expert in wine tasting, but here's a crash course on the words of wine, how to pronounce them, and what they mean, should you want to impress the locals.

APPELLATION: A legally defined grape-growing region. Alexander Valley, for example, is an appellation.

BLANC DE BLANCS (blahnk deh BLAHNK): A sparkling wine made from white grapes, usually chardonnay. Delicate and dry.

BLANC DE NOIRS (blahnk deh NWAHR): A sparkling wine made from red grapes, usually pinot noir. Sometimes faintly pink. Fruity but dry.

BLUSH: A pink or salmon-colored wine made from red grapes. Juice from red grapes is actually white. Red wine derives its color from juice left in contact with the grape skin. The longer the contact, the darker the wine.

BRUT (BROOT): The most popular style of sparkling wine. Typically a blend of chardonnay and pinot noir. Dry.

CRUSH: Harvesting and pressing of grapes. The beginning of the winemaking process.

ESTATE BOTTLED: Wines made from vineyards owned or controlled by the winery.

FERMENTATION: The conversion of grape juice into wine, using yeast to change sugar into alcohol.

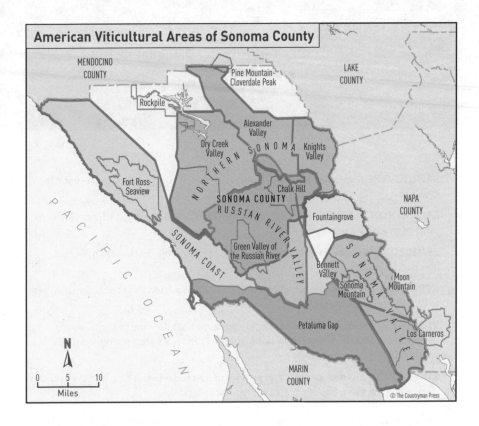

American Viticultural Areas of Sonoma County

MENDOCINO COUNTY

LAKE COUNTY

Pine Mountain-Cloverdale Peak

Rockpile

Alexander Valley

Dry Creek Valley

SONOMA

Knights Valley

NORTHERN

Fort Ross-Seaview

Chalk Hill

SONOMA COUNTY

NAPA COUNTY

RUSSIAN RIVER

Fountaingrove

PACIFIC

SONOMA COAST

Green Valley of the Russian River

VALLEY

SONOMA

Bennett Valley

Sonoma Mountain

Moon Mountain

OCEAN

Petaluma Gap

VALLEY

Los Carneros

N

0 5 10
Miles

MARIN COUNTY

© The Countryman Press

LATE HARVEST: Sweet dessert wine made from grapes left on the vine longer than usual. *Botrytis cinerea* mold forms, dehydrating the grapes and intensifying the sugar content.

MALOLACTIC FERMENTATION: A second fermentation that converts malic acids (which have a tart-apple quality) to softer lactic acids (which lend a buttery quality).

MÉTHODE CHAMPENOISE (meh-TUD sham-pen-WAHZ): Traditional French champagne-making process. Still wine is placed with sugar and yeast into a bottle, which is then sealed. The yeast devours the sugar, creating bubbles. The wine then "sits on the yeast," or ages in the bottle, several years. Finally, the yeast is extracted, and the sparkling wine—never once removed from its original bottle—is ready to drink.

OAK: Wine aged in oak barrels picks up some of the smell and taste of the wood, which also contributes to tannins and long aging. Example: "That chardonnay has too much oak for my taste."

RESERVE: A term traditionally used to mean wine held back, or reserved, for the winery owners, but the meaning has become vague in recent years. It's now sometimes used to mean better-quality grapes or wine aged longer in oak barrels.

RESIDUAL SUGAR: Unfermented sugar that remains in the wine. Wine is considered sweet if it contains more than 0.5 percent residual sugar by weight.

GRAPES RIPENING IN A RUSSIAN RIVER VINEYARD

RIDDLING: Process used to extract yeast from sparkling wine. A laborious process that slowly shakes deposits to the neck of the bottle, where they can be removed without disturbing the wine.

SPARKLING WINE: Generic term for champagne. Technically, real champagne can come only from the Champagne region of France.

TANNINS: Thought to further a wine's ability to age, tannins derive from the skin and stalk of the grapes as well as oak barrels. Wines containing an abundance of tannins (typically young reds) produce a puckery sensation in the mouth and are described as "tannic."

TERROIR: (teh-RWAHR) Literally "soil" in French, refers to the unique quality that locale—geography and climate—imparts to the wine.

VARIETAL: A wine named for the grape variety from which it's made. Example: Chardonnay is a varietal; Bordeaux is not. (Bordeaux is a region in France, but Bordeaux wine can contain a number of varietals: cabernet sauvignon, merlot, etc.)

VINTAGE: The year the grapes for a particular wine are harvested. Nonvintage wines can be blends of different years.

VITICULTURAL AREA: A wine-growing region. The Russian River Valley, for example, is a viticultural area of Sonoma County.

A BRIEF HISTORY OF
NAPA & SONOMA

History repeats itself;
that's the one thing that's wrong with history.
—Clarence Darrow

Why was it, back in school, that the worst, most monotonous teachers taught history? It didn't take long before all those dates and wars and proclamations made your brain glaze over like an Easter ham. Well, that kind of history won't repeat itself here. It helps, of course, that Napa and Sonoma counties have a lively past, busy with fascinating people and places—and, yes, dates and wars and proclamations, too. From the thunderous tremors that raised the land out of a prehistoric sea to the chic winery life of today, Napa and Sonoma counties have been twins—fraternal rather than identical. They share similar origins but have grown into distinctly different siblings.

Natural History

A vast inland sea once spanned Napa and Sonoma counties, the salt water nourishing the soil over millennia. The Mayacamas Mountains as well as coastal and other mountain ranges attest to the land's violent origins. Continental plates have fought for elbow room here for millions of years, colliding and complaining, creating a tectonic furnace of magma and spewing forth volcanoes and towering mountain spines that now divide and surround the two counties.

At 4,344 feet, Mount St. Helena is the area's tallest remnant of the volcanic era. Magma still simmers below the hills, producing the area's powerful geysers and Calistoga's soothing mineral water. Other vivid reminders occur on occasion: earthquakes. The San Andreas Fault runs up the center of Bodega Head on the coast, and the more timid Rodger's Creek Fault sits beneath Santa Rosa and Healdsburg.

When the ancient sea receded, it left bays and lagoons that became fertile valleys. The Napa and Russian rivers formed and for eons roamed back and forth over the face of the Napa and Santa Rosa plains, mixing the soil and volcanic ash. It's hard to imagine a land more made to order for wine. The soil is rich with minerals, and the rocky nature of the land creates excellent drainage. Cool air masses from the Pacific meet the dry desert air from the east, creating a unique climate. Fog chills the mornings, then burns off as the days turn ideally warm; as the sun sets, the crisp air returns. And perhaps most important: rain. Typically, Napa and Sonoma counties are drenched from December through April, and then things dry up until November.

First Inhabitants

Brave the occasionally harrowing California freeway system, and you'll inevitably see this bumper sticker: CALIFORNIA NATIVE. How natives do moan about newcomers!

It's rather silly, of course, because people are such a recent addition to Northern California—5,000 years, in the grand scheme of things, is hardly enough time to unpack.

The earliest "newcomers" crossed the land bridge that once connected Asia and Alaska, and then they wandered south. The first known inhabitants were the Pomo and Miwok tribes in Sonoma and the Wappo in Napa Valley and eastern Sonoma County. It was a plentiful place and allowed for an unhurried way of life; the men hunted and the women gathered berries, mussels, and other foods. Communities thrived. Most were small, but some villages had populations of 1,000 or more.

These early inhabitants gave special names to this land of theirs, names that remain today. Not that historians particularly agree on what the words mean. *Mayacamas* is a Spanish adaptation of a Native American word that means "howl of the mountain lion." *Napa,* depending on which story you believe, is Wappo for "grizzly bear," "fish," or "bountiful place." The first European arrivals were heavily outnumbered. As many as 12,000 Wappo lived between Napa and Clear Lake to the north, and 8,000 Pomo prospered in what are now Sonoma, Lake, and Mendocino counties. That would quickly change.

The Spanish naval officer and explorer Francisco de Bodega y Cuadra stumbled on present-day Sonoma County somewhat by accident in 1775 while piloting his ship the *Sonora* along the coast in search of San Francisco Bay. Rough seas and a damaged skiff prevented Bodega y Cuadra and crew from actually coming ashore, but Bodega's name nonetheless stuck: Bodega Bay. The Russians, however, not the Spanish, were the first to establish an outpost in the area.

By the early 1800s, the Russian-American Company, a private entity supported largely by imperial Russia, was expanding south after the Alaskan fur trade began to play out. In 1812, a colony was established on the Sonoma coast. Exploring the coast-line farther, the Russian-American Company's Ivan Kuskov selected a bluff a few miles to the north and established Fort Ross the following year. The fort became the hub of Russian activity in the region.

The Spanish were determined that their presidio in San Francisco would be the dominant force in the area. Even Mexico declaring independence from Spain in 1822 didn't lessen the importance of the land north of San Francisco. California had been explored and established largely through the mission system, which began in 1769 as a way to civilize the "heathen" Natives and convert them to Catholicism. It was also a way to establish a Spanish presence and, if a mission was successful, add greatly to the wealth and power of the church.

In 1823, Father José Altimira, an ambitious young priest at San Francisco's Mission Dolores, became convinced that a new mission was needed in the northern territory. But church authorities—cautiously considering their waning influence with the new Mexican government—balked, so Altimira turned to the Mexican governor of California, Don Luis Arguello. Seeing an opportunity to thwart the Russians, Arguello approved the idea. Altimira set out that year with a party of 14 soldiers to explore the land north of the San Francisco Bay.

On July 4, 1823, with a makeshift redwood cross, Altimira blessed the mission site in what is now the city of Sonoma, and the Mission San Francisco Solano was founded. It was California's last mission and the only one established under Mexican rule. In the early years, the mission was a great success, and despite having the reputation of being a harsh taskmaster, Altimira converted more than 700 Native Americans. In the fall of 1826, Native laborers staged a violent uprising after bringing in a bountiful harvest. The mission was partially burned, and Father Altimira fled for his life. The mission was rebuilt under another priest's leadership, and by 1834 it was at the height of its prosperity when the Mexican Congress secularized the mission system and returned

BICYCLE ENTHUSIASTS PLAN THEIR ROUTE AT THE SONOMA PLAZA

the acquired wealth to the people. It was the beginning of a new era.

Lieutenant Mariano Guadelupe Vallejo was an enterprising 28-year-old officer given the opportunity of a lifetime. The Mexican government sent him to Sonoma to replace the padres and also to establish a presidio and thereby thwart Russian expansion. Vallejo's ambitions were far greater than even that; he soon became one of the most powerful and wealthy men in California. As commandant general, Vallejo ruled the territory north of San Francisco and eventually set aside more than 100,000 acres for himself. He laid out the town of Sonoma around an eight-acre plaza—the largest in California—and for himself built the imposing Petaluma Adobe in 1836. It would be the largest adobe structure in Northern California and the first crop-producing rancho in the area.

It was Vallejo who pushed for the settlement of Napa and Sonoma counties. He found an ally in frontiersman George Yount. Others had been exploring Napa Valley since 1831, but Yount was the first to explore with the notion of settlement. Befriending the already powerful Vallejo, Yount established the 11,814-acre Rancho Caymus in 1836, now the Yountville area of central Napa County. About that same time, Vallejo was giving Sonoma land grants to family members, who established the rancho predecessors of Santa Rosa, Kenwood, and Healdsburg. Mexican influence continued to expand, particularly after 1839, when the Russians, having wiped out the otter population that was the source of their trading operation, sold Fort Ross.

Otters weren't the only inhabitants facing annihilation. Indian uprisings were not uncommon, and Yount's house in Napa Valley was half home, half fortress. Vallejo occasionally led campaigns against rebellious Indians, but perhaps the most devastating blow came in 1837, when a Mexican corporal inadvertently brought smallpox to Sonoma Valley. This disease all but wiped out Sonoma County's Native population, which had no immunity to the virus.

Bear Flag Revolt

Throughout the 1830s and early 1840s, American settlers streamed into California, lured by stories of free land. Mexican rule, however, denied Americans land ownership, and this led to confrontations. Tensions peaked in 1846 when rumors spread that Mexico was about to order all Americans out of California. At dawn on June 14, some 30 armed horsemen from Sacramento Valley and Napa Valley rode into Sonoma. Thus began the Bear Flag Revolt, 25 eventful days when Sonoma was the capital of the independent Republic of California. Few soldiers still guarded the Sonoma outpost when the riders arrived, and the insurrectionists captured Sonoma without a single shot. A new republic was declared and a makeshift flag was hoisted to the top of a pole in the plaza. Saddle maker Ben Dewel crafted this flag for the new government, using a grizzly bear as the chief symbol. (Some said it looked more like a prized pig.) The Bear Flag Republic had a short reign. In July, an American navy vessel captured the Mexican stronghold of Monterey and claimed California for itself. The Bear Flag boys immediately threw in with the Americans, and four years later, in 1850, California became a state. Eventually, in 1911, the Bear Flag was adopted as the state flag.

A First Glass of Wine

Initially, oats and wheat were the primary crops of Napa and Sonoma counties, and sheep and cattle were also dominant. Father Altimira planted 1,000 vines of mission grapes, a rather coarse variety brought north from Mexico for sacramental wine. Napa's first vineyard was planted in 1838 by Napa's first Euro-American settler, George Yount. He brought mission vines east from Sonoma and made wine for his own use. It wasn't until 1856, when a Hungarian aristocrat named Agoston Haraszthy arrived in Sonoma, that the idea of a wine industry first took root. Haraszthy had attempted vineyards in San Diego and San Mateo and immediately recognized potential in the soil and climate of Sonoma and Napa valleys. Purchasing land and a winery northeast of the plaza, Haraszthy established Buena Vista—which means "beautiful view."

Wineries began to spring up throughout Napa and Sonoma counties, the beginnings of wine dynasties such as Beringer and Inglenook that still exist today. The wine industry was small but growing in the late 1800s, although it shared the land with other important crops: hops, timber, and apples in Sonoma, and wheat in Napa. Winemaking and drinking in those days was anything but the chic activity it is today. Wine was sold almost exclusively in bulk and often wasn't even blended until it reached its selling point. It was vended from barrels in saloons and stores, with customers usually bringing their own containers. Gustave Niebaum of Inglenook and the old Fountaingrove Winery in Santa Rosa were among the first to bottle their own wines. Niebaum was also the first to use vintage dates on his wine and promote "Napa Valley" on his labels.

Winemaking received a major blow late in the century, in the form of phylloxera. A voracious microscopic aphid that infests vine roots, phylloxera first appeared in Europe in the 1860s, devastating vineyards such as Chateau Margaux, Chateau Lafite, and others. Only by grafting their vines to American rootstock were the Europeans able

THE FIRST PUBLIC TOUR OF BERINGER VINEYARDS IN 1934 COURTESY OF BERINGER VINEYARDS

to save their classic wines. While the European wine industry recovered, California wine began to receive its first world notice. Sonoma County—not Napa—had been the undisputed capital of California wine, but fate and phylloxera would change all that. Phylloxera surfaced first in Sonoma Valley in 1875, and it slowly spread north to the Russian River. By 1889, Sonoma County's vineyards were in ruins when the French invited American wines to compete in the World's Fair in Paris. Napa Valley's wines scored well, raising Napa from obscurity to fame. The crown had been snatched by the time phylloxera finally invaded Napa. Growers tried everything to kill the pest, from chemicals to flooding their fields, but nothing worked. Eventually most were forced to pull out their vines. Some planted again, using resistant stock. Others gave up and planted fruit trees.

Looming even larger on the horizon of the wine industry was Prohibition. The temperance movement in the United States had been gaining steam since the turn of the century, and by 1917 a majority of states had outlawed alcohol. The US Congress cinched it with the Volstead Act, which prohibited the manufacture, sale, and transportation of alcoholic beverages except those used for medicinal and sacramental purposes. When Prohibition began, on January 1, 1920, three million useless gallons of wine in Sonoma County alone were left to age in vats. Sebastiani in Sonoma, Beaulieu in Rutherford, and a handful of other wineries survived by making religious wine and "medicinal spirits." But most wineries closed—almost 200 in Sonoma County alone and more than 120 in Napa Valley. By the time Prohibition was repealed in 1933, the Great Depression was on, followed by World War II. It would be some time before the California wine industry recovered. But when it did, it took the world by storm (See *Know the Back Story: The Paris Tasting of 1976*, page 45).

Wine Country Today

Today Napa and Sonoma counties continue to grow, much to the chagrin of longtime residents. Tourism bureaus report that each year, about 4.7 million people travel to Napa Valley, and 7.2 million visit Sonoma County, drawn increasingly by wine, landscape, and climate. Santa Rosa is a small but blossoming metropolis. Highway 29, the main road through Napa Valley, pulses with activity. How different it is from the days of grizzly bears and the Wappo Natives.

As the designation "Wine Country" implies, the wine industry has grown exponentially in the region since the mid-twentieth century. Consider this fact: in 1976 there were 65 wineries in Napa Valley alone, and today there are roughly 400. Despite this growth, Napa and Sonoma remain full of striking natural beauty.

CITY OF NAPA

CITY OF NAPA

The city of Napa is no longer a drive-by city. Long groomed by investors, Napa has arrived. The Japanese restaurant Morimoto Napa was said to be a game-changer under the ownership of quirky celebrity chef Masaharu Morimoto. The Archer Hotel Napa, Kenzo restaurant, and the wine bar Carpe Diem are among the other establishments marking Napa's transformation into a world-class destination city.

Napa, a city of 80,000 at the southern end of Napa Valley, has truly become a cosmopolitan oasis for highbrow food and drink. Drink, we're convinced, is ultimately the big draw in welcoming curious palates to Wine Country. One local boasts that there are 20-plus tasting rooms within walking distance, the largest concentration of such venues in the country. As for restaurants, Napa is a citizen of the world, with downtown eats ranging from Italian to Thai, Vietnamese to French, and everything in between. When traveling, it's key to find your base so you can plan day trips accordingly. Do you thrive in the bustle of downtown, or would you prefer a more bucolic setting? Napa offers both.

✲ To See & Do

ART GALLERIES Napa Valley offers modern art, sculpture gardens, galleries, and more, alone or paired with wine at a winery. **Clos Pegase** and **Cliff Lede Vineyards** are also of interest to art lovers.

✪ ✐ **Di Rosa Preserve** (www.dirosaart.org, 707-226-5991, 5200 Sonoma Highway, Napa, CA 94559; open Wednesday–Saturday 10-4; tours are $15 and $20; children under 12 free; discounts for seniors, students, and the handicapped). Di Rosa Preserve is both an art gallery and a nature preserve. The nationally known collection includes more than 2,000 works of San Francisco Bay Area art, on display in a former stone winery and outdoors, amid 35 acres of rolling meadows in the scenic Carneros District of southern Napa Valley.

✪ **Hess Collection** (www.hesscollection.com, 707-255-1144, 4411 Redwood Road, Napa, CA 94558). This multitasking winery houses the most impressive collection of modern art north of San Francisco.

Artesa Vineyards & Winery (www.artesawinery.com, 707-224-1668, 888-679-9463, 1345 Henry Road, Napa, CA 94559). Artesa is a work of art in itself: built into a hillside, the winery looks like a lost tomb. Contemporary art is on display throughout the building.

BALLOONING **Napa Valley Aloft** (www.nvaloft.com, 855-944-4408, 707-944-4400, 6525 Washington Street, Yountville, CA 94599). Offers champagne flights daily and shuttle service from several local hotels. Sunrise launches daily from the parking lot of V Marketplace in Yountville.

GOLFING **Silverado Country Club and Resort** (www.silveradoresort.com, 707-257-5460, 800-362-4727, 1600 Atlas Peak Road, Napa, CA 94558). This club is private for members and guests. It offers two 18-hole championship courses, par 72; a pro; and a shop. Many consider it to be the best course in Northern California. Expensive.

GALLERY HOPPING IN NAPA VALLEY'S DI ROSA PRESERVE   TIM FISH

SCENIC TRAIN RIDE ✪ **Napa Valley Wine Train** (www.winetrain.com, 707-253-2111, 800-427-4124, 1275 McKinstry Street, Napa, CA 94559). The train itself is a gloriously restored vintage beauty, and the trip through Napa Valley is a charming and scenic adventure. Quattro Vino Tours offer a range of food and wine-centric packages that pair four-course meals with exclusive winery tours. The farm-to-table food is impressive with entrées like braised pork belly and miso-glazed fillet of salmon. A ride should be on everyone's bucket list.

TENNIS **Silverado Country Club and Resort** (www.silveradoresort.com, 707-257-5541, 1600 Atlas Peak Road, Napa, CA 94558). The courts are open to members and guests. Altogether there are 14 courts, three of them lit, and there's a pro on-site.

✳ Wineries

Yes, cabernet sauvignon is king in Napa Valley, but there are other varietals to explore in our detailed lineup of wineries as well. As mentioned, Domaine Carneros is a house of sparkling wine, but it's also well known for its sleek pinot noir. These are the best places to drink in Napa.

  Artesa Vineyards & Winery (www.artesawinery.com, 707-224-1668, 888-679-9463, 1345 Henry Road, Napa, CA 94559; tastings daily 10–5). Artesa began life in 1991 as sparkling-wine specialist Codorniu Napa. Spain's Codorniu has been making bubbly since 1872 but couldn't make a go of it in California. The winery eventually changed its name and switched to still wine: pinot noir, chardonnay, merlot, sauvignon blanc, and syrah. So far, the wines are quite promising. The mystery of the winery begins to unravel as you approach the entrance, a long staircase with a waterfall cascading down the center. Inside, it seems anything but a bunker, with elegant decor, a sunbaked atrium, and spectacular views through grand windows. It's a must for any student of architecture.

Bouchaine Vineyards (www.bouchaine.com, 707-252-9065, 800-654-WINE, www .bouchaine.com, 1075 Buchli Station Road, Napa, CA 94559; tastings daily 10:30–4). Well off the tourist path, this modern, redwood winery sits on the windswept hills of southern Carneros. Built on the vestiges of a winery that dates to the turn of the twentieth century, Bouchaine is a grand redwood barn sitting alone on rolling hills that lead to San Pablo Bay. A fire warms the tasting room on cool Carneros days. Chardonnay and pinot noir are specialties, but the riesling is also tasty.

Covert Wine Estate (www.covertestate.com, 707-224-1959, 15 Chateau Lane, Napa, CA 94558; tastings by appointment). The entire winery is underground, and its tasting room has a rustic feel with buffalo hides and barn wood. Here Bordeaux red wines take the spotlight and are made with a collaborative effort with Mother Nature. Sustainability farming is prized here; the talented Julien Fayard is both the winemaker and managing proprietor at the forefront of best farming practices.

Cuvaison Winery (www.cuvaison.com, 707-942-2455, 1221 Duhig Road, Napa, CA 94559; tastings daily 10–5). *Cuvaison* is a French term that describes the period in which the juice of grapes soaks with the skins and seeds to develop color and flavor. It's an appropriate name because Cuvaison's wines are often boldly flavored. Be sure to try the pinot noir.

Darioush Winery (www.darioush.com, 707-257-2345, 4240 Silverado Trail, Napa, CA 94558; tastings daily 10:30–5). Darioush Khaledi grew up in Iran's Shiraz region and immigrated to the United States in the late 1970s. The passionate wine lover spent the early 1990s searching for a vineyard estate and founded Darioush Winery in 1997. Darioush, which opened in the summer of 2004, is unique in Wine Country: Here East meets West. The winery has classic Persian elements blended with modern European touches, and 90 percent of the stone used in building the winery came from the ancient quarries used by King Darius of ancient Persia. Darioush focuses on the Bordeaux varietals, with small lots of chardonnay, viognier, and Shiraz.

Del Dotto Historic Winery & Caves (www.deldottovineyards.com, 707-963-2134, 1055 Atlas Peak Road, Napa, CA 94558; tastings by appointment). Dave Del Dotto, a pop culture icon of sorts, is best known for his real estate infomercials that aired in the 1980s. He came to the Napa Valley in 1989 to create a new image, and in 1998 he opened this winery, with its Italian ambience. Although varietals here include cabernet franc, merlot, and pinot noir, the winery is best known for its cabernet sauvignon. The tours take you through 120-year-old caves, with opera music piped in. A portion of this underground area dates back to 1885, when Chinese laborers dug a 350-foot cave, using only picks and shovels. Del Dotto has another winery operation in St. Helena, also with caves, but those are less rustic and more opulent, with marble floors and Venetian crystal chandeliers.

✪ **Domaine Carneros** (www.domainecarneros.com, 707-257-0101, 800-716-2788, 1240 Duhig Road, Napa, CA 94581; tastings daily 10–6). The Domaine Carneros winery is an exclamation point along Highway 12, towering on a hilltop surrounded by vineyards. Built in the style of an eighteenth-century French chateau, Domaine Carneros is no everyday winery. Owned in part by champagne giant Taittinger, Domaine Carneros makes a $14 million statement about its French heritage. The terrace of this cream-and-terra-cotta chateau overlooks the lovely rolling hills of the Carneros District. Inside are marble floors and a maple interior crowned with ornate chandeliers.

Etude (www.etudewines.com, 707-257-5782, 1250 Cuttings Wharf Road, Napa, CA 94559; tastings daily 10–4:30; a study of pinot noir tasting by appointment). The winery and tasting room were inaugurated with the 2003 vintage. The masonry buildings, which total about 40,000 square feet, were the former home of a brandy distillery. Founder and winemaker Tony Soter sold the winery to Foster's Group and is no longer

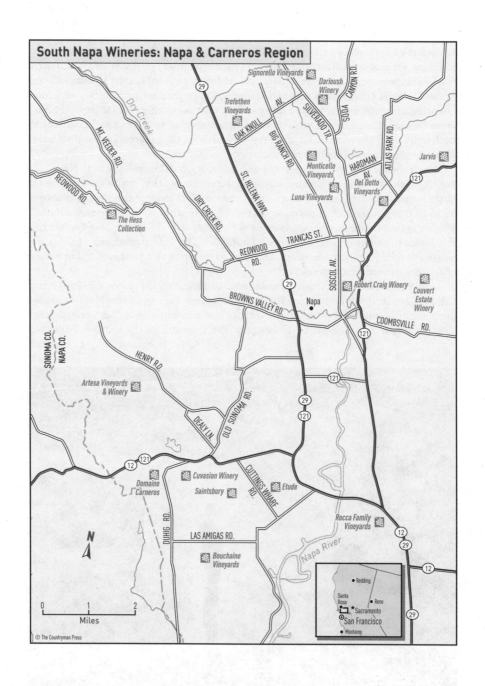

South Napa Wineries: Napa & Carneros Region

Dry Creek

29

Signorello Vineyards

Darioush Winery

Trefethen Vineyards

OAK KNOLL AV.

SILVERADO TR.

SODA CANYON RD.

MT. VEEDER RD.

ATLAS PARK RD.

Jarvis

121

REDWOOD RD.

BIG RANCH RD.

Monticello Vineyards

HARDMAN AV.

Del Dotto Vineyards

Luna Vineyards

ST. HELENA HWY.

DRY CREEK RD.

The Hess Collection

TRANCAS ST.

REDWOOD RD.

29

BROWNS VALLEY RD.

Napa

SOSCOL AV.

Robert Craig Winery

Couvert Estate Winery

121

COOMBSVILLE RD.

SONOMA CO.
NAPA CO.

HENRY RD.

Artesa Vineyards & Winery

121

DEALY LN.

OLD SONOMA RD.

29

121

12

121

Domaine Carneros

DUHIG RD.

Cuvasion Winery

Saintsbury

CUTTINGS WHARF RD.

Etude

Rocca Family Vineyards

12
29

LAS AMIGAS RD.

Napa River

12

Bouchaine Vineyards

N

0   1   2
Miles

Redding

Santa Rosa

Reno

★ Sacramento

San Francisco

Monterey

29

© The Countryman Press

involved. Etude produces a full range of wines, from cabernet sauvignon to pinot gris, but it gets the most attention for its class-act pinot noir.

⊙ **Hess Collection** (www.hesscollection.com, 707-255-1144, 4411 Redwood Road, Napa, CA 94558; tastings daily 10–5). If there's a gallery in Wine Country that deserves the title "museum," it's the Hess Collection. Swiss entrepreneur Donald Hess transformed the old Mont La Salle Winery into an ultramodern showcase for his two great passions: art and wine. The art collection spans the upper two floors and features the works of internationally known artists such as Francis Bacon, Robert Motherwell, and Frank Stella. A mix of paintings and sculpture, the works are provocative and often haunting, although humor plays a role too. Stop in at the tasting room to explore Hess's other passion. Hess concentrates on two wines: cabernet sauvignon and chardonnay, both well made. The chardonnays are stylish and oaky; the cabernets have great bones (structure) and a good concentration of fruit.

Jarvis (www.jarviswines.com, 707-255-5280, 2970 Monticello Road, Napa, CA 94559; tastings and tours by appointment). Jarvis boasts that it was the first winery in the world to put its entire facility underground. That's right—the winery is housed amid 46,000 square feet of roaming caves, complete with an underground waterfall. When digging the cave, workers found a spring that they decided to incorporate into the design to ensure an adequate level of humidity. The winery produces a full slate of wines, including mainstream cabernet as well as lesser-known petit verdot, but its best efforts are cab and chardonnay.

Luna Vineyards (www.lunavineyards.com, 707-255-2474, 2921 Silverado Trail, Napa, CA 94558; tastings daily 10:30–5:30). In 1995, George Vare and Mike Moon launched Luna, which means "moon" in Italian, with an intent to focus on Italian varietals such as pinot grigio and sangiovese. In keeping with their Italian theme, they built their

AT THE HESS COLLECTION, ART AND WINE ARE UNDER ONE ROOF   TIM FISH

V intner Donald Hess founded the winery called the Hess Collection, and the collectables? Fine wine and fine art. Hess, now retired, had an interesting procurement strategy. It typically involved a sleepless night. If he lost sleep over a piece, he was apt to buy it because he knew that it moved him (www.hesscollection.com).

winery in the California style of Craftsman architecture, with hints of Tuscan influence. Luna also produces merlot and cabernet. Don't miss the pinot grigio; it's as tasty as pinot grigios that hail from Italy.

Monticello Vineyards (www.corleyfamilynapavalley.com, 707-253-2802, ext. 18, 800-743-6668, 4242 Big Ranch Road, Napa, CA 94558; tastings daily 10–4:30). If the visitor center of this winery looks familiar, check the nickel in your pocket. It's modeled after Thomas Jefferson's Virginia home, Monticello. A Jefferson scholar, owner Jay Corley paid tribute in this way to one of America's first wine buffs. Corley began as a grape grower in the early 1970s and started making wine in 1980. Cabernet sauvignon has of late surpassed chardonnay as the winery's specialty. The cabernet is generally well structured and elegant.

Robert Craig Wine Cellars (www.robertcraigwine.com, 707-252-2250 ext. 1, tasting room: 625 Imperial Way, Napa, CA 94559; tastings by appointment). For most wine fans, visiting this boutique cabernet sauvignon producer was out of the question until Craig opened this tasting room in downtown Napa. Craig is a Napa veteran who launched his own label in 1992, and he makes three cabernets: a Bordeaux-style blend called Affinity and two wines made from the rocky slopes above the valley, Howell Mountain and Mount Veeder. The mountain wines are intense, concentrated, and rich. The tasting room is an intimate storefront.

Rocca Family Vineyards (www.roccawines.com, 707-257-8467, 129 Devlin Road, Napa, CA 94558; tastings by appointment). The vintners—Mary Rocca and her husband, Eric Grigsby—both have farming in their roots. Mary spent plenty of time in her mother's vegetable garden in Northern California, while Eric was the son of a Tennessee farmer. Both are enamored with nature and equally fond of history. The tasting room here is a historic old Victorian built by the late General Vallejo, and the outside patio is a great place to sip and take in the view of the San Pablo Bay. It all began when the couple found a 21-acre vineyard in the heart of Napa Valley, and after growing grapes, they couldn't resist the temptation of creating their own wines. They focus on red wine varietals—including cabernet, merlot, syrah, and red blends. Their four children each grace a label, and Mary likes to joke that the kids are only quiet on the label.

AT JARVIS, THE MAJORITY OF THE WINERY IS UNDERGROUND IN A CAVE COURTESY OF JARVIS

Saintsbury (www.saintsbury.com, 707-252-0592, 1500 Los Carneros Avenue, Napa, CA 94559; tastings by appointment Monday–Saturday). David Graves and Richard Ward came to Carneros in search of Burgundy. Enthused about the district's potential for Burgundian grapes chardonnay and pinot noir, in 1981 the duo formed Saintsbury, named for the author of the classic *Notes on a Cellar-Book*. With its unassuming design, weathered redwood siding, and steeply sloped roof, the winery fits snugly amid the grapevines in this rural area. We have a soft spot for Saintsbury's moderately priced Garnet pinot noir, and its Carneros pinot and chardonnay are typically lush and complex.

Signorello Vineyards (www.signorellovineyards.com, 707-255-5990, 800-982-4229, 4500 Silverado Trail, Napa, CA 94558; tastings daily by appointment). This winery's tasting room and business offices burned down in the wildfires of 2017, but both were rebuilt. It continues to garner attention for its vibrant chardonnay and semillon, a cousin to sauvignon blanc. Its stable of reds includes a powerful cabernet sauvignon as well as merlot and pinot noir. Ray Signorello's first vintage was 1985, and he prefers a low-key, natural approach to winemaking.

Starmont Winery & Vineyards (www.starmontwinery.com, 707-252-8001, 1451 Stanly Lane, Napa, CA 94559; tastings daily 10-5). Sipping through the Starmont wines is a great way to explore the Carneros. This region, at the base of Napa Valley and Sonoma County, is world renowned for its stellar chardonnay and pinot noir because of its growing conditions: foggy mornings and cool afternoon bay breezes. The Starmont chardonnay and pinot are the standouts, but the lineup also includes cabernet sauvignon, merlot, sauvignon blanc, and rosé. The Starmont story is an impressive one, a growing brand that split off from the mother ship to become its own winery. It began as part of Merryvale, a quality wine at an affordable price that over-delivered. But when Starmont grew from a single wine to a full-fledged brand, it moved out of Merryvale's St. Helena digs in 2005 and into a portion of the historic Stanly Ranch. It's a certified Napa Green Winery, clearly a draw for millennials who keep an eye on corporate environmental doings.

Trefethen Vineyards (www.trefethen.com, 707-255-7700, 866-895-7696, 1160 Oak Knoll Avenue, Napa, CA 94558; tastings daily 10–4:30). Shaded by a 100-year-old oak, this winery was built in 1886 by Hamden W. McIntyre, the architect behind Inglenook and Greystone Cellars. The Trefethen family bought the winery in 1968 and restored it, painting the redwood beauty a pumpkin orange. Tours highlight the McIntyre-designed, three-level gravity-flow system, in which grapes are crushed on the third floor, juice is fermented on the second, and wine is aged in barrels on the ground level. Since its first vintage in 1973, Trefethen has made its name with chardonnay.

WINERY COLLECTIVES These tasting rooms allow guests "one-stop sipping," pouring brands from several wineries.

✪ **Gustavo** (www.gustavowine.com, 707-257-6796, 1021 McKinstry Street, Napa, CA 94559). Gustavo Brambila brings you his signature '06 Barbera, which is an Italian varietal, as well as offerings from several other small producers. Gustavo serves as winemaker. Gustavo is one of the characters in the 2008 film *Bottle Shock,* set during the famous Judgment of Paris tasting in 1976. He is portrayed by the actor Freddy Rodriguez.

✪ **Vintners Collective** (www.vintnerscollective.com, 707-255-7150, 1245 Main Street, Napa, CA 94559). This is the crème de la crème of collectives. It's housed in a historic building and offers a range of sought-after wines, including those by Azur, D Cubed, Ancien Wines, and Flanagan. Here more than 20 of the most celebrated boutique producers are available under one roof. Open daily 11 a.m. to 7 p.m.

✳ Lodging

Andaz Napa Hotel (www.napa.andaz
.hyatt.com, 707-687-1234, 1450 First
Street, Napa, CA 94559; $$$–$$$$). This
hotel in the heart of downtown Napa
serves as an ambassador to Wine Coun-
try, giving guests valuable advice on the
best places to go, eat, and sip. It is close
to tasting rooms and not far from the
Oxbow Public Market. For ease and com-
fort, there's a restaurant on the prem-
ises—the Andaz Farmers Table, which
serves American cuisine. There are 141
guest rooms and suites on five floors,
and the hotel has some great perks: On
the second floor, there's a terrace with
cabanas and a fire pit. And intrepid
explorers can unwind by means of a com-
plimentary wine tasting and access to
the fitness center.

 ✿ **Archer Hotel Napa** (www.archer
hotel.com/napa, 707-690-9800, 855-437-
9100, 1230 First Street, Napa, CA 94559;
$$$–$$$$). This hotel is a large boutique
property nestled amid wine tasting
rooms, restaurants, and wine bars in the
heart of downtown Napa, making it a
prime spot for those looking for an urban
experience while exploring Napa Val-
ley. The Archer also is home to Charlie

Palmer Steak, which serves hefty serv-
ings of beef, as well as seafood and veg-
gies procured from the region. The hotel
has 183 rooms, and 40 suites, many with
private balconies and fireplaces. Wine
and food enthusiasts will appreciate the
offerings at The Archer. Each room has
a wine cooler and a refreshment bar, and
a rooftop bar offers 360-degree views of
Napa Valley. It has fire pits and an all-
day menu serving food and cocktails.
Best of all, if you need to recover from a
long day of imbibing and indulging, you
can book a treatment at the on-site spa.

A SOAK IN THE TUB, WINE COUNTRY-STYLE, AT ANDAZ
NAPA HOTEL COURTESY OF ANDAZ NAPA HOTEL

ROOFTOP COCKTAILS ANYONE? HERE'S A PEEK AT THE ARCHER HOTEL IN DOWNTOWN NAPA COURTESY OF THE ARCHER HOTEL

✪ **Beazley House** (www.beazleyhouse .com, 707-257-1649, 800-559-1649, 1910 First Street, Napa, CA 94559; $$$–$$$$). One of Napa's first B&Bs, this shingled, circa 1902 mansion has six charming and cozy rooms. Even more desirable is the carriage house, built in 1983, with a fireplace and two-person spa standard in each of its five guest rooms. The main house is a beauty; the dining and common rooms have coved ceilings and oak floors with mahogany inlays. The Beazleys offer a warm welcome at breakfast, and Carol—a former nurse—concocts healthful, tasty fare served buffet style.

♂ **Carneros Resort and Spa** (www .carnerosresort.com, 707-299-4900, 888-400-9000, 4048 Sonoma Highway, Napa, CA 94559; $$$$). This inn has a sun-washed, farm-style appeal, and it's quite a spread. It has two restaurants on the premises—FARM and the Boon Fly Café—and both have earned high marks from food critics. There's also a wedding and events venue called The Arbor, and the inn has become quite a popular spot for weddings with a range of bridal and elopement packages.

For the athletes and yoga enthusiasts, there's a 3,000-square-foot fitness center, two pools, hot tubs, and an expanded spa with imported mud from Italy for treatments. Its 86 rooms and 10 suites have been upgraded, and if you have a pooch, you're welcome to bring him or her along. The crown jewel of the accommodations, of course, is the expansive house, for those traveling with a group. This 2,400-square-foot, 3-bedroom home has 16-foot ceilings and a fireplace, great for entertaining a group of friends. One of the packages includes a group cooking class with an executive chef and a sommelier. With so much on its sprawling grounds, guests can enjoy a restorative stay at this resort with everything they need at their fingertips.

✪ **Cottages of Napa Valley** (www .napacottages.com, 707-252-7810, 866-900-7810, 1012 Darms Lane, Napa, CA 94558; $$$–$$$$). These cozy cottages are the ultimate in private getaways. Each of the eight master-suite cottages' 450 to 600 square feet of space has a fireplace, a whirlpool tub, a kitchenette, a deck, and an outdoor fireplace. Spa services include a relaxing, in-room massage. Breakfast—delivered to your front porch—is in a basket featuring pastries from Yountville's Bouchon Bakery.

Churchill Manor (www.churchill manor.com, 707-253-7733, 800-799-7733, 485 Brown Street, Napa, CA 94559; $$$–$$$$). From the moment you spy Churchill Manor, you'll know it's special. A National Historic Landmark, the inn was built in 1889 on a lush acre, and it has the Greek Revival columns, wraparound verandas, and grand parlors of days gone by. If you like antiques, this is your place. Hand-painted Delft tiles, 24-carat-gold trim, and an antique beaded opera gown are among the rich details in the rooms. A generous gourmet buffet-style breakfast is served in the marble-tiled solarium, where wine and cheese are offered in the evening.

🍴 **Elm House Inn, Best Western** (www .bestwestern.com, 707-255-1831, 800-780-7234, 800 California Boulevard, Napa, CA 94559; $$–$$$). This wood-shingled inn is modern but done in the style of an old European village. Italian-marble

A SCRUMPTIOUS BREAKFAST AT THE BEAZLEY HOUSE
COURTESY OF BEAZLEY HOUSE

fireplaces adorn some of the 22 rooms (all with private baths), and each has a TV, a phone, and a stocked refrigerator. An elevator makes the inn wheelchair accessible. A complimentary breakfast buffet is served in the courtyard when

THE BEAZLEY HOUSE HAS GREAT CURB APPEAL COURTESY OF BEAZLEY HOUSE

weather permits. The inn is located at a busy intersection.

Embassy Suites Napa Valley (www.embassysuites.com, 707-253-9540, 1075 California Boulevard, Napa, CA 94559; $$$–$$$$). All 205 rooms in this hotel are two-room suites with contemporary furnishings, equipped for light cooking with mini-refrigerators, coffeemakers, and microwave ovens. A daily complimentary full breakfast is cooked to order, and complimentary cocktails are served for two hours each evening. Small pets are allowed for a fee in certain rooms. This is an elegant, business-class hotel that's also ideal for leisure travelers.

Hennessey House (www.hennessey house.com, 707-226-3774, 1727 Main Street, Napa, CA 94559; $$–$$$$). This home—on the National Register of Historic Places—is a stunning example of a perfectly restored 1889 Eastlake-style Queen Anne. The main house has six rooms, all appointed with antiques and private baths. Four additional rooms are located in the carriage house. A full breakfast is served in the dining room, with its restored, hand-painted stamped-tin ceiling. The neighborhood is urban but quiet and is a short walk to downtown Napa.

🍴 **Hotel Indigo** (www.hotelindigo.com, 707-253-9300, 4195 Solano Avenue, Napa, CA 94558; $$). This former Best Western offers rooms that are modern and clean, with rates that begin at $120 for a 300-square-foot room and extend up to $1,000 for a suite of 500 square feet. The hotel has 115 rooms, four suites, a full gym, a pool, and an eclectic in-house restaurant called Cupa. North of downtown Napa, the hotel is part of the British InterContinental Hotels Group, but it manages to offer a boutique experience at a fair price. It has been credited for over-delivering, reeling in rave reviews for giving great advice to travelers who want to explore the local haunts—wineries, shops, and bars. For those in pinstripes: This hotel is particularly well suited for the business traveler.

Its business center is open 24/7, and it has a computer available, as well as a fax, a scanner, and a copy machine.

☀ **La Belle Epoque** (www.labelle epoque.com, 707-257-2161, 1386 Calistoga Avenue, Napa, CA 94559; $$$–$$$$). The stained-glass windows and fine Victorian furniture in this 10-room inn will transport you to another time and place. Built in 1893, this gingerbread beauty is near downtown, with its abundance of new restaurants and activities. Rates include gourmet breakfast served in the dining room, on the sunporch, or delivered to the room, a private wine cellar, hosted wine reception, and tasting passes to wineries. And if you're so inclined, enjoy a massage in the inn's secluded garden or your own room.

⚥ ☀ **Meritage Resort And Spa** (www.meritagecollection.com, 844-283-4588, 875 Bordeaux Way, Napa, CA 94558; $$$–$$$$). The most unique feature of the Meritage is its 22,000-square-foot underground cave, which includes a spa, a banquet facility, and a wine-tasting bar. Aboveground, the Meritage has 158 rooms, a vineyard with walking trails, and even a chapel that seats 60 for daily masses. It also manages nearby properties, which brings its room count to 460-plus. A key amenity for gatherings is the resort's estate cave that can accommodate 200 for events, including weddings. The business center offers high-speed Internet and conference and banquet rooms. An on-premises, award-winning gourmet restaurant, Siena, with Tuscan-inspired decor, features California cuisine with an Italian twist—great pastas and pizzas.

☀ ⚥ **Milliken Creek Inn & Spa** (www.millikencreekinn.com, 707-255-1197, 1815 Silverado Trail, Napa, CA 94558; $$$–$$$$). Milliken Creek is located at the base of Wine Country. Nestled between the Silverado Trail and the Napa River, the 12 rooms of this boutique luxury inn, which combines the amenities of a large resort and the intimacy of a B&B, beckon you to relax and unwind. This

A MASSAGE IN A CAVE?

The underground spa at Spa Terra of the Meritage Resort (www.meritagecollection.com) is undeniably unique. Treatment rooms, some reserved for couples, are in "the hushed serenity of the cave," with a wine tasting bar within reach. Men's and women's private lounges feature steam grottos and water walls. Services include massages and body treatments, facials, and manicures. One example is "The Duetto," which includes—first and foremost—a glass of bubbly, a 50-minute Target Massage (pinpointing areas of stress), and a 50-minute Organic Bliss Facial Massage for $250.

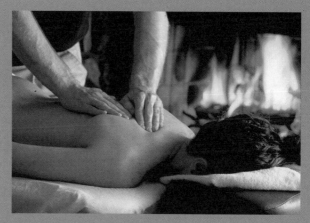

SPA TERRA PAMPERS A GUEST WITH A FULL BODY MASSAGE   COURTESY OF SPA TERRA

place is set up to pamper: spa and massage services, yoga, private wine tastings, breakfast in bed, Italian linens, and Napa River views. Great for a romantic getaway. The inn is now part of the Four Sisters Inns group.

🐾 **Napa River Inn** (www.napariverinn .com, 707-251-8500, 877-251-8500, 500 Main Street, Napa, CA 94559; $$$–$$$$). Once a mill, later a warehouse, this lovely old brick building right on the Napa River is now a luxury boutique hotel. The inn was built in the 1800s and has the charm of a fine B&B but the privacy of a hotel. It's also pet friendly. Located in the heart of Napa's downtown, the inn is not far from the historic Napa Valley Opera House and two of the city's top restaurants: Angele and Celadon. Guests receive a complimentary breakfast at Sweetie Pies Bakery, and the hotel also offers personalized complimentary breakfast delivery.

Napa Valley Marriott (www.napa valleymarriott.com, 707-253-8600, 800-228-9290, 3425 Solano Avenue, Napa, CA 94558; $$$–$$$$). With 275 rooms and suites, the Marriott is one of the largest inns in the valley. Nicer than a motel, it's not quite a hotel, either, but it's comfortably appointed and has the usual services you would expect from a chain hotel. On the north edge of the city, it's convenient to most of the valley. There is a spa, a heated outdoor pool and whirlpool, and complimentary daily wine tasting.

River Terrace Inn (www.riverterrace inn.com, 707-320-9000, 866-627-2386, 1600 Soscol Avenue, Napa, CA 94559; $$–$$$$). This three-story hotel, with an exterior design that's both stylish and rustic, appeals to vacationers and business travelers alike. The 106 rooms and 28 junior suites all have a touch of luxury, with crown moldings, ceiling fans, and granite bathrooms with whirlpool tubs. Most of the rooms have balconies, many of which overlook the river.

♻ **Senza Hotel & Resort** (www .senzahotel.com, 707-253-0337, 800-253-9203, 4066 Howard Lane, Napa, CA 94558; $$$–$$$$). The interesting twist about this hotel is its tie to diplomacy.

SENZA is co-owned by Kathryn Hall, the former ambassador to Austria under former presidents Bill Clinton and George W. Bush. Kathryn and her husband Craig are also the vintners of Hall and Walt wineries in Napa Valley. When they purchased the former La Residence in 2006, they wanted to transform the bed-and-breakfast into a luxury hotel and give their guests a glimpse of Wine Country living beyond their tasting rooms. It absolutely delivers, with some surprising perks. Among its accommodations, SENZA offers a piece of Napa history with the Parker Mansion, a renovated three-story 1870s home. The property also sports a spa and plenty of contemporary art to peruse along the pathways to the pool, cellar, or dining room. Of course, for people who travel with their four-legged friends, the pet-friendly policy may be the most attractive feature.

AN UPSCALE BEDROOM AT NAPA'S SENZA HOTEL

This is a gorgeous piece of property with plenty of vineyard views. Here you are truly amid the vines.

✪ Silverado Resort (www.silverado resort.com, 707-257-0200, 800-532-0500, 1600 Atlas Peak Road, Napa, CA 94558; $$$$). Golf is king at Silverado. Its two courses are prized in Napa Valley. With more than 750 regular members, the resort is constantly bustling with activity. The main house, an imposing mansion built just after the Civil War, was remodeled in 1992. Today, there are 390 rooms scattered over the 1,200-acre estate. All rooms are comfortably furnished to feel like home, and the kitchenettes contain just about everything you need for light cooking. The concierge staff is perhaps the best in the valley.

✪ Westin Verasa Napa (www.westin napa.com, 707-257-1800, 888-627-7169, 1314 McKinstry Street, Napa, CA 94559; $$$). The hotel has 180 spacious guest rooms and suites—studios, one-bedroom, and two-bedroom—many with kitchenettes. This kind of condo hotel has been around for decades in resort towns, but visitors are just starting to see more of them in Northern California. The Westin provides views of the Napa River or historic downtown Napa. There is an outdoor heated pool and a gym.

✳ Where to Eat

Angele (www.angelerestaurant.com, 707-252-8115, 540 Main Street, Napa, CA 94558; $$$; cuisine: French). This French-style bistro, located in a former boathouse on Napa's booming riverfront, has an elegant but unstuffy atmosphere, with concrete floors and walls and rough-hewn wood rafters. There are some serious players behind it; owners include Claude Rouas, who built Auberge du Soleil, and Bettina Rouas, the former manager of The French Laundry. The menu is classic to a tee, with filet mignon, duck, roasted chicken, and veal chop. The wine list is modest but deftly

WHY NOT DRAW A HOT BATH AND POUR YOURSELF A GLASS OF WINE AT THE SENZA HOTEL?

selected, with a fine grouping of French and Napa wines.

✪ **Azzurro Pizzeria e Enoteca** (www .azzurropizzeria.com, 707-255-5552, 1260 Main Street, Napa, CA 94559; $; cuisine: Italian). This restaurant offers tasty Italian food at a great price. Azzurro is a good idea for lunch or for those much-needed casual dinners during your Wine Country vacation. Located in a storefront in downtown Napa, Azzurro has a smart, functional atmosphere and limited side-walk dining. There's a short list of salads, pasta, and pizzas, and so far, we haven't found a dud on the menu. The roasted mushroom pizza with taleggio cheese and thyme is addictive, and salads such as Caesar and spinach with goat cheese and dried fruit vinaigrette are light but flavorful. The wine list is small but well suited to the menu.

✪ **Bistro Don Giovanni** (www .bistrodongiovanni.com, 707-224-3300, 4110 Howard Lane, Napa, CA 94558; $$–$$$; cuisine: Italian). The seduction begins the moment you approach Bistro Don Giovanni. Inside, the setting is romantic, a high-ceilinged room done in warm tones, white linen, and modern art with vineyard views through tall windows. Bistro Don Giovanni is Napa's most popular Italian restaurant, and the menu includes the requisite salads, pasta, and risotto as well as pizza from a wood-burning oven. Salads are first-rate, and the antipasto is a generous and flavorful plate. House specialties include

silk handkerchiefs (thin sheets of pasta with pesto), a robust braised lamb shank, and fillet of salmon pan-seared with a thin crust to protect its moist and flaky heart. The wine list is from Napa and Italy mostly and rather pricey. Service is attentive. This place is a find. Don't miss it!

Boon Fly Café, at Carneros Resort and Spa (www.boonflycafe.com, 707-299-4870, 4048 Sonoma Highway, Napa, CA 94559; $$–$$$; cuisine: California). Location is this café's major appeal—it's in the heart of rural Carneros Wine Country—but the food is stylish and hearty, perfect for a wine-tasting lunch or dinner in shorts or jeans. The interior is high-tech-meets-retro-California, a barn setting with towering ceiling, exposed metal beams, tin tabletops, and wood floors. The food shares similar sensibilities: modern yet full of comfort, stocked with artsy BLTs, Kobe burgers, chicken and waffles, and towering stacks of French fries and onion rings. Breakfast is rich enough to feed a farmhand, with eggs Benedict, "Green Eggs and Ham" (special ingredient: lemon leek cream), breakfast flatbread, and the like. The wine list is modest and focused largely on wines from the surrounding Carneros region, and the prices are generally a steal.

Bounty Hunter Wine Bar & Smokin' BBQ (www.bountyhunterwinebar.com,

THIS DELECTABLE PIE CAME STRAIGHT OUT OF THE PIZZA OVEN AT BISTRO DON GIOVANNI

THIS PLACE REELS IN 20-SOMETHINGS WITH CHAMPAGNE, WINE, BEER, AND CIDER

707-226-3976, 975 First Street, Napa, CA 94559; $$–$$$; cuisine: California). This wine bar has a comfortably eccentric atmosphere, with exposed brick walls, a towering, tin-covered ceiling, and various bear and ram heads decorating the walls. Wine is the key player here, but the food hardly plays second fiddle. There are more than 30 wines available by the glass, and many come in themed flights of three. The wine list is both international and domestic, and there are about 400 selections, ranging from bargains to major investments. The menu is wine friendly, as you might expect, ranging from small plates of olives and charcuterie to beer can chicken and ribs.

✪ **Cadet Wine Bar** (www.cadetbeer andwinebar.com, 707-224-4400, 930 Franklin Street, Napa, CA 94559; $$). This is the brainchild of co-founders Colleen Fleming and Aubrey Bailey, game to celebrate beer and wine from California and beyond. There is a definite pro-California stance at this sleek, modern wine bar, a hub that reels in plenty of 20-somethings. The revolving menu often includes rare champagne among its wine, beer, and cider picks. The Belgian beers are particularly appealing, and foodies will be delighted with the house specialty—the Cadet Cubano—ham and pork loin on a roll with spicy pickles. One of the coolest aspects of this spot is the

way the founders want their guests to rub shoulders with the next generation of producers—vintners, brewers, and chefs. In fact, they invite the experts in to take over the joint to host talks and tastings. These events highlight a range of bottlings that include Oregon wines, champagne, and flights from Austria and Hungary. The Cadet is also happy to host a party for people looking for a sassy backdrop for a gathering. The Cadet has been called the hippest joint in all of Napa because it plays to boutique producers—both locally and internationally—and gives a retro nod to the record player. Here you can play an album on the bar's record player with each bottle you buy.

✪ **Carpe Diem Wine Bar** (www.carpe diemwinebar.com, 707-224-0800, 1001 Second Street, Napa, CA 94559). A hip and friendly sipping and dining environment that gets great reviews from locals and visitors alike. The wine list is weighted to California offerings, and the menu features light fare: artisanal cheeses and charcuterie, soups and salads, grilled flatbreads, and a selection of signature dishes.

Celadon (www.celadonnapa.com, 707-254-9690, 500 Main Street, Napa, CA 94559; $$$; cuisine: California). Celadon masters the art of balance better than most restaurants. Its food is top-rate, its service is intelligent and well paced, and its decor is refreshing. Celadon's most impressive offering is its food. Recommended dishes include the ahi tuna and the Moroccan-inspired braised lamb shank. The wine list has a good selection by the glass, and prices across the board are reasonable. The restaurant's name refers to a type of pottery with a pale green glaze, and throughout this smart restaurant, there are touches of pale green, pleasing and subtle.

Charlie Palmer Steaks (www .charliepalmersteak.com/locations/ napa, 707-819-2500, 1260 First Street, Napa, CA 94559; $$$–$$$$; cuisine: steakhouse). Celebrity chef and Healdsburg resident Charlie Palmer knows a thing or two about high style, and this glitzy spot in the brand-new Archer Hotel Napa delivers glamour along with its $100, four-ounce A5 Wagyu steak sourced from the Miyazaki Prefecture of Japan. It's a see-and-be-seen-in-the-dark, wood-and-stone-column-decorated spot that gets loud when busy (which it always is). All-day menus are ambitious—Pig Ear Pad Thai for dinner, anyone? It also offers well-crafted signatures like a mountain of donuts and bottomless mimosas at brunch, or a supper of Snake River Farms strip steak dressed in apple-horseradish cream. Seafood is exceptional as well, such as pan-roasted black cod dressed in chorizo-white bean bouillabaisse. The polished staff has expert knowledge of the lengthy Cal-centric wine list, guiding guests to wines that work best with clever dishes, such as short rib pastrami laced with candied lemon and curried almond. And while expense account guests are pampered, it is worth noting that Palmer caters to locals, too, offering friendly touches like complimentary corkage on the first bottle of Napa wine and a bargain happy hour that brings in the fashionable set.

Cole's Chop House (www.coleschop house.com, 707-224-6328, 1122 Main Street, Napa, CA 94559; $$$$; cuisine: steakhouse). Cole's Chop House is slick.

A quiet storefront from the outside, inside it's a bustling, cosmopolitan nightclub with a jazz trio playing in the balcony. This place has a pulse. Located inside a circa 1886 building with loft-like 35-foot ceilings, it's a big restaurant with lots of tables and lots of people, but the service is seamless. Besides, Napa is cabernet country, and that's a wine that demands a slab o' meat. The New York and porterhouse steaks are all top-of-the-line, dry-aged Chicago. The à la carte side dishes are family-style huge, so two people can share. The wine list has a good selection of half-bottles and more than 50 offerings by the glass. There's a good showing of French wines and some older California library wines.

Farm at Carneros (www.farmat carneros.com, 707-299-4880, 4048 Sonoma Highway, Napa, CA 94559; $$–$$$$; cuisine: American). Farm, the restaurant at Carneros Resort, is rustic-chic. The building is barnlike, with a high-pitched ceiling and exposed rafters, but it also has a contemporary feel, with clean lines, numerous windows, and dramatic lighting. As for the food, it's quite good.

A NIGHT CAP AT CARPE DIEM WINE BAR IS A FINE END TO A GREAT DAY IN NAPA VALLEY

Farm also has a decent wine list, focusing on Napa and Sonoma bottlings, and it has 21 wines by the glass. The bar is upscale with an urban feel. Best of all, the resort offers a place to stay after dinner (see listing under *Lodging*).

✪ **Kenzo** (kenzonapa.com, 707-294-2049, 1339 Pearl Street, Napa, CA 94559; $$$$; cuisine: Japanese). Kenzo and Natsuko Tsujimoto also own the beyond-opulent, $100 million Kenzo Estate winery in Napa, and they take the same meticulous approach with this upscale restaurant. No decor detail is overlooked, from the perfect handcrafted pottery and chopstick rests to the minimalist but stunning teakwood, clear maple, and stone dining room design. Guests can plan to pay a pretty penny ($225 per person) for the pristine multicourse kaiseki dinners, and the world-class cuisine is worth it. Fish comes from Tokyo's Tsukiji Market, to be pampered in treatments like straw-smoked Chiba Golden Eye snapper owan (dashi broth), or rice cracker–crusted, bekko-an–glazed Aomori sawara (mackerel) dusted in shichimi pepper. The beef is true Satsuma Wagyu, the salmon roe and scallops come from Hokkaido, and meals start the authentic Japanese way, with hassun, an assortment of seasonal tiny bites, such as exquisite sesame tofu with wasabi gelee, sweetened kumquat, cherry blossom carrot, and mizuna. There are just 10 seats in the 400-square-foot dining room, but the intimate sushi bar is a more relaxed choice, and the private dining room to the side offers another sushi bar. This is also a rare opportunity to enjoy Kenzo's remarkable wines, if your wallet is ready—the Murasaki Bordeaux blend, for example, is an eye-popping $70 per glass.

✪ **The Kitchen Collective** (www.kitchencollective.club, 707-690-9381, 1650 Soscol Avenue, Napa, CA 94559). It bills itself as "America's first urban cooking club in the heart of Napa Valley." The idea is to appeal to foodies with an epicurean experience they can only dream about. Members have incredible support; they get to cook in a fully-stocked, state-of-the-art kitchen, with coaching from a professional chef. But you can still partake in the fun, even if you're a non-member. There are plenty of themed events for the public like Pizza Night with pies made in wood-burning ovens, and A Taste of Italy, with an Italian menu of antipasta, braised short ribs, fettuccini, and more.

✪ **La Toque** (www.latoque.com, 707-257-5157, 1314 McKinstry Street, Napa, CA 94559; $$$–$$$$; cuisine: French). La Toque is a popular restaurant because it's more accessible than The French Laundry and easier on the wallet, and yet the experience is sublime. Chef Ken Frank learned to cook in France, and he's a genius in the kitchen. If you can afford the splurge, opt for the Chef's Table Menu. Frank offers nine courses, six savory dishes, cheese, and two desserts. The wine list is smart and the service is nimble. Located in the upscale Westin Verasa Napa (see listing under *Lodging*), La Toque has a dress code and it doesn't permit shorts, flip flops, or ball caps. But in the hotel lobby, you'll experience the casual side of Frank's cooking at Bank Café & Bar.

✪ **Morimoto Napa** (www.morimotonapa.com, 707-252-1600, 610 Main Street, Napa, CA 94559; $$$$; cuisine: contemporary Japanese). Morimoto Napa is a hot spot. The celebrity chef Masaharu Morimoto is known to millions as the star of TV's *Iron Chef* and *Iron Chef America,* and he has garnered critical acclaim for his seamless integration of Western and Japanese ingredients. The restaurant serves contemporary Japanese cuisine and includes a sushi bar, a lounge, and outdoor dining overlooking the River Walk. Do not miss this spot, even though it's spendy.

Oenotri (www.oenotri.com, 707-252-1022, 1425 First Street, Napa, CA 94559; $$$; cuisine: Italian). Here you can travel to Italy by palate rather than passport. The menu features artisanal pizza Testarossa (compliments of a wood-fueled

BEST DAY IN SAN FRANCISCO

The opening of the Golden Gate Bridge in 1937 made Napa and Sonoma counties easily accessible to and from San Francisco, and today many Wine Country travelers visit this celebrated city at some time during their stay. Our tour of San Francisco below offers its share of culinary delights, while immersing you in the culture of what's been called the Paris of the West.

1. First stop: the Ferry Building Marketplace (www.ferrybuildingmarketplace.com, 1 Ferry Building at the Embarcadero and Market Street). If possible, come on a Tuesday, Thursday, or Saturday, when you'll find the Ferry Plaza Farmers Market in full swing. A great variety of fresh fruits and vegetables are on offer, as well as artisanal creations.

2. Next stop, lunch at Ton Kiang (www.tonkiangsf.com, 415-752-4440, 5821 Geary Boulevard, San Francisco, CA 94121). The highlight here is dim sum, which literally means "to touch your heart" and comes in the form of dumplings, steamed dishes, and other goodies served in small portions. Favorites include barbeque pork buns and shrimp & spinach dumplings.

3. Now it's time to play tourist. Ride the Powell-Hyde Cable Car (at Powell and Market streets, the Powell-Hyde line). Visit Lombard Street (Lombard Street between Hyde and Leavenworth streets), known as the "crookedest street in San Francisco." Go for a sundae at Ghirardelli Ice Cream & Chocolate Shop (415-474-3938, Ghirardelli Square, 900 N. Point Street, San Francisco, CA 94109).

4. Next up, be a culture vulture and explore the city's museums. Top picks include the graceful palace of the Legion of Honor (legionofhonor.famsf.org, 415-750-3600, 100 34th Avenue, San Francisco, CA 94122; at Clermont Street, in Lincoln Park).

5. Time for good eats. Here are two great options: Greens (www.greensrestaurant.com, 415-771-6222, Building A, Fort Mason Center, San Francisco, CA 94123) is a destination for the health conscious, with some of the most inspired vegetarian cooking around. The decor is warm and inviting, the views are stunning, and the wine list is smart, and worldly but playing to a local strength—California wine. Michael Mina (www.michaelmina.net, 415-397-9222, 252 California Street, San Francisco, CA 94111) offers the signature dishes of the eponymous celebrity chef, including black mussel soufflé and Maine lobster pot pie. Great Union Square location.

6. Rest your head at the Westin St. Francis (www.westinstfrancis.com, 415-397-7000, 335 Powell Street at Geary Street, San Francisco, CA 94102), a prized property that is both luxurious and well situated, right on Union Square. The revolving flags outside give you a clue as to what dignitary is currently a guest.

Acino oven imported from Naples), and pasta and handcrafted salumi are among the dishes taking their inspiration from Campania, Calabria, Basilicata, and Puglia. The wine list highlights the southern Italian region, and the restaurant also has a full bar and features unique cocktails.

✳ Entertainment

⊙ **Blue Note Napa** (www.bluenotenapa .com, 707-880-2300, 1030 Main Street, Napa, CA 94559). This hot spot for jazz lovers is the West Coast outpost for the famous New York City jazz bar. Blue Note is the first-floor tenant of the Napa Valley Opera House, and it's not only a live music venue focusing on live nightly jazz from local, national, and international acts, but it is also a full-service gourmet restaurant, making it an entertainment destination for locals and music-loving visitors alike. Performers such as Spyro Gyra, David Sanborn, and Yolanda Brown flock to the intimate venue, which has just over 150 seats, including

BLUE NOTE NAPA PAIRS LIVE JAZZ WITH A FULL-SERVICE GOURMET RESTAURANT

cabaret-style tables, booths, and bar seating. Watch a live performance while dining on the creations of executive chef Quentin Garcia, which include a large array of seasonal small plates and hearty entrées, both for meat-eaters and vegetarians. Dinner and music is paired with a full bar serving local spirits, beer, and wine. Larger concerts, featuring more diverse acts like George Clinton & the Parliament Funkadelic or Train, take place in the upstairs ballroom.

Napa Valley Opera House (www.nvoh .org, 707-226-7372, 1030 Main Street, Napa, CA 94559). Built in 1879, this Italianate beauty is a solid structure that rolls in theater and musical performances, from pop to classical. The first-floor tenant is Blue Note, a jazz and supper club, while the second floor is the restored JaM Cellars Ballroom at the Margrit Mondavi Theatre, which hosts community gatherings, concerts, and private parties.

✪ **Uptown Theatre** (www.uptown theatrenapa.com, 707-259-0123, 1350 Third Street, Napa, CA 95449). This theater has been welcoming guests to Napa's West End for entertainment since 1937. An art deco masterpiece, the Uptown offers nightly live music

and comedy from acclaimed national acts. It's an intimate setting, with a mere 860 seats and not a bad view in the house. You can grab a preshow meal at nearby Grace's Table, which offers

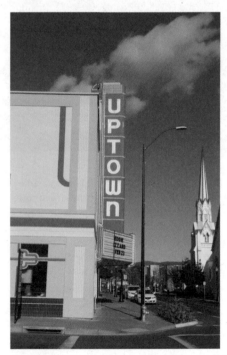

UPTOWN THEATRE IS AN ART DECO MASTERPIECE OFFERING LIVE MUSIC AND COMEDY

globally inspired cuisine, or a bite at Zuzu, a tapas restaurant. Afterward, purchase a glass of local wine at Uptown's bar, whose proceeds help maintain the historical heritage of the building, then settle in for a night of entertainment. Recent performers include Eddie Izzard, Snoop Dogg, Chris Isaak, Rosanne Cash, Keb' Mo, Tears for Fears, and the Indigo Girls.

✳ Selective Shopping

First Street Napa is a thriving mecca for shoppers and restaurant-goers, a three-block spread bookended by Franklin and Coombs streets. Formerly the Napa Town Center, this enterprise is anchored by Archer Hotel Napa, with a generous amount of office space, retail shops, and restaurants in the mix. The most notable of these include Charlie Palmer Steaks in Archer Hotel Napa, with the restaurant's focus on red meat and red wine; Compline, which offers California cuisine and specializes in wine and food pairings; Mecox Gardens, which features furniture and accessories; Kalifornia Jean Bar, which sells jeans and clothes for men and women; State & First, which features high-end women accessories; Lush Cosmetics; Mayacamas Vineyards Tasting Room; Napastäk, which offers boutique condiments, foods, and table top accessories; and Tommy Bahama, which features casual wear for men and women. Formerly located in Yountville, there is also Overland Sheepskin Co., which offers leather and sheepskin coats and rain gear for men and women, as well as rugs and accessories.

✪ **Oxbow Public Market** (707-266-6529, 644 First Street, Napa CA 94559) is the place for gourmet fare. Like San Francisco's Ferry Building Marketplace, its appealing range of food purveyors includes Model Bakery, Three Twins

A FRONT ROW SEAT AT THE UPTOWN THEATRE

Organic Ice Cream, Hog Island Oyster Bar, and Kara's Cupcakes. Check out Whole Spice, offering 300-plus different spices, along with a broad range of salts and mushroom powders.

The Beaded Nomad (707-252-3060, 1149 First Street, Napa, CA 94559) You

THERE'S AN AMPLE SUPPLY OF DELECTABLE CHEESE AT THE OXBOW MARKET

BEYOND WINE COUNTRY

The sights farther afield . . .

TO THE SOUTH

The striking countryside and tony hamlets of Marin County are directly south of Wine Country. In San Rafael, just east of Highway 101, don't miss the dramatic Marin Civic Center, one of the last buildings designed by Frank Lloyd Wright. If you're not in a hurry, consider trekking north or south on Highway 1, the winding two-lane road that hugs the rugged coastline. It will take you by Muir Woods, home to some of the tallest redwoods north of the Bay, and also to the majestic Mount Tamalpais. Drive to its 3,000-foot summit for a spectacular view of San Francisco (clear weather permitting, that is). Point Reyes Lighthouse is also worth a stop along Highway 1, as are the oyster farms near Marshall.

Farther south—just a one-hour drive from Wine Country—is one of the most intriguing, romantic, and ethnically diverse cities in America: San Francisco. (Check out our "Best Day in San Francisco" for the full tour.) Across the Bay are Oakland and the ever-eclectic Berkeley, both stops worth making.

TO THE EAST

While motoring your way to Sacramento along I-80, your thoughts may turn to . . . onions. The aroma of onions and other commercially grown produce fills the air in fertile Sacramento Valley, where fruits and vegetables are tended in endless flat fields. The city of Sacramento, the state capital and once a major hub for rail and river transportation, is proud of its historic center: Old Town, a faithful re-creation of the city's original town center, with a multitude of shops, restaurants, and museums.

TO THE NORTH

Not to be outdone by Napa and Sonoma counties, Mendocino County is also a major player in the game of fine wine, with several premium wineries along Highway 101 and in beautiful Anderson Valley. The coastal hamlet of Mendocino, one of Hollywood's favorite movie locations, is also a treasure trove for shoppers. Its art galleries, antiques shops, and fine dining, as well as its New England–like atmosphere, make it a popular second destination for Wine Country visitors.

don't have to be a child of the 1960s to relish the wares here. This shop features jewelry and imported items such as masks and bronze statues. **Copperfield's** (707-252-8002, 3740 Bel Aire Plaza, Napa, CA 94558) is an all-purpose bookstore, a fun stop for readers.

Napa Premium Outlets (707-226-6219, 629 Factory Stores Drive, Napa, CA 94558) has a maze of stores, including Cole Haan, J. Crew, Michael Kors, Tommy Hilfiger, American Eagle Outfitters, Ann Taylor, the Gap, Calvin Klein, Skechers, Banana Republic, and Coach.

YOUNTVILLE & STAGS LEAP DISTRICT

YOUNTVILLE & STAGS LEAP DISTRICT

The town of Yountville was named after pioneer George Calvert Yount (1794–1865), a Midwestern farmer who left his family to become a fur trapper and ultimately planted the first vineyard in Napa Valley. (His grave is in the cemetery on the corner of Jackson and Washington streets.)

Today this region is known in all of Wine Country as the cradle of cuisine. It's home to the world-renowned French Laundry, and the lineup of other restaurants—from Bouchon to Bistro Jeanty to Bottega—confirms that this is a foodie's paradise. Snagging a spot at some of these restaurants is not easy. Best to make a reservation (months ahead of time, in some cases) and say a prayer. Here chefs like Thomas Keller (The French Laundry, Bouchon, Ad Hoc) and Michael Chiarello (Bottega) are revered. Americans are not a patient people by nature, but they know great food is worth the wait. Accommodations in the region serve both seekers of chic and the value-oriented. All will provide a welcome place to hang your hat, and some are destinations unto themselves.

As for wine, this is a region with an impressive pedigree. The first vines in Yountville were planted in 1836, and the appellation is best known for cabernet, even though the biggest winery, Domaine Chandon, is a house of sparkling wine. This chapter includes

SCULPTURE AT CLIFF LEDE VINEYARDS: *TWIN VENUSES FROM THUNDER* BY JIM DINE COURTESY OF JENN FARRINGTON STUDIOS

wineries from the nearby Stags Leap District, a region that garnered international recognition when a cabernet sauvignon from Stag's Leap Wine Cellars outscored French producers Mouton-Rothschild and Haut-Brion, among others, in the Paris Tasting of 1976. A Who's Who of French wine cognoscenti selected cabernet in a blind tasting over the best of Bordeaux, and this win jolted the wine world.

Some describe cabernet from Stags Leap District as "an iron fist in a velvet glove." The best are good on two counts: they're tasty when released, and they're capable of aging well.

✳ To See & Do

ART GALLERIES ✪ **The Gallery at Cliff Lede Vineyards** (www.cliffledevineyards .com, 800-428-2259, 707-944-8642, 1473 Yountville Cross Road, Yountville, CA 94599; open 10–4). The gallery, in the winery's original fermentation room, has a modern feel, with concrete floors and crisp walls. The outside collection includes Jim Dine's *Twin 6' Hearts* and a bronze sculpture by Lynn Chadwick that sets the stage for the work inside.

BALLOONING **Napa Valley Aloft** (www.nvaloft.com, 855-944-4408, 707-944-4400, 6525 Washington Street, Yountville, CA 94599). This hot-air balloon outfit offers pickup from San Francisco and Napa Valley hotels, a champagne breakfast, and daily flights. Napa Valley's oldest balloon company launches daily from the grounds of the V Marketplace in Yountville.

Napa Valley Balloons (www.napavalleyballoons.com, 707-944-0228, 800-253-2224, 4086 Byway E., Napa, CA 94559). This highly regarded hot-air balloon company was founded in 1980. It offers a champagne brunch following the flight. The meeting location is Yountville's Domaine Chandon.

MUSEUMS ✐ **Napa Valley Museum** (www.napavalleymuseum.org, 707-944-0500, 55 Presidents Circle, Yountville, CA 94599; open Wednesday–Sunday 11–4, closed Monday and Tuesday; admission: adults over 17, $10, seniors and children under 17, $5). Since its debut in 1997, this has been an impressive addition to the valley. Housed in a stylishly modern take on an old California barn, the $3.5-million-dollar museum devotes itself to the history, culture, and art of Napa, with standing and touring exhibitions.

PARKS ✐ **Yountville City Park** (just off Madison Street on the north edge of town). If you're touring Wine Country with tykes, they need their share of fun too. Sometimes 30 minutes on a playground can go a long way. Grab a picnic or a snack and head to Yountville City Park, which features one of the best playgrounds in Napa Valley, as well as recreational equipment for the kids. The park also offers plenty of shade for Mom and Dad. Best of all, it's free.

✳ Wineries

Chimney Rock Winery (www.chimneyrock.com, 707-257-2641, 866-279-4637, 5350 Silverado Trail, Napa, CA 94558; tastings daily 10–5). The design of this winery is Cape Dutch–inspired; South Africa was once home to the winery's founder, the late Sheldon "Hack" Wilson. Today, Chimney Rock is owned by wine importer Tony Terlato, who has invested millions in upgrading the facility. The emphasis here is on cabernet sauvignon, which prospers in the Stags Leap District. The winery's best cabernets are sleekly structured, but they age beautifully.

✪ **Cliff Lede Vineyards** (www.cliffledevineyards.com, 800-428-2259, 707-944-8642, 1473 Yountville Cross Road, Yountville, CA 94599; tastings daily 10–4). Canadian Cliff Lede has made a major impact on Napa Valley. He bought the old S. Anderson Winery, where sparkling wine had been the focus, and began producing cabernet sauvignon and sauvignon blanc, and right out of the gate his wines were competing with the valley's best. Lede added a gracefully elegant California bungalow-style visitor center and art gallery. In the hills east of the winery, Lede opened the Poetry Inn, a small, upscale, and exclusive inn that just may be the best in the valley (see entry under *Lodging*).

Clos Du Val (www.closduval.com, 707-261-5212, 800-993-9463, 5330 Silverado Trail, Napa, CA 94558; tastings daily 10–5). Bernard Portet was raised among the casks and vines of Château Lafite-Rothschild, where his father was cellar master. The Bordeaux influence is strong here, in both the wines and the winery. An elegant and understated building surrounded by vineyards, Clos Du Val resembles a small country winery, with red roses marking the end of each vine row, in typical French fashion. The tasting room has a vaulted ceiling and windows that open into the cellar. Established in 1972, Clos Du Val was an early Napa pioneer, and the cabernets are typically elegant and complex. The winery's roster includes a wonderfully fleshy zinfandel, but the merlot and pinot noir can be inconsistent.

✪ **Domaine Chandon** (www.chandon.com, 707-944-2280, 888-242-6366, 1 California Drive, Yountville, CA 94599; tastings daily 10–5). The turning point for California sparkling wine came in 1973, when the famed French Champagne house Moët Hennessy built this ultramodern winery in the hills west of Yountville. Domaine Chandon is a museum of sorts, with artifacts and explanations of *méthode champenoise,* the classic French process of making bubbly. Domaine Chandon makes a variety of sparkling wines, from a round and refreshing brut to the expensive and intense Etoile.

Hestan Vineyards (www.hestanvineyards.com, 707-945-1002, 6548 Washington Street, Yountville, CA 94559; tastings daily 10:30–6). This winery is known for its Bordeaux red blends and the interesting vintner behind the operation. Stanley Cheng is well known for his global cookware company, Meyer, and he even produces a Meyer bottling. Aside from tasting the lineup of wines, the perk in visiting the winery is getting a peek at its striking property. There's an 11-acre pond amid the 56-plus acres of rolling vineyards. Stanley and his wife Helen bought the property in 1996, began planting in 1997, and released their first wines in 2005. They also produce a Stephanie label, named after their only daughter.

✪ **JCB Tasting Salon & Atelier** (www.jcbcollection.com, 707-967-7600, 6505 Washington Street, Yountville, CA 94599; tastings by appointment). The Francophiles among us won't be able to resist this spot, a celebration of the finer things in life. The tasting room and epicurean boutique make a classy combo, and it's not surprising that vintner/owner Jean-Charles Boisset is behind this operation. The tasting room is dramatic, with crystal, gold, leopard print, red velvet, and gilded mirrors on the ceiling. One interesting note for the wine geeks who double as techies: there are interactive digital tables that reveal which wines are on hand in the tasting room. Flights of four or five wines include some highbrow labels priced up to $350. The delectable Atelier nearby offers an incredible assortment of tasty treasures: caviar, cheese and charcuterie, confections, truffles, foie gras, and anchovies. JCB Tasting Salons are chic spots in Wine County, sometimes dressing up rustic barrel rooms with chandeliers. They give people a taste of the good life in the glass and beyond. Additional salons are at St. Helena's Raymond Vineyards and at Santa Rosa's DeLoach Vineyards.

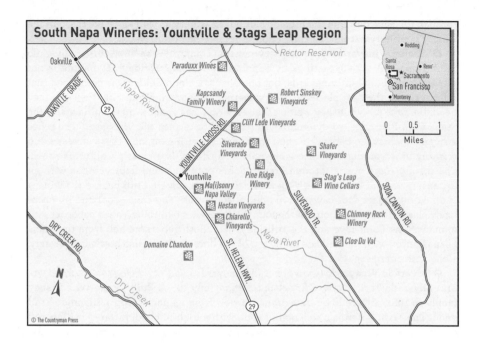

Kapcsándy Family Winery (www.kapcsandywines.com, 707-948-3100, 1001 State Lane, Yountville, CA 94559; tastings by appointment). The Bordeaux-styled reds and the dry rosé produced here are worth a stop. Lou Kapcsándy has true grit: After the brutal crushing by the Soviet Army of the 1956 Hungarian Revolution, he fled his country, coming to America without knowing a single word of English and dirt-poor as well. Lou gave the general contracting business a shot, but a trip to Bordeaux in 1998 altered his destiny, making wine his day job.

✪ **Paraduxx Napa Valley** (www.paraduxx.com, 707-945-0890, 7257 Silverado Trail, Yountville, CA 95448; tastings by appointment). Here blends completely fill the tasting menu. Duckhorn Wine Company, the owner of Paraduxx, wanted to explore blends while keeping Duckhorn's focus on Bordeaux varietals in check. The Paraduxx winery opened in 2005. Its most unique feature is its 10-sided fermentation building, which looks like a round barn. The design of the entire winery property was intended to resemble the historic farmsteads in the region.

Pine Ridge Vineyards (www.pineridgevineyards.com, 800-575-9777, 5901 Silverado Trail, Napa, CA 94558; tastings daily 10:30–4:30). Pine Ridge is an unassuming winery sequestered among the hills along the Silverado Trail. From the tasting room, take your glass onto the patio or explore the shady grounds. Tours begin in the vineyard and trek through the aging caves; on some tours, samples from oak barrels are offered. The winery's cabernet sauvignon is rich and focused.

Robert Sinskey Vineyards (www.robertsinskey.com, 707-944-9090, 6320 Silverado Trail, Napa, CA 94558; tastings daily 10–4:30). On a rise overlooking the Silverado Trail, this winery blends a modern design with the warmth of stone and redwood. The ceiling of the tasting room stretches 35 feet high, wisteria entwines courtyard columns, and through a huge glass window you can get a good view of the winery at work. There are a number of tours offered, but visitors generally get an extensive trip through the cave dug into the hillside behind the winery as well as a hike through the winery's culinary garden. The pinot noir is among the best in Napa.

✪ **Shafer Vineyards** (www.shafervineyards.com, 707-944-2877, 6154 Silverado Trail, Napa, CA 94558; tastings by appointment Monday–Friday). Dynamite is not often required to plant vineyards, but back in 1972, John Shafer was convinced that hillsides were the best places to grow cabernet sauvignon. Mountain vineyards may be all the rage now, but they weren't then. The soil was shallow on the hills below the Stags Leap Palisades, so dynamite was required to terrace the vineyards. The vines struggle against the bedrock to find water and nourishment, and these stressed and scrawny vines produce intense wines. Shafer's winery is a classic California ranch. The tasting room opens through French doors onto a second-floor veranda with an expansive view of lower Napa Valley. Under the vine-covered hill behind the winery is an 8,000-square-foot cave, carved out of solid rock. The cave—cool and immaculately clean—is the high point of the tour. Shafer makes two Napa Valley cabernet sauvignons: One Point Five and the Hillside Select. Both cabernets hail from the Stags Leap District, with the Hillside at the top of the line. Merlot is also bottled separately, along with chardonnay.

✪ **Silverado Vineyards** (www.silveradovineyards.com, 707-257-1770, 855-270-1770, 6121 Silverado Trail, Napa, CA 94558; tastings daily 10–5). Built by the Walt Disney family in 1981, Silverado offers a dramatic view from its perch atop a Silverado Trail knoll. The tasting den is a welcoming spot, with a high-pitched, raftered ceiling and plenty of seats outside to enjoy the landscape. Here the focus is on cabernet sauvignon, but the winery also makes merlot, sangiovese, chardonnay, and sauvignon blanc, along with some less mainstream varietals.

✪ **Stag's Leap Wine Cellars** (www.cask23.com, 707-261-6410, 5766 Silverado Trail, Napa, CA 94558; tastings daily 10–4:30). Founded by the Winiarski family in 1972, the winery is famous in Wine Country. This is the place, after all, responsible for the cabernet that stunned the French judges at the Paris Tasting of 1976, putting California wine on the map. The winery was purchased in late 2007 by the Washington-based Ste. Michelle Estate and Italian vintner Piero Antinori. It offers tastings out of its FAY Outlook & Visitor Center. A wine educator will walk you through a picturesque setting, historic vineyards, and the Stags Leap Palisades. Just an insider tip—the Estate Collection Tasting Flight often includes the winery's revered CASK 23.

✲ Lodging

✪ 🐾 **Bardessono** (www.bardessono.com, 707-204-6000, 6526 Yount Street, Yountville, CA 94599; $$$$). This 62-room hotel courts eco-conscious travelers with its earth-friendly design: the architecture, the heating and cooling systems, and the lighting and landscaping are all certifiably "green." But this doesn't mean that guests forgo luxury. Quite the opposite, in fact. Among the low-impact indulgences are luxurious suites with organic bed linens and robes as well as champagne bubble baths for two. Lucy Restaurant is on the premises, as is the B Spa Therapy Center. Oh yes, and man's best friend is also welcome here. Of course, there's a cleaning fee of $150 per stay. But isn't your four-legged beast worth it?

Hotel Yountville Resort & Spa (www.hotelyountville.com, 707-967-7900, 6462 Washington Street, Yountville, CA 94599; $$$–$$$$). Prefer a full-service hotel but can't afford the sky-high rates of some of the nearby lodgings? This inn is a good alternative. Set on a peaceful creek and featuring mature landscaping, the hotel has an elegantly rustic feel to it. There are 80 rooms, each featuring a fieldstone fireplace. Many of the top rooms have vaulted ceilings and

OUR TOP OVERALL PICKS FOR YOUNTVILLE AND STAGS LEAP DISTRICT

The French Laundry (www.thomaskeller.com)
Bardessono (www.bardessono.com)
Bottega (www.botteganapavalley.com)
Domaine Chandon (www.chandon.com)
Ad Hoc (www. thomaskeller.com)
Cliff Lede Vineyards (www.cliffledevineyards.com)
Redd (www.reddnapavalley.com)
Stag's Leap Wine Cellars (www.cask23.com)
Bouchon & Bouchon Bakery (www. thomaskeller.com)
Villagio Inn & Spa (www.villagio.com)
JCB Tasting Salon & Atelier (www.jcbcollection.com)
Bistro Jeanty (www.bistrojeanty.com)

ATELIER IS AN EPICUREAN BOUTIQUE WITH CHEESE, CHARCUTERIE, CONFECTIONS, AND CAVIAR

private patios. A 4,000-square-foot spa is also on-site. A continental breakfast is served.

Lavender (www.lavendernapa.com, 707-944-1388, 800-522-4140, 2020 Webber Street, Yountville, CA 94599; $$$$). A little bit of Provence in the heart of Napa Valley. Surrounded by its namesake flowering herb, the inn has nine guest rooms in all, including two in the main house—a lovely old farmhouse with a wide porch—and the others in three cottages. The decor is done in French country furnishings and fabrics, and all rooms have fireplaces. In the breakfast room a Parisian-style bistro breakfast is served. Guests have pool privileges at nearby sister inn Maison Fleurie.

Maison Fleurie (www.maisonfleurie napa.com, 707-944-2056, 800-788-0369, 6529 Yount Street, Yountville, CA 94599; $$$$). French for "flowering house," Maison Fleurie is a lovely complex of vine-covered buildings blessed with a colorful past—built in 1873, it was a bordello and a speakeasy. Today, it is a 13-room inn in the heart of the increasingly chic burg of Yountville, but it has the feel of a French country inn, featuring provincial antiques and reproductions. A full breakfast is

served family-style in the fireside dining room.

Napa Valley Lodge (www.napavalley lodge.com, 707-944-2468, 888-944-3545, 2230 Madison Street, Yountville, CA 94599; $$$$). This delightful lodge has 55 well-appointed and spacious rooms and suites—33 with fireplaces—decorated with ceiling fans and tropical plants and offering postcard views of the valley. It is styled like a Spanish hacienda, with a red-tiled roof and balconies or terraces off every room. This is a restful location surrounded by ripening grapes in the vineyards, and it's an easy walk to Yountville's shops. Special hot-air balloon and romance packages are also available.

North Block Hotel (www.northblock hotel.com, 707-944-8080, 6757 Washington Street, Yountville, CA 94599; $$$–$$$$). Nestled in Yountville's epicurean village, the North Block Hotel is walking distance from many of its prized restaurants, tasting rooms, and boutique shops. It has a contemporary design and calls itself an "unpretentious wine country escape." The hotel has a communal courtyard and fireplace area, offering a spot for guests to mingle. The pool area also includes a hot tub, a large cabana area, and plenty of chaises and umbrellas. North Block has 20 rooms with either a patio or a balcony, and many rooms have fireplaces, as well.

🍃 **Petit Logis Inn** (www.petitlogis .com, 877-944-2332, 6527 Yount Street, Yountville, CA 94599; $$–$$$). This inn has a culinary edge. It's within walking distance of The French Laundry—by many accounts the best restaurant in America—and it's also near some other top-rated restaurants, including Bouchon and Bistro Jeanty. All five guest rooms feature a fireplace and a double Jacuzzi. The shingled lodge with a trellis of vines has a French country, minimalist feel. The inn is simple and lovely, and the price is right.

✪ **Poetry Inn** (www.poetryinn.com, 707-944-0646, 6380 Silverado Trail, Napa, CA 94558; $$$$). Cliff Lede, a Canadian businessman, established Cliff Lede Vineyards in 2002 and opened the nearby Poetry Inn in 2005. The inn, on a hillside in the Stags Leap District, has stunning views of the Napa Valley. The six rooms have king-sized beds, private balconies, and wood-burning fireplaces. A popular spa treatment is a massage in the open air. Breakfasts include kale and chorizo hash—decadence at its best.

✪ **Villagio Inn & Spa** (www.villagio .com, 707-944-8877, 800-351-1133, 6481 Washington Street, Yountville, CA 94599; $$$–$$$$). Villagio Inn & Spa has 112 spacious guest rooms, each featuring a wood-burning fireplace, a patio or balcony, and a refrigerator. Of course, the main draw here is the 13,000-square-foot Spa Villagio, with seven treatment rooms and five private spa suites that include oversized infinity tubs, fireplaces, and wet bars. Yet another plus is the nearby V Marketplace, offering upscale specialty shops, galleries, cafés, a complete wine cellar, and a hot-air balloon company—all housed within a 148-year-old restored brick winery.

Vintage House (www.vintagehouse .com, 707-944-1112, 800-351-1133, 6539 Washington Street, Yountville, CA 94599; $$$$). This is an exceptional inn designed with villa-style units clustered around a common waterway. The 80 spacious and beautifully decorated rooms have oversized beds, whirlpool-spa tubs, ceiling fans, in-room coffeemakers and

VINTAGE HOUSE IS A LUXURIOUS INN DESIGNED LIKE A VILLA WITH ELEGANT ROOMS.

FRANCOPHILES WILL LOVE BISTRO JEANTY

refrigerators, private verandas, and wood-burning fireplaces. Second-story rooms cost a little more but are worth it for the vaulted ceilings and, especially, the views. California bubbly is served with the breakfast buffet. The V Marketplace shopping complex is next door.

✳ Where to Eat

✪ **Ad Hoc** (www.thomaskeller.com, 707-944-2487, 6476 Washington Street, Yountville, CA 94599; $$$, prix fixe $55; cuisine: traditional American comfort food). Celebrity chef Thomas Keller, best known for his award-winning restaurant The French Laundry, is also behind this first-rate eatery. Here comfort food reigns. Irresistible dishes, served in generous portions, include buttermilk fried chicken, spiced hanger steak, lobster mac and cheese, and braised beef short ribs. The menu, which changes daily, is limited to a single four-course meal (no-stress ordering!), and food is served family style. The wine list includes imports but focuses on Napa Valley labels, with a few bottlings from Sonoma.

This is a great spot in Wine Country—and it may be as close as you can get to Thomas Keller's ingenuity, given that The French Laundry requires a lengthier wait.

✪ **Bistro Jeanty** (www.bistrojeanty .com, 707-944-0103, 6510 Washington Street, Yountville, CA 94599; $$$; cuisine: French). Having for years prepared the meticulously elaborate creations at Domaine Chandon, chef Philippe Jeanty returned to his roots in 1998 and opened this delightful bistro. The idea, he said, was to create the French country comfort food he grew up with in Champagne. It's hard not to be won over by Jeanty's menu, which is ripe with classics such as cassoulet, *daube de boeuf*, and ratatouille. A favorite is coq au vin, a hearty red wine stew of moist chicken and mushrooms: delicious. The wine list won't impress stuffy collectors; it's a small and impeccable list selected strictly with the menu in mind.

✪ **Bottega** (www.botteganapavalley .com, 707-945-1050, inside the V Marketplace, 6525 Washington Street, Yountville, CA 94559; $$$; cuisine: Italian). This place is hot hot hot. Celebrity chef

BOUCHON IS A FRENCH BISTRO THAT TRANSPORTS YOU TO PARIS

Michael Chiarello, the Emmy Award–winning host of the Food Network's *Easy Entertaining* and vintner of Chiarello Family Vineyards, is doing something very right with Bottega. The restaurant shines a light on Chiarello's signature bold Italian flavors and elegant style. The menu highlights artisanal and house-made ingredients, as well as local produce. The ambiance is vintage Napa Valley, rustic and elegant; the restaurant is located in one of the oldest wineries in the region, the Groezinger Estate.

✪ **Bouchon** (www.thomaskeller .com, 707-944-8037, 6534 Washington Street, Yountville, CA 94599; $$$; cuisine: French). If Bistro Jeanty down the road is trying to corner the market on French country bistros, then Bouchon has Paris in mind. The mood is distinctly urban. Noted New York designer Adam Tihany—famous for Cirque 2000, among others—created a chic den with burgundy, velvet, bold mosaics, and a zinc raw bar handcrafted in France. If this sounds elaborate even by Napa Valley standards, there's good reason: the man behind it is Thomas Keller of The French Laundry in Yountville and Per Se in New York. Bouchon is truly one of the best dining experiences in Wine Country. If Bouchon has the authentic feel of an upscale brasserie, it has a menu to match. Specialties include an incredible *steak frites* (French for "steak with fries"); equally delectable is the roasted chicken with Savoy cabbage, roasted parsnips, and bacon lardons. To begin, why not sample from the raw bar? The oysters are impeccable. The wine list is sharply focused on wines that bring out the menu's best, and prices are average. The service is first-rate, and Bouchon stays open late; the bar is one of the busiest and classiest in the valley.

✪ **The French Laundry** (www.thomas keller.com/tfl, 707-944-2380, 6640 Washington Street, Yountville, CA 94599; $$$$; cuisine: French). The French Laundry is arguably the best restaurant in the country, and it has an international reputation for quality. Owner-chef Thomas Keller has become a celebrity, and the rich and famous flock here. This place is hot. Is it worth all the fuss? Yes, if you can afford it. It's easily the most expensive restaurant in Wine Country—a dinner for two with a bottle of wine, tax, and tip can exceed $800. The grand stone house, which was built in 1900, was a bar and brothel before becoming a French-style laundry. Keller purchased it in 1994 and his version is upscale; the atmosphere is formal and you might call his cuisine "California labor-intensive." You can order a 12-course feast, which changes daily. Keller sends out his famous Oysters and Pearls appetizer, heady with poached oysters and

THE FRENCH LAUNDRY'S SECRET GARDEN

Arrive at The French Laundry with sufficient time before your reservation so that you can stroll across Washington Street and see the restaurant's two-and-a-half-acre garden. It's farmed year-round and, depending on the season, you'll see edible blossoms, tomatoes, greens, and squash, among other items destined for the dinner table. The garden also supplies fresh fare to chef Thomas Keller's other restaurants in Yountville: Ad Hoc and Bouchon. ✪

caviar atop richly sauced tapioca, but from there, the cuisine takes a bolder approach, often touched with hints of Asia. That might mean nubbins of sake-poached Japanese yagara fish glazed in cherry leaf gelee or a dainty sautéed fillet of Japanese blue nose medai with creamed parsnip purée, wilted arrowleaf spinach, and Rumi spice-saffron pudding. As always, the vegetarian menu shines, too, in dishes such as morel mushroom farci fanned with winter radishes, broccoli, miner's lettuce, and potato purée. Then there's the signature dessert, coffee and doughnuts. You've never had cinnamon-sugared doughnuts so tasty, and they're served with a "cup of coffee"—cappuccino-flavored mousse complete with foam. The wine list is impressive, with a superb offering of California and French wines, and there are 400-plus half-bottles in the mix. Save up your allowance, and make a reservation well in advance.

Mustards Grill (www.mustardsgrill .com, 707-944-2424, 7399 St. Helena Highway, Yountville, CA 94558; $$–$$$; cuisine: California). After all these years, Mustards Grill still lives up to its reputation. The secret of Mustards isn't actually a secret at all: hearty bistro food prepared with style, at a moderate price and in a lively atmosphere. "Truck-stop deluxe," they call it. The open kitchen takes center stage, dominating an intimate dining room. The tables are packed in close, but trust us: the resulting din lends an air of privacy. While servers seem harried, they're efficient and friendly. Chef-owner Cindy Pawlcyn, who

also runs Cindy's Backstreet Kitchen in St. Helena, creates comfort food with flair. House specialties include a juicy Mongolian pork chop, smoked duck, plus braised lamb shanks and grilled rabbit. A must are the onion rings, a heaping pile that comes thinly sliced and highly seasoned. The wine list is well focused and priced fairly. The wine-by-the-glass selection is also first-rate.

✪ **Redd** (www.reddnapavalley .com, 707-944-2222, 6480 Washington Street, Yountville, CA 94599; $$$$; cuisine: California). Richard Reddington made a name for himself at Masa's and Jardinière in San Francisco and Auberge du Soleil in Napa Valley, and then stepped out on his own with this classy restaurant. The interior is sleekly urban, with polished wood and aqua-blue highlights. The menu shows Asian

THE CHIC LOUNGE AT THE RESTAURANT REDD.

and French influences and showcases Reddington's passion for putting a high polish on what's ordinarily considered rustic comfort food. Excellent signature dishes include glazed pork belly with apple purée, burdock, and soy caramel, as well as Liberty Farms duck breast and Alaskan halibut. The wine list is on the expensive side, but it's loaded with Old and New World collectibles (California and French), and the wine service is first-rate. If you're in the mood to splurge, Redd is an excellent choice.

✳ Selective Shopping

✪ ✒ **Bouchon Bakery** (707-944-2253, www.thomaskeller.com, 6528 Washington Street, Yountville, CA 94599). Score Parisian treats like muffins, pastries, cookies, and chocolates from Thomas Keller's acclaimed bakery. Also sandwiches, which Bouchon describes as "the French version of fast food—delicious ingredients between excellent bread."

Domain Home & Garden (707-945-0222, 6525 Washington Street, Yountville, CA 94599). This store has everything from fountains and furniture to wine racks.

✪ **Finesse, The Store** (finessethestore .com; 6540 Washington Street, Yountville, CA 94599). The shop carries everything for the well-equipped kitchen and more, handpicked by owner/creator Thomas Keller of The French Laundry fame. The 450-square-foot store features an assortment of Keller's most favorite kitchen tools and accessories. Items include cooking kits and cookbooks by Keller, as well as knives and wooden spoon sets. The Thomas Keller Restaurant Group is an umbrella organization that includes the famed French Laundry, Bouchon, and Ad Hoc and Addendum of Yountville, as well as Per Se of New York.

Lemondrops (707-947-7057, 6525 Washington Street, Yountville, CA 95499). The business outfits babies, girls up to 16, and boys up to 12. The toys are inventive, and the service is friendly.

OPPOSITE: NICKEL & NICKEL MAKES A PRICEY CAB THAT'S TURNING HEADS

OAKVILLE & RUTHERFORD

OAKVILLE & RUTHERFORD

The villages of Oakville and Rutherford are a cross-section of delectable cabernet country. The "Rutherford Bench" describes the middle of Napa Valley, where cabernet reigns. "Rutherford dust" is said to imbue wine with a dusty, berry, spicy quality.

While wine tasting, people often stop at Oakville Grocery for highbrow picnic fixings: duck pâté, cold cuts, and caviar. Since when did picnics become so glamorous? When in Napa Valley . . .

The most prized resort in the area is Auberge du Soleil or "Inn of the Sun," which also has a restaurant and spa, a great place to relax after a marathon tasting.

Roam these villages with an eye on cabernet and you'll find the top names—Robert Mondavi, Beaulieu, and Rubicon, to name a few.

Now we take a peek at this wine region through the eyes of wine lovers. In Oakville and Rutherford, cabernet sauvignons are powerful, with a clear sense of place. There are many cult cabernet producers in this area; here we give only those that are open to the public. The bigger players included in our listings make killer cab and are definitely worth a stop.

✲ To See & Do

ART EXHIBITIONS **Mumm Napa** (www.mummnapa.com, 707-967-7700, 8445 Silverado Trail, Rutherford, CA 94573). The long hallways of this winery are devoted to art, and it's a lovely space. A permanent exhibition is Ansel Adams's *Story of a Winery*, along with other rotating exhibitions of photography and/or art.

A GORGEOUS STRETCH OF VINEYARDS AT ROBERT MONDAVI WINERY

Robert Mondavi Winery (www.robertmondaviwinery.com, 888-766-6328, 7801 St. Helena Highway, Oakville, CA 94562) This is one of the first wineries to show art. Rotating shows are on display in the Vineyard Room.

✲ Wineries

Beaulieu Vineyard (www.bvwines.com, 707-967-5233, 800-373-5896, 1960 St. Helena Highway, Rutherford, CA 94573; tastings daily 10–5). If you could sum up the early history of Napa Valley winemaking with a single bottle of wine, it would be the Georges de Latour Private Reserve cabernet sauvignon by Beaulieu.

MONDAVI FEUD OVER A FUR COAT

Few know that a one-two punch was behind the breakup of the late Robert and Peter Mondavi. The brothers were originally vintners of Charles Krug Winery in St. Helena, and the feud was reportedly instigated by Robert's extravagant purchase of a fur coat for his wife. Robert opened his namesake winery in 1966 while Peter remained at Charles Krug (www.robertmondaviwinery.com).

REDS ARE THE STRONG SUIT OF THIS SPANISH MISSION–STYLE WINERY

Although no longer the best cabernet in the valley, it has been at times the yardstick against which all other cabernets have been measured. Pronounced "bowl-YOU" and called BV for short, Beaulieu is one of Napa's most distinguished wineries, dating back to 1900, when Frenchman Georges de Latour began making wine. In 1938, Latour hired a young Russian immigrant, André Tchelistcheff, who went on to revolutionize California cabernet. Today, though, Beaulieu struggles to maintain that rich tradition. Built of brick and covered with ivy, the winery isn't particularly impressive, but a tour can be an eye-opener, particularly when it passes the forest of towering redwood tanks. A video in the visitor center briefs guests on Beaulieu's past and present. Three or four wines are offered; sip as you browse through the museum of old bottles and memorabilia.

○ **Cakebread Cellars** (www.cakebread.com, 707-963-5221, 800-588-0298, 8300 St. Helena Highway, Rutherford, CA 94573; tastings by appointment 10–4). The Cakebread clan runs this winery set in prime cabernet sauvignon territory. Jack and Dolores Cakebread began making wine in 1973 and have won a loyal following. This striking winery looks like a modern rethinking of a historical California barn and is surrounded by gardens and vineyards. While you're in the tasting room, try the melony sauvignon blanc—one of the best. Cakebread's cabernet sauvignons and chardonnay, lean and crisp on release, bloom after a few years.

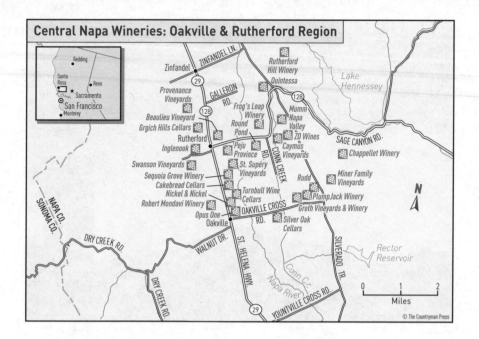

✪ **Caymus Vineyards** (www.caymus.com, 707-967-3010, 8700 Conn Creek Road, Rutherford, CA 94573; tastings daily 10–4 by appointment). In the past, no American wine was more highly regarded than the Caymus Special Selection cabernet sauvignon. Upon its release, people would crowd the winery for the honor of paying $130 a bottle. While the Caymus SS remains a signature cabernet in Wine Country, it has lost its standing to other highbrow cult cabs. The winery is still a no-frills family outfit and tampers little with its wines. The main 40-acre vineyard lies east of the Napa River, in the heart of Napa Valley's cabernet country—a blessed location. The tasting room is in a modern winery made of sturdy fieldstone. Wines are poured at a seated tasting, and in addition to the cabernets, Caymus samples its zinfandel and sauvignon blanc, sold only at the winery.

✒ **Frog's Leap Winery** (www.frogsleap.com, 707-963-4704, 8815 Conn Creek Road, Rutherford, CA 94573; tastings daily 10–4 by appointment). It's rare to find a winery with a sense of humor as well oiled as Frog's Leap's. Printed on every cork is the word *ribbit,* and the weathervane atop the winery sports a leaping frog. The name, a take-off on Stag's Leap Wine Cellars, was inspired by the winery's original site, an old St. Helena frog farm. Founders Larry Turley and John Williams parted ways in 1994, and Williams moved Frog's Leap south to restore a winery that dates to 1884. All five wines—Rutherford cabernet sauvignon, zinfandel, merlot, chardonnay, and sauvignon blanc—are reliable and often superb. Tasting takes place in the vineyard house behind the winery.

✪ **Grgich Hills Estate** (www.grgich.com, 707-963-2784, 800-532-3057, 1829 St. Helena Highway, Rutherford, CA 94573; tastings daily 9:30–4:30). French wine lovers worship the land, but in California, the winemaker is king. Cult followings have a way of developing—as with Mike Grgich, one of Napa Valley's best-known characters. The scrappy immigrant from the former Yugoslavia first gained renown as the winemaker at Chateau Montelena in Calistoga. Later, Grgich joined with Austin Hills and

While the 2008 film *Bottle Shock* gives full credit to Jim Barrett for producing the winning chardonnay of the Paris Tasting of 1976, it was actually Mike Grgich who crafted the 1973 Chateau Montelena. Stop in at Grgich Hills Estate to taste his striking chardonnays.

opened this winery. An ivy-covered stucco building with a red-tiled roof, Grgich's winery remains a house devoted to chardonnay. Grgich also makes a fumé blanc and has considerable luck with zinfandel, cabernet sauvignon, and merlot. However, over the years, the wines have become inconsistent.

Groth Vineyards & Winery (www.grothwines.com, 707-944-0290, 750 Oakville Cross Road, Oakville, CA 94562; tastings Monday–Saturday 10–4 by appointment). This California mission-style winery is a grand sight along the Oakville Cross Road. It's also home to a top-notch cabernet sauvignon, the Groth Reserve. Dennis Groth began making wine in 1982, and his graceful winery was completed a few years later. The tour is enlightening, beginning on a terrace that overlooks the vineyards, giving you a glimpse of the insectary garden, continuing past the bottling line and the cavernous barrel-aging room, and ending at the tasting bar. Groth cabernets typically have a lush elegance married to a firm backbone.

✪ **Inglenook** (www.inglenook.com, 707-968-1161, 800-RUBICON, 1991 St. Helena Highway, Rutherford, CA 94573; tastings and tours daily at 11 a.m., 2 p.m., and 3 p.m., with reservations strongly recommended). Film director Francis Ford Coppola rescued the Inglenook chateau from potential oblivion in the mid-1990s and lovingly restored the property to the romantic ideal of what a Napa Valley winery should look like: a sturdy stone castle, shrouded in ivy and enveloped by vineyards. Visitors approach the winery through a long, tree-lined driveway. Coppola's affections for Inglenook date to the mid-1970s, when he bought the former home of Inglenook's founder, Gustave Niebaum, which is next to the winery. Coppola released his own wine, Rubicon, a stout yet elegant Bordeaux-style blend, beginning with the 1978 vintage. Coppola's movie memorabilia, formerly on display at Inglenook, can be found at Francis Ford Coppola Winery in Sonoma County.

Miner Family Winery (www.minerwines.com, 707-944-9500, 800-366-9463 ext. 17, 7850 Silverado Trail, Oakville, CA 94562; tastings daily 10–5). Miner is making some impressive cabernet sauvignons and zinfandels. David Miner, a former software salesman, purchased a 60-acre vineyard high above the valley in 1989. The winery, situated above Silverado Trail, is a smart-looking edifice, done in rich golden hues and a modern, Mediterranean style. The tasting room, sleek in its polished wood tones, offers a grand view of the valley. Visitors can watch the winery in action through wide windows that overlook the barrel and fermentation rooms.

✪ **Mumm Napa** (www.mummnapa.com, 707-967-7700, 800-686-6272, 8445 Silverado Trail, Rutherford, CA 94573; tastings daily 10–6). Mumm Napa may have a French pedigree, but it's a California child through and through. The winery is a long, low ranch barn with redwood siding and a green slate roof. Mumm blends traditional French *méthode champenoise* with the distinctive fruit of Napa Valley, and the result is some of California's best sparkling wines. The winery tour offers a detailed look at the French way of making sparkling wine. Brut Prestige is the main release, a snappy blend of pinot noir and chardonnay, and a zesty Brut Rosé. The salon is quaint and country, with sliding glass doors that allow easy views of the Rutherford countryside.

Nickel & Nickel (www.nickelandnickel.com, 707-967-9600, 8164 St. Helena Highway, Oakville, CA 94562; tastings daily 10–4 by appointment). Nickel & Nickel was established by the partners of Far Niente, and the winery opened in July 2003. The idea was to produce 100-percent single-vineyard wines that best express the personality of each vineyard and varietal. Visiting the tasting room is like stepping back in time. It's housed in a building that dates back to 1882. Nickel & Nickel produces high-end chardonnay, merlot, syrah, cabernet, and zinfandel, but it's best known for cab—and these pricey cabs are typically well worth the price.

✪ **Opus One** (www.opusonewinery.com, 707-944-9442, 800-292-6787, 7900 St. Helena Highway, Oakville, CA 94562; tastings daily by appointment 10–4). A joint venture between Robert Mondavi and France's Château Mouton-Rothschild, Opus One is an elegant temple, a cross between a Mayan palace and the *Battlestar Galactica*. Designed by the firm that created San Francisco's Transamerica Pyramid, the winery opened in 1991 but was largely inaccessible to the public until 1994. It's apropos that the winery makes a vivid architectural statement. Opus One has been one of Napa Valley's highest-profile wines since its first vintage in 1979. The wine—a blend of cabernet sauvignon, cabernet franc, petit verdot, malbec, and merlot—is a classic: rich, oaky, and elegant. The tasting room fee is extravagant (what do you expect for highbrow wine?), but the pour is generous. Few people know that the balcony off the tasting room has one of the best views of Napa Valley for miles around. Step out with your glass and take a peek.

Peju Province (www.peju.com, 707-963-3600, 800-446-7358, 8466 St. Helena Highway, Rutherford, CA 94573; tastings daily 10–6). The grounds of this family-owned estate are lovely. There's good reason: Tony and Herta Peju ran a nursery in Los Angeles before coming north in the early 1980s. A row of beautiful sycamores leads to the French provincial winery, which is enveloped in white roses and other flowers. There is also a fine collection of marble sculptures. The tour doesn't take long; it's a small place. Cabernet sauvignon and cab franc are the specialties. Enjoy a rotating art exhibition while tasting.

✪ **PlumpJack Winery** (www.plumpjackwinery.com, 707-945-1220, 620 Oakville Cross Road, Oakville, CA 94562; tastings daily 10–4). PlumpJack is named for the roguish spirit of Shakespeare's Sir John Falstaff. In the mid-1990s, the company bought a century-old Napa Valley vineyard property renowned for producing cabernet of exceptional quality. Cabernet is still PlumpJack's flagship wine. The tasting room has Shakespearean whimsical touches, an uneven wavering fence outside, and iron decanters filled with flowers inside. You might spy the dashing politico and founder Gavin Newsom on your visit. Newsom is well known in Wine Country for his entrepreneurial spirit; he was one of the first to use screw caps for high-end bottlings.

Provenance Vineyards (www.provenancevineyards.com, 707-968-3633, 1695 St. Helena Highway, Rutherford, CA 94573; tastings daily 10–5). Provenance Vineyards makes appealing cabernet, sauvignon blanc, and merlot, getting particularly high marks for the latter. It's no wonder: winemaker Tom Rinaldi cut his teeth at Duckhorn Vineyards as founding winemaker, and he spent 22 vintages at the winery that exemplifies the best in merlot. Ironically, Rinaldi wanted to be a veterinarian, but because he worked with so many dissatisfied doctors who wanted to be winemakers, he opted for the latter. The modern-looking winery has a tasting room that's known for its French and American oak flooring constructed from strips of barrels—quite a conversation piece at the horseshoe-shaped tasting bar.

Quintessa (www.quintessa.com, 707-967-1601, 707-286-2730, 1601 Silverado Trail, Rutherford, CA 94573; tastings and tours daily 10–4 by appointment). This winery is somehow both inconspicuous and dramatically styled. Arching like a crescent moon from a wooded knoll in Rutherford, most of the winery is underground. The facade is rugged stone, and inside is a state-of-the-art, gravity-flow winery in which the grapes arrive on the roof and end up as wine in oak barrels in the underground cellar. On the rolling hills surrounding the winery are 170 acres of vineyards, mostly cabernet, and owners Valeria and Agustin Huneeus produce just one wine: Quintessa, the elegant red Bordeaux-style blend.

✪ **Robert Mondavi Winery** (www.robertmondaviwinery.com, 888-766-6328 option 2, 7801 St. Helena Highway, Oakville, CA 94562; tastings daily 10–5). We never thought we'd see it in our lifetime: the Robert Mondavi family without its namesake winery. Of course, Mondavi began to loosen his grip when the winery went public in 1993, but he and his family lost ownership interest after a $1.36 billion buyout by Constellation Brands of New York. The late Robert Mondavi was an innovator, such a symbol of the "new" Napa Valley that it's hard to believe he founded his winery in 1966. Once too flamboyant for conservative Napa County, the Spanish mission–style winery now seems as natural as the Mayacamas Mountains. After breaking away on his own from family-owned Charles Krug, Mondavi became the most outspoken advocate for California and its wines. Few Napa wineries are busier on a summer day than Mondavi, which offers one of the most thorough tours in the valley. Mondavi bottles one of the valley's most extensive lists of wines. Reds seem to be the winery's strong suit. The reserve cabernet sauvignons and pinot noirs become more magnificent every year—and so do the prices. Of course, the regular bottlings are hardly slackers.

✪ **Round Pond Estate** (www.roundpond.com, 707-302-2575, 888-302-2575, 875 Rutherford Road, Rutherford, CA 94573; tastings daily 11–3:30 by appointment). The MacDonnell family has been selling cabernet sauvignon grapes to the likes of Beaulieu and Franciscan for decades and owns more than 400 acres in the Rutherford area. A few years ago, the family decided to build their own winery and start making wine. The cabernets are polished yet concentrated. The winery is a showplace, and there are a number of tastings and tours available, including an exploration of the olive oil press.

Rudd Winery and Vineyards (www.ruddwines.com, 707-944-8577, 500 Oakville Cross Road, Oakville, CA 94562; tastings and tours Tuesday–Saturday by appointment). The late Leslie Rudd knew a thing or two about luxury. He owned Oakville Grocery and several restaurants around the country, and even a high-end gin distillery, and he once owned upscale retailer Dean & DeLuca. In the mid-1990s, Rudd came to Napa and transformed an underperforming winery into a showpiece. He replanted the vines on the 55-acre estate and created a stone winery with a 22,000-square-foot cave. Cabernet is the star attraction, and the wines are powerful and polished. The tour is an extensive affair, offering a thorough overview of Rudd and ending with a seated tasting.

Rutherford Hill Winery (www.rutherfordhill.com, 707-963-1871, 200 Rutherford Hill Road, Rutherford, CA 94573; tastings daily 10–5). The winery here is a mammoth barn, albeit a stylishly realized one, covered in cedar and perched on the hills overlooking Rutherford. Carved into the hillside behind are among the largest man-made aging caves in California, winding a half mile into the rock. The titanic cave doors are framed by geometric latticework that recalls the work of Frank Lloyd Wright. A trek through the cool and humid caves is the tour highlight. Merlot is the star here, and it's typically fleshy, with a tannic backbone.

✪ **St. Supéry Vineyards & Winery** (www.stsupery.com, 707-963-4507, 8440 St. Helena Highway, Rutherford, CA 94573; tastings daily 10–5). Wineries, on the whole, aren't the best places to take kids. St. Supéry is an exception. It adds a touch of science-museum adventure, with colorful displays, hands-on activities, and modern winery gadgetry. Windows reveal the bottling line, the barrel-aging room, and the like. A highlight is the "smellavision," where noses are educated on the nuances of cabernet sauvignon and sauvignon blanc. Ever hear cabernet described as cedar or black cherry? Hold your nose to a plastic tube, and smell what these descriptions mean. Another display gives you a peek under the soil to see the roots of a grapevine. St. Supéry offers a solid cabernet sauvignon, Meritage, and an exceptional sauvignon blanc, among other wines.

✪ **Sequoia Grove Winery** (www.sequoiagrove.com, 707-944-2945, 800-851-7841, 8338 St. Helena Highway, Napa, CA 94558; tastings daily 10:30–5). Dwarfed by century-old sequoia trees, this winery is easy to overlook along Highway 29, but the cabernet sauvignons are worth the stop. Wine was made in the 150-year-old redwood barn before Prohibition, but the wine and the winery had been long forgotten when the Allen family began making wine here again in 1980. The chardonnay is solid, but the regular and reserve cabernets can achieve greatness.

✪ **Silver Oak Cellars** (www.silveroak.com, 707-942-7022, 800-273-8809, 915 Oakville Cross Road, Oakville, CA 94562; tastings Monday–Saturday 9–5, Sunday 11–5). Not many wineries can live off one wine, but then Silver Oak isn't just any winery. Here cabernet sauvignon has been raised to an art form. Low-profile by Napa Valley standards, Silver Oak is known to cabernet lovers around the country, and that's all that matters. The Alexander Valley (Sonoma County) cabernet is typically more accessible than the Napa Valley bottling, but both are velvety and opulent and done in a distinctly California style. Silver Oak was established in 1972 on the site of an old Oakville dairy. A fire destroyed much of the original cellar in 2006 and the winery rebuilt it from scratch, hoping to pay tribute to the past while looking toward the future.

SILVER OAK CELLARS IS A POPULAR DESTINATION FOR THOSE WHO FANCY CABS

OUR TOP OVERALL PICKS FOR OAKVILLE AND RUTHERFORD

St. Supéry Vineyards & Winery (www.stsupery.com)
Oakville Grocery Co. (www.oakvillegrocery.com)
Opus One (www.opusonewinery.com)
Auberge du Soleil (www.aubergedusoleil.com)
Robert Mondavi Winery (www.robertmondaviwinery.com)
Inglenook (www.inglenook.com)
Lake Berryessa (www.visitnapavalley.com/plan/town/lake-berryessa/)
Mumm Napa (www.mummnapa.com)
PlumpJack Winery (www.plumpjackwinery.com)
Round Pond Estate (www.roundpond.com)

Swanson Vineyards (www.swansonvineyards.com, 707-754-4018, 1271 Manley Lane, Rutherford, CA 94573; tastings daily by appointment). The Swanson family moved to Napa Valley after Clarke Swanson realized that wine had more allure for him than banking and journalism. The winery produces a cabernet blend, merlot, and pinot grigio. The petite sirah is great, but it's not produced every year; when it is produced, it's made in small batches. On the upside, there's a great supply of Alexis, the Bordeaux blend, so keep your eye out for that. The tasting room is extravagant, inspired by the sumptuous salons of eighteenth-century Paris. And don't forget to visit the Sip Shoppe, which is considered a candy store for adults, featuring fine wines, bonbons, caviar, and cheeses.

Turnbull Wine Cellars (www.turnbullwines.com, 707-963-5839, 800-887-6285, 8210 St. Helena Highway, Oakville, CA 94562; tastings daily 10–5). This small redwood winery in the heart of cabernet sauvignon country was designed by award-winning architect William Turnbull, a former partner in the winery, which originated in 1979. The cabernet is known for its distinct minty quality.

Zd Wines (www.zdwines.com, 707-963-5188, 800-487-7757, 8383 Silverado Trail, Napa, CA 94558; tastings daily 10–4). Chardonnay, pinot noir, cabernet sauvignon: ZD has a way with all three. The winery began its life in 1969 in Sonoma Valley and was transplanted to Napa 10 years later. Crowned with a roof of red tile, the winery was expanded a few years back by the de Leuze family. The star is chardonnay, with its opulent beauty, while cabernets are dense and powerful. The pinots are light but intensely fruity.

Lodging

✪ **Auberge du Soleil** (www.aubergedusoleil.com, 707-963-1211, 800-348-5406, 180 Rutherford Hill Road, Rutherford, CA 94573; $$$$). Auberge du Soleil is Napa Valley's most luxurious experience, and it has a great perk: a world-class restaurant on the property (see listing under *What to Eat*). The style throughout the inn is distinctly southern France, with deep-set windows and wood shutters and doors. Each room or suite has a terrace and private entrance, and most rooms have spectacular views of the valley. All furnishings are chic yet casual. The 7,000-square-foot Auberge Spa (866-228-2490) is one of the most luxurious in the valley. Pampering takes on new meaning with the signature Head to Toe massages, which include a scalp and foot treatment. After indulging yourself, take in the sculpture garden set along a half-mile path.

BEST DAY IN NAPA VALLEY

Our tour of Napa Valley takes in the cities of Napa and Yountville as well as Oakville and Rutherford; see the individual city chapters for full listings. Here we set you up with a 24-hour itinerary, featuring wine tasting, an exotic Japanese dinner, and a show at Uptown Theatre.

You can easily tailor this tour to the Napa Valley "home base" of your choice. We'll escort you to the most interesting places, offering plenty of options so you can create your own Best Day.

1. To begin, we sweep you off to Paris, or so it seems, but no passport is necessary at Bouchon Bakery (Yountville; www.thomaskeller.com). You'll find exceptional treats, like melt-in-your-mouth croissants and coffee éclairs. (Overslept? No worries. Grab a sandwich. The bread is divine.)

2. Time to trade up from a latte to a glass of wine. Morning sipping? You bet, and here are some great options.

Domaine Chandon (Yountville; www.chandon.com). As the house that Moët Hennessy built, Chandon knows sparkling wine. This ultramodern winery in the hills west of Yountville is the setting for informative tours as well as tastings. Outstanding exhibitions by local artists rotate throughout the year.

Cliff Lede Vineyards (Yountville; www.cliffledevineyards.com). Canadian Cliff Lede bought the old S. Anderson Winery, where sparkling wine had been the focus, and transformed it into a producer of cabernet sauvignon and sauvignon blanc. Right out of the gate, the wines were competing with the valley's best.

Stag's Leap Wine Cellars (Napa; www.cask23.com). This is the place that put California wine on the map in 1976, when its 1973 cabernet won the famous Paris Tasting. For wine lovers, a visit to Stag's Leap Wine Cellars is a pilgrimage.

3. After a morning of sipping, you'll need to refuel with a hearty lunch. Oakville Grocery Co. (Oakville; www.oakvillegrocery.com) fills the bill. Don't let the country-store facade fool you (the place has been in business since 1881): this is a gourmet grocery. Fare includes duck pâté, cold cuts, and caviar. Sandwiches include turkey with pesto and a glorious muffuletta.

✳ Where to Eat

☺ **Auberge du Soleil** (www.auberge dusoleil.com, 707-963-1211 800-348-5406, 180 Rutherford Hill Road, Rutherford, CA 94573; $$$$; cuisine: California, French). If you want a picture-postcard view of Napa Valley, a tapestry woven of vineyards, make a reservation at Auberge du Soleil, located at the inn of the same name (see *Lodging*). Then make sure you slip in early enough to grab a table on the outside deck. The check may cause a double take, but the experience is worth it. Auberge du Soleil, or "Inn of the Sun," has a French country style, with provincial antiques, but the rooms are also infused with modern California touches. What arrives on the plate rivals the atmosphere, with rich dishes such as roasted Liberty Farms duck and seared ahi tuna. Although pricey, the wine list is one of the best in Northern California, with an extensive selection of wine by the glass, including champagne. The service, too, is impeccable but never overly attentive. For those looking for lighter fare throughout the day, there's a Bistro & Bar menu that offers 15-plus small plates with items like Blue Crab Cakes, Grouper Ceviche, Chicken Wings, and Mediterranean Spiced Lamb Skewers.

4. Prepare for another round of sipping—Wine Tasting, Part II—with plenty of options. Go ahead, be choosy.

Inglenook (Rutherford; www.inglenook.com). Film director Francis Ford Coppola rescued the Inglenook chateau from potential oblivion in the mid-1990s. It is now lovingly restored, the romantic ideal of what a Napa Valley winery should look like: a sturdy stone castle, shrouded in ivy and enveloped by vineyards.

Opus One (Oakville; www.opusonewinery.com). Call it visually distinctive or just plain cool, the building housing this winery is a must-see because it looks like something out of *Battlestar Galactica*. Opus One has been one of Napa Valley's highest-profile wines since its first vintage in 1979. The wine—a blend of cabernet sauvignon, cabernet franc, and merlot—is a classic: rich, oaky, and elegant.

Robert Mondavi Winery (Oakville; www.robertmondaviwinery.com). Once too flamboyant for conservative Napa County, the Spanish mission–style winery now seems as natural as the Mayacamas Mountains. After setting out on his own in 1966 from the family-owned Charles Krug vineyard, Mondavi was the most outspoken advocate for California and its wines until his death in 2008.

5. Now for an exotic dining experience at one of Napa Valley's newest and most exciting locales: **Morimoto Napa** (Napa; www.morimotonapa.com). This restaurant, under the direction of Iron Chef Masaharu Morimoto, serves contemporary Japanese cuisine (with a California twist, of course) in a sleek, dynamic space overlooking the River Walk.

6. Why not follow dinner with a show? **Uptown Theatre** (Napa; www.uptowntheatrenapa.com) is the venue for live performance in Napa Valley. It's also been restored to its former art deco splendor. Check out current offerings on the website.

7. End the day with a nightcap at the swanky **Carpe Diem Wine Bar** (Napa; www.carpediemwinebar.com). Pair your libation with a light bite: yummy cheeses and charcuterie, grilled flatbreads, or perhaps you'd prefer something sweet.

8. A romantic getaway is in order. Prepare to be indulged at **Milliken Creek Inn & Spa** (Napa; www.millikencreekinn.com). Guest rooms at the inn beckon you to relax and unwind. This place is set up to pamper: spa and massage services, yoga, breakfast in bed, Italian linens, and Napa River views. Sweet dreams.

Rutherford Grill (www.rutherfordgrill.com, 707-963-1792, 1180 Rutherford Road, Rutherford, CA 94573; $$–$$$; cuisine: American). So you discovered a big burly cabernet sauvignon while wine tasting. What do you eat with it? California cuisine is not always cabernet friendly, but this restaurant fills that niche with steak. The prime rib and filet mignon may not be the best you've ever had, but the beef is tasty and generally tender, and the portions are generous. Steaks and baby-back ribs are grilled over hardwood, and even the hamburgers are worth trying. The homemade Oreo ice cream sandwich with chocolate sauce is a worthy indulgence.

DECADENT CHEESES AT THE OAKVILLE GROCERY WILL MAKE YOU SWEAR OFF YOUR DIET

The atmosphere is classy in a casual sort of way, with a decor that's steakhouse-meets-nightclub: dark wood and leather. The wine list is narrow but well focused on Napa, and the service is deft.

✳ Selective Shopping

✪ **Oakville Grocery Co.** (www.oakville grocery.com, 707-944-8802, 7856 St. Helena Highway, Oakville, CA 94562). This iconic country store houses a gourmet grocery. The fare is well suited to a Wine Country picnic basket, with everything from duck pâté and caviar to hearty sandwiches. The store also offers coffee by the cup, bakery treats, and local wines. It's open daily for coffee at 7:30 a.m. This is a great stop before or after wine tasting. Vintner Leslie Rudd owns Oakville Grocery.

OPPOSITE: A HAVEN FOR FOODIES AND WINE GEEKS, THE CULINARY INSTITUTE OFFERS PROGRAMS FOR CULINARY PROFESSIONALS

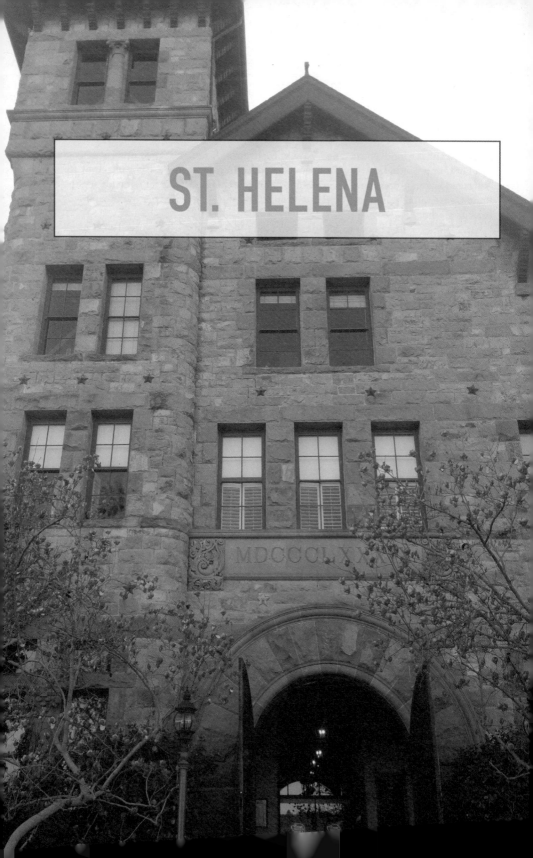

ST. HELENA

St. Helena is a food mecca. The Culinary Institute of America at Greystone is housed here, in a castle that was once the Christian Brothers winery. It's a big draw for rookies and professionals who want to improve their craft. As for wine lovers, the Rudd Center on the premises (which was once a distillery) has two tasting theaters for serious sipping.

St. Helena is also home to Meadowood Napa Valley, perhaps the swankiest of all Wine Country resorts. Every year it hosts Auction Napa Valley, one of the most successful wine charity auctions in the country, second only to the Naples Winter Wine Festival in Florida.

Travelers here soon realize that food and wine dominate the itinerary, with perhaps the possibility of squeezing in some golf and tennis between palate adventures. Unique restaurants play to both California cuisine and comfort food, and top-name chefs include Hiroyoshi Sone and Cindy Pawlcyn, who have made food, quite simply, edible art.

Tasting rooms and wineries are plentiful, with vineyards not far from the center of town. Spottswoode is a favorite, but there are many wineries worth exploring.

A STREET SCENE IN DOWNTOWN ST. HELENA

The town, which seems quaint at first glance, is surprisingly sophisticated. Shoppers will enjoy downtown St. Helena's chic strip of stores. In fact, when you slip into some of the shops, for a split-second you think you're on Madison Avenue. Woodhouse Chocolate, for example, resembles a highbrow jewelry store, but instead of jewels under glass, you'll find delectable confections. Accommodations, meanwhile, cater to a variety of interests and budgets: there are bargains here as well as luxe resorts, for which you'll pay a premium.

St. Helena is a great destination for wine tasting because there's quite a range to explore, from big to boutique, from old to new. For example, we've listed Charles Krug Winery, a historic winery, along with Hall Winery, which has only been in the area since 2007.

✳ To See & Do

BIKING **St. Helena Cyclery** (www.st helenacyclery.com, 707-963-7736, 1156 Main Street, St. Helena, CA 94574)

O prah Winfrey, *Tonight Show* host Jay Leno, and *American Idol* host Ryan Seacrest have frequented **Auction Napa Valley**, a charity event in which $10 million is routinely raised in a single afternoon. When Oprah was here she said, "Napa Valley is my new favorite place. This is how people are supposed to live—sipping a glass of wine on a patio in the afternoon, looking out over a vineyard" (www.napavintners.com).

advertises its rental bike fleet as the best in Napa Valley. With terrain that varies from meandering valleys to steep mountains and a spectacular coastline, there are roads and trails to satisfy everyone from the most leisurely sightseers to ambitious cycling fanatics.

GALLERIES AND MUSEUMS 🎨 ✒ ✪ **Aerena Gallery** (www.aerenagalleries.com, 707-963-8800, 1354 Main Street, St. Helena, CA 94574; open daily 10–6). This is an excellent gallery with serious intentions about art, specializing in contemporary paintings, photography, and crafts by emerging American artists. *Contemporary* does not necessarily read *abstract*; here the emphasis is on realist imagery. Exhibitions feature single artists, but a wide range of artists is continuously shown.

✒ 🎨 **Stevenson Museum** (www.stevensonmuseum.org, 707-963-3757, 1490 Library Lane, P.O. Box 23, St. Helena, CA 94574; open Tuesday–Saturday 12–4). Writer Robert Louis Stevenson was taken with Napa Valley. In 1880, the author of *Dr. Jekyll and Mr. Hyde* and *Treasure Island* honeymooned with his wife in a cabin near the old Silverado Mine. He wrote about the area in *The Silverado Squatters*. He called Napa's wine "bottled poetry," and Mount St. Helena was the inspiration for Spyglass Hill in *Treasure Island*. Although Stevenson spent only a few months in Napa Valley, he has been accepted as an adopted son. Part of the St. Helena Library Center, the museum has the feeling of a small chapel. Founded in 1969, on the 75th anniversary of Stevenson's death, it's more a library than a museum. It contains more than 8,000 artifacts, including dozens of paintings and photographs, as well as original Stevenson letters and manuscripts. There are also hundreds of books and first printings.

GOLF **Meadowood Napa Valley** (www.meadowood.com, 707-963-3646, 877-963-3646, 900 Meadowood Lane, St. Helena, CA 94574). This executive golf course is private for members and guests. It offers 9 holes, par 31, on a tree-lined, narrow course.

✳ Wineries

✪ **Beringer Vineyards** (www.beringer.com, 707-257-5771, 866-708-9463, 2000 Main Street, St. Helena, CA 94574; tastings daily 10–5). There's something almost regal about the Rhine House, the circa 1874 mansion that forms the centerpiece of Beringer Vineyards. Sitting amid manicured lawns and meticulously restored, the Rhine House suggests that Beringer doesn't take its past or its reputation lightly. This is one of the few wineries that has it all. A prime tourist attraction with a historical tour, it's also one of Napa's most popular makers of cabernet sauvignon and chardonnay. For a quick taste of wine, visit the Old Winery for Beringer Classics Old Bottling, where you can take in vino and history. The room is decorated with artifacts such as a photo of Clark Gable. To taste Beringer's top wines, climb the staircase of the Rhine House to the private reserve tasting room. The reserve cabernet is stunning.

Buehler Vineyards (www.buehlervineyards.com, 707-963-2155, 820 Greenfield Road, St. Helena, CA 94574; tastings by appointment). "We're not at the end of the world," John Buehler Jr. likes to say, "but you can see it from here." The winery, a complex of handsome Mediterranean buildings, is not that remote, although it is secluded above the rocky hills that overlook Lake Hennessey. The spotlight here is on cabernet, but zinfandel is also making noise. Don't miss a pour of both.

Burgess Cellars (www.burgesscellars.com, 707-963-4766, 800-752-9463, 1108 Deer Park Road, St. Helena, CA 94574; tastings by appointment). Built atop the vestiges of a stone winery that dates to the 1880s, Burgess has a low profile and likes it that way. High on the western slopes of Howell Mountain, the two-story stone-and-redwood winery is not one that tourists often happen upon. Tom Burgess began it in 1972 and built a reputation for cabernet, merlot, and syrah.

✪ **Cade Winery** (www.cadewinery.com, 707-965-2746, 360 Howell Mountain Road S., Angwin, CA 94508; tastings by appointment). California lieutenant governor Gavin Newsom and entrepreneur Gordon Getty are behind this winery atop Howell Mountain, at an altitude of 1,800 feet. The motto here is "Think Green. Drink Green." The winery is ecofriendly, and the vineyards have earned their organic certification. The focus here is on cabernet sauvignon, but the sauvignon blanc will turn your head. So will the view. On a clear day, you can spy Mount Diablo.

Chappellet Winery (www.chappellet.com, 707-963-7136, 707-286-4219, 1581 Sage Canyon Road, St. Helena, CA 94574; tastings and tours by appointment). Styled like a pyramid, this winery would make a striking statement along Highway 29. Instead, it's hidden among the rustic hills east of the valley. Built in the late 1960s by Donn and Molly Chappellet, the winery was only the second to open in the county after Prohibition ended. The vineyards are steeply terraced and produce a striking cabernet sauvignon and a Bordeaux red blend called Las Piedras.

✪ **Charles Krug Winery** (www.charleskrug.com, 707-967-2229, 800-682-KRUG, 2800 Main Street, St. Helena, CA 94574; tastings daily 10:30–5). After working under Agoston Haraszthy in Sonoma, Charles Krug built Napa Valley's first winery in 1861. This massive stone winery was gutted by fire the day after it was finished, but Krug rebuilt it. When the Mondavi family bought Krug in 1943, another Napa dynasty began. Robert Mondavi began his own winery in 1966 after a falling-out with his brother Peter. In disrepair for many years, the historic winery building has regained much of its former glory. The winemaking takes place in a facility just behind the first site. The winery bottles one of the valley's most exhaustive wine menus, and its cabernet sauvignons have recently regained their former stature.

Corison Winery (www.corison.com, 707-963-0826, 987 St. Helena Highway, St. Helena, CA 94574; tastings by appointment). Winemaker Cathy Corison is a pioneer, among the first women winemakers in the valley. She's been making wine for more than 30 years, and her background includes a decade as winemaker for Chappellet Vineyards. At Corison the specialty is cabernet, and stylistically the wines are complex but elegant. The winery resembles a nineteenth-century barn with gables, and the modest tasting room is in the middle of the cellar, with temperatures ranging from 55 degrees to a high of 70 degrees—both quaint and chilly.

Del Dotto Estate Winery & Caves (www.deldottovineyards.com, 707-963-2134, 1445 St. Helena Highway S., St. Helena, CA 94574; tastings daily 11–5 by appointment). Dave Del Dotto, once the infomercial king of late-night television, is now a vintner with some of the most opulent caves in Wine Country. They are highbrow, lined with Italian marble and ancient tiles, with mosaic marble floors underfoot and, overhead, Venetian crystal chandeliers. The winery focuses on small-lot production of high-end wines. It produces a full range, but its Bordeaux varietals are the most interesting in the lineup.

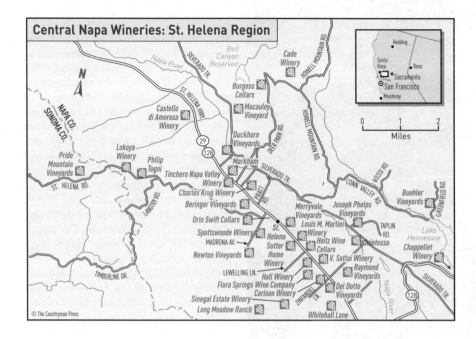

Central Napa Wineries: St. Helena Region

Duckhorn Vineyards (www.duckhorn.com, 707-963-7108, 866-367-9945, 1000 Lodi Lane, St. Helena, CA 94574; tastings daily 10–4). Duckhorn has long reigned as the king of merlot in Napa, and the winery's cabernet sauvignon and sauvignon blanc are first-rate as well. The tasting room, set in the majestic estate house, is a chic den with a fireplace, done with polished wood and granite. Since its first release in 1978, Duckhorn has been a major presence on restaurant wine lists around the country.

Flora Springs Wine Company (www.florasprings.com, 707-967-8032, 866-967-8032, tasting room: 677 St. Helena Highway, St. Helena, CA 94574; tastings daily 10–5). This tasting room on the heavy tourist path of Highway 29 is a comfortable space, decorated with humorous murals, and there's a garden in the back where you can sip from a glass on a sunny day. The winery itself, on Zinfandel Lane, is a handsome stone edifice that dates to 1888, and current owners Jerome and Flora Komes arrived in 1977. After some shaky years, the wines are now coming into their own, with a lineup that includes several solid chardonnays, an exotic sauvignon blanc named Soliloquy, and an intriguing red blend dubbed Trilogy.

✪ **Hall Winery** (www.hallwines.com, 707-967-2626, 800-688-4255, 401 St. Helena Highway S., St. Helena, CA 94574; tastings daily 10–5:30). This winery offers a glimpse into the lives of Kathryn Walt Hall, former U.S. ambassador to Austria, and her husband, Craig Hall, a Texas businessman. The duo has a focus on keeping the highest environmental standards in both the vineyards and the winery facility. As for the wine, Hall has had good success with cabernet sauvignon, merlot, and sauvignon blanc. The winemaker, Steve Leveque, is well respected, beginning his career with 16 years of crafting wine at Robert Mondavi Winery.

Heitz Wine Cellars (www.heitzcellar.com, 707-963-3542, 436 St. Helena Highway S., St. Helena, CA 94574; tastings daily 11–4:30). Driving along Highway 29, you might spot a line outside the tasting room, the wine faithful clamoring for a bottle of Heitz's Martha's Vineyard, the internationally acclaimed cabernet sauvignon. Curmudgeon and maverick Joe Heitz worked at Beaulieu before going his own way in 1961. Within

FLORA SPRINGS IS WELL KNOWN FOR ITS TASTY RED BLEND NAMED TRILOGY

a few years, he'd refurbished a stone winery in the hills of the valley's east side, keeping the old winery on Highway 29 as a tasting room. Joe died in 2000, but the winery is thriving with the second generation. The tasting room, in native stone and mahogany, showcases a library of old wines for sale, and typically two or three current wines are poured—although seldom the good stuff. Heitz also produces a chardonnay, and grignolino, a stout Italian varietal, has considerable charm.

Joseph Phelps Vineyards (www.joseph phelps.com, 707-963-2745, 800-707-5789, 200 Taplin Road, St. Helena, CA 94574; tastings by appointment). This winery pioneered Bordeaux blends in California with its Insignia bottling, and it remains among the best of the breed. Bordeaux blends use the traditional grapes of that region: cabernet sauvignon, merlot, petit verdot, and the like. Phelps built his large and elegant redwood barn in 1973 and drew immediate attention. The current offerings include some of the best cabernets in Napa Valley and a viognier.

✪ **Lokoya** (www.lokoya.com, 707-948-1968, 3787 Spring Mountain Road, St. Helena, CA 94574; tastings by appointment). The cabernet sauvignons produced here are crafted with mountain-grown fruit, so it's no wonder they're showstoppers. The gothic stone winery and tasting room have been renovated, and they offer gorgeous views. The Jackson Family wine group founded Lokoya in 1995, and it has succeeded in its mission to make cult cab.

✪ **Long Meadow Ranch Winery and Farmstead** (www.longmeadowranch.com, 707-963-4555, 738 Main Street (entrance on Charter Oak Avenue), St. Helena, CA 94574; tastings daily 11–6). Long Meadow Ranch is not just a winery, it's an agricultural experience, a place to stop for a drop-in tasting, and a place to enjoy a lingering 2-hour lunch at Farmstead. Nestled on 650 acres atop the Mayacamas Mountains, the ranch has a history that dates to the 1870s. Today, it's owned by the Hall family, and it has devoted to organic farming and produce a little of everything: eggs, olive oil, grass-fed beef, organic produce, and—of course—wine. All this shows up on the plate at Farmstead, a crossroads of great farming practices and impressive gourmet cooking. The cabernet is the main selection, and it's a burly red that usually requires a few years in the cellar. Long Meadow Ranch offers one tour, three times daily (10 a.m., 1 p.m., and 3 p.m.), called the Mayacamas Estate Experience, in which you view the estate from the comfort of a Mercedes Sprinter.

✪ **Louis M. Martini Winery** (www.louismartini.com, 707-968-3362, 800-321-WINE, 254 St. Helena Highway, St. Helena, CA 94574; tastings daily 10–6). Run by the third generation of Martinis, but owned since 2002 by the wine behemoth E&J Gallo, this large but unostentatious winery is one of Napa Valley's best-known spots. That's one of the charms of visiting Wine Country: you know the label, why not visit the source? Martini is one of the valley's great overachievers, producing a voluminous roster that runs from cabernet sauvignon to port and other dessert wines. They're all capable and good values. Its top cabernets, Monte Rosso and Lot 1, have recently regained much of their glory. Coming from Kingsburg, California, in 1922, Martini moved to St. Helena in 1933. Napa's first post-Prohibition success story, the winery flourished under founder Louis M. Martini, one of the valley's great characters. Son Louis P. Martini brought the winery into the modern era.

Macauley Vineyard (www.macauleyvineyard.com, 707-963-1863, 3520 Silverado Trail N., St. Helena, CA 94574; tastings by appointment). This is second-generation winemaking at its best. Ann Macauley Watson set the stage in the 1980s by producing a highly touted late-harvest sauvignon blanc with the help of the esteemed winemaker Rick Forman. In 2000, Ann's son Mac revived the label. Collaborating with his friend Kirk Venge, their first vintage was 2001. They say their goal is to source from the highest-quality fruit in the Napa Valley, and their great scores prove they're on the right track.

Markham Vineyards (www.markhamvineyards.com, 707-963-5292, 2812 St. Helena Highway N., St. Helena, CA 94574; tastings daily 10–5). Founded in 1978, Markham quietly went about its business until the Japanese firm Sanraku took over in 1988. Since then, the wines have been on a roller-coaster ride of quality. Once known for its elegant merlot, the winery has had more recent success with whites such as chardonnay and sauvignon blanc. Following a multimillion-dollar facelift in the early 1990s, the winery became a popular tourist attraction. Beyond large fountains out front is an expansive and affluent tasting room.

Merryvale Vineyards (www.merryvale.com, 707-963-7777, 1000 Main Street, St. Helena, CA 94574; tastings daily 10:30–5:30). As Sunny St. Helena Winery, this historic stone cellar was the first winery built here after Prohibition, and in 1937 it was the Mondavi family's first venture in Napa Valley. It became home to Merryvale in 1985, when the building was renovated; the renovation updated its wine technology while retaining much of its historic charm. Done in rich wood, the tasting room feels like a large cabin, and behind the iron gates you'll see the cask room, with its massive 100-year-old cask. Profile, a cabernet blend that's the winery's flagship, is a wine to watch.

Newton Vineyard (www.newtonvineyard.com, 707-204-7423, 2555 Madrona Avenue, St. Helena, CA 94574; tastings by appointment). Perched high on Spring Mountain, this is one of the most spectacular wineries to visit in the valley, offering an eclectic mix of elaborate English gardens, Chinese red lanterns, and gates and vineyards carved into steeply terraced hillsides. Beneath all of this is an extensive cave system that extends several stories beneath the surface of the earth. As part of the tour, tastings are offered in a barrel-aging corridor deep inside one cave. The merlot and chardonnays are worth a taste.

Orin Swift Cellars (www.orinswift.com, 707-967-9179, 1325 Main Street, St. Helena, CA 94574; tastings daily 10–5). David Swift Phinney is producing crazy good artisan blends from Rhone and Bordeaux varietals. One tasty example is Abstract, a blend of grenache, petite sirah, and syrah. Phinney made a name for himself with his popular Prisoner and Saldo labels, which he sold in 2011. Prisoner was a particularly inventive zinfandel blend, with cabernet sauvignon, petite sirah, and charbono in the mix. Phinney fell in love with wine on a lark, taking a friend up on an offer to go to Florence and study in 1995. He came back, worked at Robert Mondavi Winery, and decided that if he was going to work that hard, he was going to have to work for himself. He founded Orin

Swift Cellars in 1998. For the curious, Orin is his father's middle name while Swift is his mother's maiden name.

Philip Togni Vineyard (www.philiptognivineyard.com, 707-963-3731, 3780 Spring Mountain Road, St. Helena, CA 94574; tastings by appointment). Creating a name for himself as winemaker for Mayacamas, Chappellet, Chalone, and Cuvaison, Togni began making his own wine in 1983. His cabernet sauvignon is an assertive beauty that has a legion of fans. Togni is a meticulous and hands-on winemaker, and the winery is a modest affair.

✪ **Pride Mountain Vineyards** (www.pridewines.com, 707-963-4949, 4026 Spring Mountain Road, St. Helena, CA 94574; tastings by appointment). Some 2,100 feet up, on the crest of the Mayacamas Mountains, this estate straddles Napa and Sonoma counties. In fact, the county line is laid out on the crush pad, so visitors can stand with one foot in each county. The current winery may just be a modest wood-beam affair, but the wines produced inside are exceptional.

✪ **Raymond Vineyard & Cellar** (www.raymondvineyards.com, 707-963-3141, 849 Zinfandel Lane, St. Helena, CA 94574; tastings daily 10–4). Here vintner Jean-Charles Boisset has put his touch on a family winery that was founded in 1970, and the result is a whimsical spin on wine and everything that goes into making it. The goal here is to teach visitors something, with some hands-on, experiential fun. There's plenty to do, from the Corridor of the Senses, where you explore aromas, to the swanky Crystal Cellar, where you learn the art of decanting, to the Theatre of Nature, where you walk through examples of biodynamic farming to explore soils, vines, etc. Raymond is certified organic and biodynamic, and 100 percent of the winery's power comes from renewable solar energy. Boisset grew up in Burgundy, and he said his late grandmother, the ultimate gardener who believed in homeopathic remedies, taught him to be a good steward of the land.

✪ **Sinegal Wine Estate** (www.sinegalestate.com, 707-244-1187, 2125 Inglewood Avenue, St. Helena, CA 94574; tastings by appointment). This is a place for cabernet-lovers and history buffs. The cabernets produced here are top-rate, and the property has a stone winery, a Victorian house, and a sprawl of gardens. Vintner David Sinegal is the former CEO of Costco, and his father, Jim, was the founder of the retail giant. Together they bought the historic Inglenook Estate in 2013 and renovated it. A walking tour of the grounds reveals how impressive their pursuit has been.

✪ **Spottswoode Winery** (www.spottswoode.com, 707-963-0134, 1902 Madrona Avenue, St. Helena, CA 94574; tastings by appointment). The first Spottswoode wines were made in 1982 in the basement of this estate's 1882 Victorian. Intense and impeccably balanced, Spottswoode's cabernet sauvignon was quickly regarded as among the best in the 1980s, a stature it retains. The cabernet's success is nearly matched by the sauvignon blanc, a wine typically intense in citrus and mineral character. Run by the Novak family, Spottswoode is a small enterprise.

Stony Hill Vineyard (www.stonyhillvineyard.com, 707-963-2636, 3 miles north of St. Helena off Highway 29; tastings by appointment; the winery will provide exact address upon appointment). The white wines, and in particular the chardonnay, give this winery its cachet. These wines strike a balance between intense fruit and crisp acidity. The wines here manage to have great bones (structure) and fleshy fruit. And to think all this comes from an old goat farm that dates back to 1943. The founders were smitten with white Burgundy and were thrilled to find an ideal place to grow chardonnay. The 160-acre property sits on the western slope of Napa Valley, between 700 and 1,200 feet above the valley floor. Now the lineup of wines includes riesling, gewürztraminer, and semillon, among others.

Sutter Home Winery (www.sutterhome.com, 707-963-3104, ext. 4208, 800-967-4663, 277 St. Helena Highway, St. Helena, CA 94574; tastings daily 10–5). Who'd have thought back in the 1970s that a simple, sweet rosé would become the Holy Grail—some would say Unholy Grail—of California wine? Since white zinfandel became one of Wine Country's hottest commodities, Sutter Home has grown from one of Napa Valley's smallest wineries to one of its biggest. In 1972, winemaker Bob Trinchero began tinkering with a rosé-style zinfandel. Sutter Home called it white zinfandel, and it became one of the best-selling varieties in America. There's no tour here—the wine is made elsewhere—but Sutter Home's tasting room is an expansive space that doubles as a folksy museum of wine and Americana. Visitors should try the red zinfandel as well as the white; it's sturdy and tasty.

Trinchero (www.trincheronapavalley.com, 707-963-1160, 3070 N. St. Helena Highway, St. Helena, CA 94574; tours by appointment). Keep your eye on single-vineyard bottlings here with the tasting option "A Taste of Terroir." The property dates back to 1948, and a tour of it gives you a good feel for the 22-acre spread, which offers striking views. The family-owned winery has built an impressive portfolio of brands over the years, with Trinchero at the forefront.

○ **Viader** (www.viader.com, 707-963-3816 option 110, 1120 Deer Park Road, Deer Park, CA 94576; tastings daily by appointment). Argentine-born Delia Viader prefers

THESE RIBBED VINEYARDS NEAR ST. HELEN'S SPOTTSWOODE WINERY CATCH YOUR EYE

Old World wines, so she imported Bordeaux-style winemaking to Northern California's Wine Country. She planted rows of vines up and down the mountain, a European design that had never been tried in the area. Her scores from reviewers showed that her instincts—to chase the sun for the optimal exposure and to plant amid rocky soils with good drainage—were spot-on. This makes the vines struggle, producing concentrated fruit and, in the end, striking wines.

V. Sattui Winery (www.vsattui.com, 707-963-7774, 1111 White Lane, St. Helena, CA 94574; tastings daily 9–6). Just about every winery has a picnic table tucked somewhere, but V. Sattui is Lawn Lunch Central. The tasting room doubles as a deli shop. The front lawn is shaded by tall oaks and filled with frolicking kids. Picnickers won't find a heartier welcome in Napa Valley. While some wineries prefer simply to make wine and not deal with the public, V. Sattui is just the opposite. Its wines are available only at the winery. It's a busy place, yet the atmosphere is cordial, not frantic. The winery produces solid chardonnays and zinfandels, but for good picnic wines, try the light and fruity Johannisberg Riesling and Gamay Rouge.

Whitehall Lane Winery (www.whitehalllane.com, 707-963-9454, 800-963-9454 ext. 19, 1563 St. Helena Highway S., St. Helena, CA 94574; tastings daily 10–5:45). This handsomely modern winery is seemingly designed with geometric building blocks, and it's worth a visit, thanks to the Leonardini family of San Francisco, who took control of the winery in 1993. The family updated the winemaking, instituted a new barrel-aging program, and was very particular when sourcing vineyards. The winery produces first-rate cabernet sauvignon and merlot.

✳ Lodging

✪ **Adagio Inn** (www.adagioinn.com, 707-963-2238, 1417 Kearney Street, St. Helena, CA 94574; $$$$). The sun-soaked porch at this 1904 Victorian cottage offers relaxation after a day of shopping and wine tasting. It has a one-bedroom suite with a two-person jetted tub and a separate apartment that sleeps up to four. The inn is spacious and done in romantically antique decor. The location is nearly ideal, in a quiet residential neighborhood a few steps from St. Helena's Main Street.

🍃 **El Bonita Motel** (www.elbonita .com, 707-963-3216, 800-541-3284, 195 Main Street, St. Helena, CA 94574; $$–$$$$). Don't let the "motel" in the name fool you. The 1950s meets the new millennium at El Bonita, a chic, art deco, pastel-hued classic. It's also Napa's best bargain. Built in 1953, the motel was renovated and newly landscaped in 1992. The garden and lawn span 2.5 acres, all sheltered from busy Highway 29. Trees and hedges also help muffle the steady hum of traffic. There's continental breakfast service in the lobby or—weather permitting—on the patio.

Harvest Inn (www.harvestinn.com, 707-963-9463, 800-950-8466, 1 Main Street, St. Helena, CA 94574; $$$–$$$$). There's a bit of Old England in Napa Valley at the Harvest Inn, a stately English Tudor–style lodge built from the bricks and cobblestones of old San Francisco homes. The lush landscaping also helps to create the aura of another time and place. The inn overlooks a 14-acre working vineyard and is within strolling distance of many wineries.

✪ **Meadowood Napa Valley** (www .meadowood.com, 707-963-3646, 877-963-3646, 900 Meadowood Lane, St. Helena, CA 94574; $$$$). Meadowood never falters in its interpretation of luxury. Its white-trimmed buildings, tiered with gabled windows and porches, are reminiscent of New England's turn-of-the-twentieth-century cottages. The staff pampers with style, and a soothing sense of privacy prevails. Most of the resort's 85 cottages, suites, and lodges—scattered around a gorgeous, wooded 250-acre property—have cathedral ceilings, skylights, ceiling fans, and air-conditioning. Breakfast is not included; however, a continental repast can be delivered to your door or a full feast is available at the Grill. Better yet, try a light breakfast by the pool during the summer months only, surrounded by lush lawns and trees. Meadowood also has one of the finest health facilities in the valley, with aerobic and exercise rooms and a full spa.

Shady Oaks Country Inn (www .shadyoaksinn.com, 707-963-1190, 399 Zinfandel Lane, St. Helena, CA 94574; $$$). Oak and walnut trees surround this friendly country inn consisting of three guest rooms with private baths, all furnished with antiques. A full gourmet

THE COURTYARD AT THE HARVEST INN WHERE MANY COUPLES SAY "I DO"

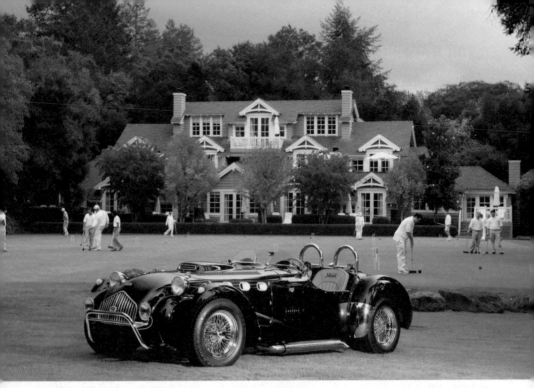

CROQUET ANYONE? THE IMMACULATE GROUNDS OF MEADOWOOD RESORT

champagne breakfast—eggs Benedict or Belgian waffles are the norm—is served in your room or in the dining room and on the garden patio, which is guarded by Roman columns. Wine and cheese are served in the evening. For those who are up for a little recreation, there's a bocce ball court in front of the inn.

Southbridge Napa Valley (www .southbridgenapavalley.com, 707-967-9400, 855-967-9400, 1020 Main Street, St. Helena, CA 94574; $$$$). A classy addition to St. Helena, this inn complex is a sleekly modern Italianate design. All 21 rooms are on the second floor and done in handsome ivory white and cream hues with sophisticated wood accents. Just off the lobby is a family-style Italian restaurant called Pizzeria Tra Vigne; it's not bad for a quick pizza (see listing under *Restaurants*). Also part of the complex is the Health Spa Napa Valley. A continental breakfast is included.

Vineyard Country Inn (www.vineyard countryinn.com, 707-963-1000, 201 Main Street, St. Helena, CA 94574; $$$–$$$$). This lovely inn takes its inspiration from a French country village. Surrounding a central court, the buildings are crowned with steeply pitched roofs and intricate brick chimneys. There are 21 suites with exposed-beam ceilings, redbrick fireplaces, king- or queen-sized beds, and wet bars with refrigerators. Many have balconies with vineyard views. For the breakfast buffet, small tables are grouped around the large dining room fireplace. The inn is on busy Highway 29, but the rooms are relatively quiet.

✪ **Wine Country Inn & Cottages** (www.winecountryinn.com, 707-963-7077, 1152 Lodi Lane, St. Helena, CA 94574; $$–$$$$). Set on a vineyard property, this inn offers striking views and amenities like wine receptions on Friday and Saturday nights, in-room spa treatments, and a welcome policy with pets. Check out the special packages and you'll see why this is such a great romantic escape.

✳ Where to Eat

Gillwood's Café (www.gillwoodscafe.com, 707-963-1788, 1313 Main Street, St. Helena, CA 94574). This is a great stop for breakfast and lunch. There are delicious burgers, sandwiches, and salads, and if you're a breakfast person, Gillwood's serves it all day long.

Giugni's (707-963-3421, 1227 Main Street, St. Helena, CA 94574). This fun Italian deli offers classic deli meats, including corned beef and pastrami, as well as a great chicken salad sandwich.

Goose & Gander (www.goosegander.com, 707-967-8779, 1245 Spring Street, St. Helena, CA 94574; $$$; cuisine: American). With its dark, pub-like dining room, its gourmet grub, and its basement bar that stays open until midnight on weekends, this spot is rustic-chic. The cuisine is American, with full entrées as well as plenty of bar bites in the mix. Chef Nic Jones makes savvy comfort food, with popular dishes like the G&G burger and the Sakura Farms pork chop. For those looking for a lighter meal, there are plenty of fish and vegetarian options. While the food is top-rate, this place has made a name for itself because of its great cocktails and wine list, with Scott Beattie in charge. Some favorite cocktails include the Scarlet Gander, the Cucumber Collins, and the Live Mint Mojito.

🍽 Gott's Roadside Tray Gourmet (www.gotts.com, 707-963-3486, 933 Main Street, St. Helena, CA 94574). This is a classic old drive-in restaurant—although you have to walk to the window these days—but average joes and gourmands alike flock to Gott's for its updated, 1950s-style, fast-food menu. The burgers, fries, milkshakes, and onion rings are top notch. There's also beer on tap and wine by the glass or the bottle. Seating is strictly picnic table, but that's half the fun. A burger joint like this can only survive in a fancy-pants food haven like Napa Valley by acting like a fancy-pants restaurant. It's particular when it sources ingredients—egg buns from Sciambra Bakery in Napa, fresh halibut for the fish tacos, and sushi-grade tuna for ahi burgers.

◐ The Charter Oak (www.thecharteroak.com, 707-302-6996, 1050 Charter Oak Avenue, St. Helena, CA 94574; $$$$; cuisine: California). When the three-Michelin-star Restaurant at Meadowood St. Helena is fancier (and pricier) than everyday cravings allow, this casual-chic eatery offers feasts from the same celebrity executive chef, Christopher Kostow. He and acclaimed restaurant director Nathaniel Dorn actually "stole" their own Meadowood chef de cuisine Katianna Hong for this inventive foray into California cooking. Expect bright, bold flavors for dishes such as crispy Brussels sprouts draped in Petaluma-made water buffalo mozzarella, grilled buttermilk brined chicken with Napa grape leaves and fresh and dried grapes, or the signature succulent beef rib that's hearth-grilled over cabernet sauvignon barrel wood and presented with roasted beets bathed in the meat's own rendered fat. This restaurant, formerly Tra Vigne, is lovely to look at, sporting a new, open-hearth kitchen, minimalist wood tables, an elegant brick-back bar, and stark charcoal-color walls warmed up with sepia photo murals. While the huge wine list impresses, cocktails are another must, in delicious mixes like the Cold Brew and Rum—of aged rums, cold brew coffee, honey, Bénédictine, and chocolate bitters. Family-style quaffs? Yes, please. Shareable, large-format cocktails include creative items such as "A Handle of Boulevardier" that serves six with brown butter bourbon, cocoa nib, Amaro Montenegro, and Aperol.

Model Bakery (www.themodelbakery.com, 707-963-8192, 1357 Main Street, St. Helena, CA 94574). Everything here is baked in a big brick oven. Sweet or sour baguettes are stacked like kindling in tall wicker baskets, and scones, muffins, and croissants compete for shelf space.

Behind the counter are burly loaves of rye, powdered with white flour on top. There's a full coffee bar, and lunch items—sandwiches, pizzas, and salads—are offered.

Pizzeria Tra Vigne (www.pizzeria travigne.com, 707-967-9999, 1016 Main Street, St. Helena, CA 94574; $$; cuisine: Italian). This family-friendly house of pizza has a stylishly casual atmosphere and reasonable prices, which make it a good lunch stop while you're touring the valley. The dining room is big and airy, with a brick, wood-fired pizza oven in full view. There are cozy booths and large communal tables that seat 12 or more. Don't let the laid-back veneer fool you, though. This place makes a sophisticated pizza pie. The menu is the same at lunch or dinner, and if you don't feel like eating the usual pizza, try something called *piadine*, a basic pizza topped with salad, which you fold and eat like a taco. The lemon chicken version is wonderful. The wine list is appealingly no-nonsense.

○ **Press** (www.pressnapavalley.com, 707-967-0550, 587 St. Helena Highway, St. Helena, CA 94574; $$$$; cuisine: steakhouse). This is a first-class steakhouse. In fact, the 14-ounce, dry-aged ribeye is one of the best steaks we've ever tasted. It's pricey, but decadence this tasty is hard to resist, plus it's big enough for two. The menu is a carnivore's delight, but there are also tasty seafood options. The eclectic all-Napa wine list is impressive but fairly expensive. The service is first-class and the decor is inviting, uncluttered sophistication at its best: high ceilings, expansive glass, and black walnut accents. Good tip: If it's warm enough, sit outdoors by the fireplace.

Villa Corona (www.villacorona catering.com, 707-963-7812, 1138 Main Street, St. Helena, CA 94574). Homemade flour tortillas and specialty sauces make for tasty burritos, particularly the super burrito. Some good breakfast dishes include the huevos rancheros.

✳ Entertainment

Cameo Cinema (www.cameocinema .com, 707-963-9779, 1340 Main Street, St. Helena, CA 94574). This charming theater in downtown St. Helena shows first-run films. The fare is mostly American, although occasional art and foreign films come for a stay.

✳ Selective Shopping

Amelia Claire (www.ameliaclaire.com, 707-963-8502, 1230 Main Street, St. Helena, CA 94574) carries upscale shoes from Aquatalia—100-percent waterproof shoes.

Calla Lily (707-963-8188, 1222 Main Street, St. Helena, CA 94574) is the consummate bed-and-bath shop, offering furniture, jewelry, linens, lotions, etc.

Dean & DeLuca (www.deandeluca .com/sth-ca, 707-967-9980, 607 St. Helena Highway S., St. Helena, CA 94574). This gourmet food store has a large and superb selection of California wines. Prices are the going rate.

Fideaux (www.fideaux.net, 707-967-9935, 1312 Main Street, St. Helena, CA 94574) is where PetSmart meets Fifth Avenue. In Wine Country, even dogs are connoisseurs with highbrow tastings; there's a lineup of biscuits in buckets so that dogs can pick out their favorite treat. The biscuits run the gamut—sweet potato, honey-glazed chicken with apple, and turkey with apple and cheese. Among the avant-garde items you'll find here is a wine-barrel doghouse. There's also a branch in Healdsburg.

Jan de Luz (www.jandeluzlinens.com, 707-963-1550, 1219 Main Street, St. Helena, CA 94574). The owner of this shop is French. His namesake store features his custom-designed linens, chandeliers, fountains, etc.

○ **Napa Valley Olive Oil Manufacturing Co.** (www.nvoliveoilmfg.com, 707-963-4173, 835 Charter Oak Avenue, St.

The specialty wine shops in Napa and Sonoma counties are, as you might imagine, among the finest in the nation, offering a huge variety as well as hard-to-find treasures. You'll be surprised to learn that wine is seldom less expensive at the wineries than it is at local retail shops, unless you catch a sale or buy by the case. You also run the risk, of course, of not being able to find a wine you love at the winery. It's your gamble.

Helena, CA 94574). Entering this faded white barn feels like going into a glorious time warp. The shop dates to the 1920s, when Napa Valley was largely populated by Italian farmers. You're as likely to hear Italian inside as English, and the deli counter looks like your grandmother's kitchen—if your grandmother were from Naples. There are picnic tables outside.

St. Helena St. Helena Antiques (707-963-5878, 1231 Main Street, St. Helena, CA 94574)—yes, "St. Helena" *is* stated twice in the store name: a bit unusual, but then so is the shop. It has a large collection of corkscrews and eighteenth- and nineteenth-century antiques.

St. Helena Wine Center (www.shwc.com, 707-963-1313, 1321 Main Street, St.

Helena, CA 94574). One of Napa's oldest, dating to 1953, this shop believes in the notion of "only the best," offering few bargains. It has a small but extremely select library of current Napa and Sonoma wines. There's also a tasting bar.

✪ **Woodhouse Chocolate** (www.woodhousechocolate.com, 707-963-8413, 800-966-3468, 1367 Main Street, St. Helena, CA 94574). This bright and airy house of chocolates resembles a highbrow jewelry store, but the prized gems here are, thankfully, edible. Woodhouse specializes in European-style fresh crème chocolate with no preservatives. Exotic treats include the Thai Ginger chocolate and the Diva, a spiced pecan in rich caramel surrounded by a milk chocolate shell. Don't miss this classy shop.

WOODHOUSE CHOCOLATE SHOWCASES ITS CANDIES LIKE PRIZED JEWELS

GET PAMPERED

The Spa at Meadowood (www.meadowood.com, 707-967-1275, 877-963-3646, 900 Meadowood Lane, St. Helena, CA 94574). Want to be pampered? The Spa at Meadowood Resort is the place. One of Napa Valley's best spas, it comes at a price, yet a basic massage is priced competitively. Meadowood specializes in face and body treatments as well as wellness programs. The setting alone soothes the soul. The spa is set in the lush foothills of Howell Mountain, and the outside pool and Jacuzzi are surrounded by towering trees. Treatments are varied and include "culinary" options using fried fruits, grains, and nuts. Massage rooms are dimly lit, and light music is piped in. Treatments are available to resort guests and members only. The 90-minute Essential Journey experience is a 60-minute massage and a body treatment or facial: $225. ✪

✷ Special Events

Auction Napa Valley (www.auctionnapa valley.org, 707-963-3388, Meadowood Resort, St. Helena, CA 94574). *The* chic wine outing, this three-day June event is busy with extravagant parties, dances, and dinners. Auction tickets cost a fortune but are in high demand. All the big names of the Napa wine industry attend, and the auction raises millions for local charities.

✪ **The Culinary Institute of America at Greystone** (www.ciachef.edu, 707-967-1100, 2555, Main Street, St. Helena, CA 94574). The school offers a variety of continuing-education programs for the food and wine enthusiast, in one of Napa Valley's most magnificent properties. Your classroom is in a castle!

Hometown Harvest Festival (www .cityofsthelena.org, 707-968-2222, downtown St. Helena, CA 94574). A rich Napa tradition, celebrating the end of the growing season and the summer's bountiful harvest. One weekend in late October, there's scads of food, wine tasting, arts and crafts, music featuring local bands, a kids' carnival, and even a pet parade.

OPPOSITE: THE WINNING CHARDONNAY THAT JOLTED THE WINE WORLD AT THE PARIS TASTING OF 1976

CALISTOGA

When you come to Calistoga, the goal is to relax at a spa and render yourself a noodle al dente. "To spa" is, of course, a verb, and in Wine Country it's practically considered a form of exercise.

The downtown strip is lined with trees, and there are local shops to explore, volcanic mud baths to experience, and outdoor bistros that allow you to take it all in. Calistoga has small-town charm combined with the sophistication of a world-class wine region. It's surrounded by vineyards and highbrow wineries, including the famous Chateau Montelena, which is featured in the 2008 film *Bottle Shock*. Chateau Montelena jolted the wine world by winning the legendary Paris Tasting in 1976. In fact, a bottle of the winery's 1973 chardonnay is in the Smithsonian, a testament to the way the blind-tasting upset led to the discovery of California wine, and in particular Napa Valley wine.

Another winery that history buffs won't want to miss is the architecturally adventurous Castello di Amorosa. The postmodern Italianate castle took 14 years to build, not to mention lots of *dinero*—$30 million, to be exact.

Wineries aside, this resort town has always been popular for its natural hot springs, drawing residents and visitors to the Napa Valley for over a hundred years.

✳ To See & Do

BIKING **Getaway Adventures** (www.getawayadventures.com, 707-568-3040, 800-499-2453, 2228 Northpoint Parkway, Santa Rosa, CA 95407). This outfit offers a day-long bicycle wine tour led by professional local guides. The tour follows scenic country roads with stops at several wineries. There are a variety of organized tours and route suggestions for the Calistoga region. The tour price includes hybrid bike and helmet rental and a gourmet picnic lunch. A great way to explore Wine Country.

Calistoga Bike Shop (707-942-9687, 1318 Lincoln Avenue, Calistoga, CA 94515). Another place offering daily rentals. Many inns also allow guests the use of bicycles for casual day trips.

🖋 **Old Faithful Geyser** (www.oldfaithfulgeyser.com, 707-942-6463, 1299 Tubbs Lane, Calistoga, CA 94515; 1 mile north of Calistoga). One of just three regularly erupting geysers in the world, it shoots steam and vapor 40 to 50 feet into the air for 3 minutes, and repeats this feat every 40 minutes. Because seismic activity influences the frequency of the eruptions, many believe Old Faithful predicts earthquakes. The site includes picnic grounds and a petting zoo with llamas and goats. Admission: $15 adults, $13 seniors, $9 children 4–12, free for children under 4. Open daily including holidays, 8:30–5 (winter) and 8:30–7 (summer).

PARKS 🖋 **Bothe-Napa Valley State Park** (www.napavalleystateparks.org, 707-942-4575, 3801 St. Helena Highway N., Calistoga, CA 94515; midway between St. Helena and Calistoga, off Highway 29). This 1,920-acre state park has 50 developed campsites. Campers up to 31 feet and trailers to 24 feet can be accommodated; no sanitation station is provided. For those who prefer a solid roof over their heads, there are 10 yurts

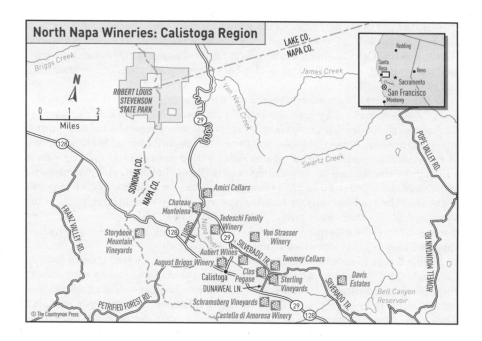

North Napa Wineries: Calistoga Region

Briggs Creek

LAKE CO.
NAPA CO.

James Creek

Redding

Santa Rosa
Reno
Sacramento
San Francisco
Monterey

N

0 1 2
Miles

ROBERT LOUIS STEVENSON STATE PARK

Van Ness Creek

29

SONOMA CO.
NAPA CO.

128

Swartz Creek

POPE VALLEY RD.

Amici Cellars

Chateau Montelena

Tedeschi Family Winery

Storybook Mountain Vineyards

128

TUBBS LN.

Napa River

29

Von Strasser Winery

SILVERADO TR.

FRANZ VALLEY RD.

Aubert Wines

August Briggs Winery

Twomey Cellars

Clos Pegase

Calistoga

DUNAWEAL LN.

Sterling Vineyards

Davis Estates

HOWELL MOUNTAIN RD.

SILVERADO TR.

Bell Canyon Reservoir

PETRIFIED FOREST RD.

Schramsberg Vineyards

Castello di Amorosa Winery

29

128

© The Countryman Press

to choose from in two sizes, and several restored historic cabins. Services include horseback-riding trails, hiking, swimming pool, picnic area, and exhibitions. Handicapped accessible in all areas. Park admission: $8 for parking. There is an additional fee for horseback riding and the use of the swimming pool, to be paid at the park entrance.

Pioneer Park (Cedar Street just off Lincoln Avenue) If you're touring Wine Country with tykes, you'll want to grab a picnic or snack and head to Pioneer Park. It's free, and there's a pleasant little playground. The kids will thank you.

✻ Wineries

✪ **Amici Cellars** (www.amicicellars.com, 707-967-9560, 3130 Old Lawley Toll Road, Calistoga, CA 94515; tastings by appointment). A group of friends decided to share their passion for winemaking and surprised themselves by ultimately creating a winery. They named the winery Amici, Italian for "friends," because it was a clan

GRAPES EVENTUALLY BECAME THE DEFAULT CROP IN NAPA AND SONOMA TIM FISH

that created all the magic. In 1990, they set out to crush a few tons of grapes for their personal cellars, but now they're producing wines for the public. The owners are John Harris, Bob and Celia Shepard, and Bart Woytowicz. They continue to focus on artisanal winemaking, with small batches of cabernet sauvignon, chardonnay, pinot noir, and sauvignon blanc.

⊕ Aubert Wines (www.aubertwines.com, 707-942-4333, 333 Silverado Trail, Calistoga, CA 94515; tastings by appointment). Vintner Mark Aubert makes chardonnays that have explosive fruit, groomed in vineyards that harvest about half of what normal vineyards produce. Aubert learned from the best and the brightest, at one time serving as the winemaking assistant to rock star Helen Turley when she was making wine at Calistoga's Peter Michael Winery. Aubert credits Ulises Valdez, his vineyard manager and viticultural partner, for helping him produce class-act fruit. His first vintage was in 2004, and he produces roughly 4,000 cases a year. If you want to buy a bottle of the cult chardonnay, patience is a virtue. Aubert grew up in St. Helena, the son of a pharmacist who owned a cabernet vineyard. He jokes that when he was a teenager, other kids were beer drinkers when he was sipping champagne.

August Briggs (www.augustbriggswinery.com, 707-942-4912, 1307 Lincoln Avenue, Calistoga, CA 94515; tastings daily 11–5 except for Tuesday, which is by appointment only). Here the mainstay is pinot noir and chardonnay. Long known as a talented consulting winemaker, August "Joe" Briggs founded this namesake winery in 1995, but now nephew and co-winemaker Jesse Inman, among other partners, run the day-to-day operations.

🍷 **⊕ Castello di Amorosa Winery** (www.castellodiamorosa.com, 707-967-6272, 4045 St. Helena Highway N., Calistoga, CA 94515; tastings daily 10–6). The wineries of Napa have often been called "castles," but in the case of Castello di Amorosa, it's true.

THE MEDIEVAL-STYLE CASTELLO DI AMOROSA IN CALISTOGA

THE COLORFUL INTERIOR OF CASTELLO DI AMOROSA

Daryl Sattui, who owns the tourist-friendly V. Sattui Winery, spent 14 years and $30 million building this extravagant, 121,000-square-foot, medieval-style fortress. With 107 rooms on eight levels, it has towers, turrets, a moat, a dungeon, and even a torture chamber. The tour is exhaustive but fascinating, rich with colorful frescoes and a barrel cellar room underground with a dramatically arched ceiling. Appropriately, the winery makes Italian-style wines, from pinot grigio to "Super Tuscan" blends, as well as mainstream wines like chardonnay and merlot and everything in between.

✪ **Chateau Montelena** (www.montelena.com, 707-942-5105, 1429 Tubbs Lane, Calistoga, CA 94515; tastings daily 9:30–4). "Not bad for a kid from the sticks," was all Jim Barrett said when Chateau Montelena stunned the wine world by winning the legendary Paris Tasting in 1976. A Who's Who of French wine cognoscenti selected Chateau Montelena's 1973 chardonnay in a blind tasting over the best of Burgundy. Chateau Montelena's star has been shining brightly ever since. No serious wine lover would think of leaving Chateau Montelena off the tour list. The wines are first-rate, and the winery is an elegant and secluded old estate at the foot of Mount St. Helena. Alfred Tubbs founded the original Chateau Montelena in 1882, and its French architect used the great chateaux of Bordeaux as inspiration. The approach isn't too impressive, but walk around to the true facade, and you'll discover a dramatic stone castle. During Prohibition the winery fell into neglect, but in 1958, a Chinese immigrant, Yort Franks, created the Chinese-style Jade Lake and the

THE FAMED CHATEAU MONTELENA HELPED PUT NAPA VALLEY ON THE MAP

CLOS PEGASE LOOKS LIKE A BABYLONIAN TEMPLE

surrounding garden. It's shaded by weeping willows, with swans and geese, walkways, islands, and brightly painted pavilions.

✪ **Clos Pegase** (www.clospegase.com, 707-942-4981, 1060 Dunaweal Lane, Calistoga, CA 94515; tastings daily 10:30–5). Clos Pegase is architecturally flamboyant, a postmodern throwback to the Babylonian temple—a shrine to the gods of art, wine, and commerce. This commanding structure of tall pillars and archways in shades of gray is the work of noted Princeton architect Michael Graves. The name *Clos Pegase* derives from Pegasus, the winged horse that, according to the Greeks, gave birth to art and wine. Pegase's wines include a ripe and complex cabernet sauvignon and a chardonnay that's typically refined but with plenty of forward fruit. If you like tasting exotic wines not available on the market, join Pegase Circle, their wine club. As a member, you'll receive regular shipments of special reserve wines.

Envy Wines (www.envywines.com, 707-942-4670, 1170 Tubbs Lane, Calistoga, CA 94515; tastings daily 10–4:30). This winery's patio gives you a taste of Tuscany, a great picnic spot. Inside the tasting room, which doubles as an art gallery, is a lovely place to taste pours as well. As for the wine, it continues to garner good reviews. Veteran Napa winemaker Nils Venge and vintner Mark Carter offer an impressive range of wines, from sauvignon blanc to cabernet to rosé to petite sirah, among an assortment of blends.

Frank Family Vineyards (www.frankfamilyvineyards.com, 707-942-0859, 800-574-9463, 1091 Larkmead Lane, Calistoga, CA 94515; tastings daily 10–5, by appointment Friday–Sunday). Rich Frank, a longtime Disney executive, couldn't find the time to take long vacations, so he settled for short trips to Napa Valley and soon fell in love with Wine Country. Housed in the historic Larkmead Winery, the tasting room focuses on cabernet and zinfandel, but it also produces some tasty chardonnay and sangiovese. The tasting room is located in the original yellow Craftsman house on the property.

✪ **Schramsberg Vineyards** (www.schramsberg.com, 707-942-4558, 800-877-3623, 1400 Schramsberg Road, Calistoga, CA 94515; tastings and tours daily by appointment). No winery symbolizes the rebirth of Napa Valley better than Schramsberg. The late Jack and Jamie Davies were the quintessential post-Prohibition wine pioneers in their day. When they bought the old Schramsberg estate in 1965, it was rich in history but near ruin. Jacob Schram had established Napa's first hillside vineyard and winery in 1862 and, with the help of Chinese laborers, built a network of underground cellars. After a few years of sweat equity, Jack and Jamie became the country's premier producers of *méthode champenoise* sparkling wine. With their passing, son Hugh has taken over the business. As a tribute to Jack, the winery has been making a Diamond Mountain cabernet called J. Davies that's worth trying. The lovely grounds of Schramsberg are also worth exploring. The tour offers insight into the winery's history and the art of making bubbly. The highlight is the old cellar caves lined with walls of bottles.

✒ ✪ **Sterling Vineyards** (www.sterlingvineyards.com, 707-942-3344, 800-726-6136, 1111 Dunaweal Lane, Calistoga, CA 94515; tastings daily 10–5). Sterling isn't just a winery, it's an experience. A modern white villa perched atop a tall knoll, it just may be Napa Valley's most dramatic visual statement. Every 15 minutes you'll hear the bells ring from the towers. A little-known fact is that the ancient bells hail from across the pond—from London's Church of St. Dunstan's, which was destroyed during the bombing of World War II.

Sure, there's a touch of Disneyland—you ascend on an aerial tramway—but that's Sterling's appeal, and from the top the view is unsurpassed. Sterling retains such a contemporary look that it's hard to believe it was built in 1973. A well-marked, self-guided tour allows a leisurely glimpse of the winery's workings and leads you ultimately to one of Napa's most relaxing tasting rooms. Although its offerings have been inconsistent, Sterling occasionally achieves greatness, particularly with its Reserve Cabernet.

✪ **Storybook Mountain Vineyards** (www.storybookwines.com, 707-942-5310, 3835 Highway 128, Calistoga, CA 94515; tastings and tours by appointment). With a dramatic gate along Highway 128 and tucked amid rolling hills, Storybook Mountain earns its romantic name. The winery is best known for its heady zin, complex and zesty, but it also makes cabernet sauvignon, a red blend, and viognier. The regular and the reserve bottlings are typically powerful and long-lived. Jacob and Adam Grimm—the brothers Grimm, thus the Storybook name—made wine on the property back in the late nineteenth century. Jerry Seps restored it in 1976, and this small and unpretentious winery remains his baby. The wines reveal a hands-off attitude: the vineyards are organic, and Seps tinkers little with the wine in the cellar.

Tedeschi Family Winery (www.tedeschifamilywinery.com, 707-501-0668, 2779 Grant Street, Calistoga, CA 94515; tastings by appointment). The Tedeschi family has been in the Napa Valley for several generations. Eugene Tedeschi planted the first grapes on their Calistoga property in the 1960s. Today, Emil Tedeschi produces handcrafted wines in the tradition of his Italian heritage. The winery is bicycle friendly, located in the north part of Napa Valley.

TAKE A RIDE ON A GONDOLA TO THE MOUNTAIN TOP TASTING ROOM AT STERLING VINEYARDS TIM FISH

Twomey Calistoga (www.twomey.com, 707-942-2489, 1183 Dunaweal Lane, Calistoga, CA 94515; tastings daily). Founded in 1999, this winery specializes in pinot noir, merlot and sauvignon blanc. It's owned by the Duncan family, whose other brand is Silver Oak Cellars, the label that produces a single varietal: cabernet sauvignon. There's also a Twomey Healdsburg, whose pinot noir is as impressive as its sister winery's Silver Oak cab.

von Strasser Winery (www.vonstrasser.com, 707-942-9500, 965 Silverado Trail, Calistoga, CA 94515; tastings and tours daily 10–4:30). Its first release arrived in 1993, and since then von Strasser has caught the eye of cabernet sauvignon fans. Rudy and Rita von Strasser own prime vineyard space on Diamond Mountain, a stone's throw from the famous Diamond Creek Vineyards. The cab is intense and production is small, with the von Strassers personally tending the vineyards and hand-sorting the grapes.

✳ Lodging

The Bergson (www.thebergson.com, 707-942-5755, 1010 Foothill Boulevard, Calistoga, CA 94515; $$$–$$$$). This stylish inn has 21 rooms, all with private baths. Many of the rooms feature fireplaces and whirlpool tubs. A modest continental breakfast is delivered to your room or served in the garden. Location is both an advantage and a bit of a disadvantage. Guests can walk to town, but Highway 29 can be noisy during the day. It's practically a moot point, however, because all the rooms are soundproofed.

Calistoga Ranch (www.calistogaranch.aubergeresorts.com, 707-254-2800, 855-942-4220, 580 Lommel Road, Calistoga, CA 94515; $$$$). Set on a 157-acre spread in the forested hills outside Calistoga, this luxury resort opened in the summer of 2004. It includes 50 individual guest lodges ranging in size from 600 to 2,400 square feet. The living areas open up onto mahogany decks that have retractable roofs, which create an indoor-outdoor atmosphere. Activities center on the pool and health-spa bathhouse, but there are also 4 miles of hiking trails.

✪ **Chateau de Vie** (www.cdvnapavalley.com, 707-942-6446, 877-558-2513, 3250 Highway 128, Calistoga, CA 94515; $$$–$$$$). Surrounded by 2 acres of vineyards, this bed-and-breakfast has an understated elegance which will be appreciated by discerning guests. The inn has excellent views of Mount St.

Helena and great gourmet breakfasts: freshly baked scones, breads, and muffins; country sausage; and vegetable quiches. All rooms have king- or queen-sized beds and private baths. A lap pool and an eight-person whirlpool spa are outside by the garden. A perk for wine lovers: the inn produces its own Chateau de Vie label for guests.

✪ **Cottage Grove Inn** (www.cottagegrove.com, 707-942-8400, 1711 Lincoln Avenue, Calistoga, CA 94515; $$$–$$$). This delightful collection of cottages is part of the Unique Hotels group, one that prizes both charm and adventure. This hub of the 16 cottages is an interesting little village. Rooms are set up studio style, with reclaimed hardwood floors from an old whiskey distillery, vaulted ceilings, and a front porch with wicker rockers. Here, breakfast is a feast with delectable offerings like frittatas, homemade waffles, and fried egg bagel sandwiches. This place is truly rustic-chic, a rare find.

Embrace Calistoga (www.embracecalistoga.com, 707-942-9797, 1139 Lincoln Avenue, Calistoga, CA 94515; $$$–$$$$). A nineteenth-century Victorian with a wraparound porch, this charming inn is located in the heart of Calistoga. There are five rooms in all, each with a private bath and gas fireplace. The king suite offers a deep soaking tub and sitting room with a bay window overlooking the garden. A continental breakfast is served in your room or on the porch, weather permitting.

OUR TOP OVERALL PICKS FOR CALISTOGA

Chateau Montelena (www.montelena.com)
Indian Springs Resort and Spa (www.indianspringscalistoga.com)
Aubert Wines (www.aubertwines.com)
Cottage Grove Inn (www.cottagegrove.com)
Clos Pegase (www.clospegase.com)
Brannan's Grill (www.brannansgrill.com)
Mount View Hotel (www.mountviewhotel.com.)
Solbar at Solage (www.solage.aubergeresorts.com)
Chateau de Vie (www.cdvnapavalley.com)
Castello di Amorosa Winery (www.castellodiamorosa.com)
Sterling Vineyards (www.sterlingvineyards.com)

Hideaway Cottages (www.hideaway cottages.com, 707-942-4108, 1412 Fairway, Calistoga, CA 94515; $$–$$$$). These 17 units are comfy but utilitarian, and all are set amid tall, mature trees on 2 acres on a quiet residential street close to Lincoln Avenue restaurants and shops. It's a good spot if you're planning an extended stay. Three deluxe cottages are available, and one of the cottages can accommodate groups of four or six. Air-conditioning and televisions are standard, and most units have kitchenettes.

✪ **Mount View Hotel** (www.mount viewhotel.com, 707-942-6877, 800-816-6877, 1457 Lincoln Avenue, Calistoga, CA 94515; $$$–$$$$). Restored mission revival and on the National Register of Historic Places, this elegant lodge was originally a European-style hotel, built in 1917. There are 29 units and three cottages, including nine luxurious suites. It's in the heart of Calistoga shopping and dining. The hotel has its own superb spa, and others are just a step away.

Pink Mansion (www.pinkmansion .com, 707-942-0558, 800-238-7465, 1415 Foothill Boulevard, Calistoga, CA 94515; $$$–$$$$). Postcard views of Napa Valley and lush forests await visitors who stay at this 1875 Victorian. The home's pink exterior will catch your attention, while the flowers, rare plants, and exotic palms will hold your interest. The inn features two rooms and four suites with fireplaces. There is also a 1,000-square-foot cottage with a loft and fireplace. The inn also has an indoor pool. Wine and cheese are available to cap off the afternoon.

✪ **Solage** (www.solage.auberge resorts.com, 707-266-7531, 866-942-7442, 755 Silverado Trail, Calistoga, CA 94515; $$$$). This is one of the most cutting-edge of the spa retreats in Napa Valley. A 22-acre complex includes 89 accommodations, from one-room studios to deluxe suites, as well as the Spa Solage and Solbar (see entry under *Restaurants*). The hip bistro offers healthful entrées as well as rich comfort food. Breakfasts are not part of the room rate, but the rate does include decadent dishes such as lemon-ricotta pancakes. This is a green resort, which means all the water is recycled and all the cleaning products are environmentally friendly. Solage Calistoga offers great views of the Palisades and the Mayacamas mountains.

✱ Where to Eat

All Seasons Bistro (www.allseasons napavalley.net, 707-942-9111, 1400 Lincoln Avenue, Calistoga, CA 94515; $$$; cuisine: California, Mediterranean). All Seasons has a soothing bistro menu matched with a modest but urbane setting. Ceiling fans spin slowly over stained-glass lights; the floor is done

S ome local establishments offer lodging/spa discount packages. (*Spa* in this context refers to Calistoga's natural hot springs and mineral pools; in some cases, massage treatments are also offered.)

Calistoga Motor Lodge & Spa (www.calistogamotorlodgeandspa.com, 707-942-0991, 1880 Lincoln Avenue, Calistoga, CA 94515; $$–$$$). This inn has been everything from a motel to what some refer to as a Moonie indoctrination camp (it was once owned and run by the Rev. Sun Myung Moon's Unification Church). The 50 rooms are appointed in retro-chic decor. Some suites have whirlpool tubs. Two outdoor mineral pools offer an expansive view of the mountains. The lodge offers an inside mineral whirlpool and sauna.

✪ Calistoga Spa Hot Springs (www.calistogaspa.com, 707-942-6269, 1006 Washington Street, Calistoga, CA 94515; $$). Relaxed and unpretentious, this inn has the amenities of a resort but at more affordable prices. All 56 family-oriented units have kitchenettes, air-conditioning, TVs, and telephones. Features include a fitness room and four outdoor mineral pools. Children are welcome.

Dr. Wilkinson's Hot Springs (www.drwilkinson.com, 707-942-4102, 1507 Lincoln Avenue, Calistoga, CA 94515; $$$). This spa has 42 spacious and functional rooms, many with kitchenettes. There are two outdoor mineral pools plus an indoor mineral whirlpool. Shopping and dining are within walking distance. Rooms, grounds, and pools have been upgraded and are very appealing.

EuroSpa & Inn (www.eurospa.com, 707-942-6829, 1202 Pine Street, Calistoga, CA 94515; $$–$$$). Each of the 13 rooms at this inn and spa is decorated in country contemporary fur-

in black, white, and green tile; and two walls of windows let you watch downtown Calistoga go by. The lunch menu focuses on salads, pizzas, pastas, and sandwiches, while dinner emphasizes upscale dinners of grilled fish, duck, beef, and chicken. The wine selection is fabulous, and service is professional and warm.

Boskos Trattoria (www.boskos.com, 707-942-9088, 1364 Lincoln Avenue, Calistoga, CA 94515; $$; cuisine: Italian). This Italian eatery serves basic and hearty food, and the price is right. The atmosphere is warm but casual and perfect for families. The lunch and dinner menus are the same, and the portions are generous. Pastas range from the basic spaghetti and meatballs to fettuccine Alfredo to pizza from a wood-burning stove. The beer and wine list is adequate.

✪ **Brannan's Grill** (www.brannansgrill .com, 707-942-2233, 1374 Lincoln Avenue, Calistoga, CA 94515; $$$; cuisine: California, American). Brannan's Grill is more adventuresome than it seems at first glance. With seating for 200, we expected the menu to be less exciting. The food is lively and the atmosphere has a club-like coziness, with large windows that swing wide open when the weather is right. Seafood is something Brannan's does particularly well; consider starting your meal with a selection of local oysters on the half shell. For hearty eaters, there's a good selection of steaks. The wine list showcases Napa Valley wines, but it's careful to include some less-traditional varietals. Rhone reds and whites, in particular, have a nice showing. The list is a bit pricey, but there's a good by-the-glass selection.

⚭ 🍴 **Café San Marco** (707-942-0714, 1408 Lincoln Avenue, Calistoga, CA 94515). This recently expanded café still makes an uncompromising cup of coffee; fruit, ice cream, and milkshakes are also offered.

🍴 **Calistoga Roastery** (www.calistoga roastery.com, 707-942-5757, 1426 Lincoln nishings. Many rooms have private whirlpools and gas-burning stoves. There is an outdoor pool as well as a whirlpool. It's close to downtown, yet it's away from the main-street bustle.

⚜ **Golden Haven Hot Springs Spa and Resort** (www.goldenhaven.com, 707-942-8000, 1713 Lake Street, Calistoga, CA 94515; $–$$$). Amid towering oak trees and lush gardens, this inn and spa isn't fancy but offers 28 rooms, several of them two-room suites. Rooms with whirlpools and saunas are also available.

✪ **Indian Springs Resort and Spa** (www.indianspringscalistoga.com, 707-709-8139, 844-378-3635, 1712 Lincoln Avenue, Calistoga, CA 94515; $$$–$$$$). Numerous white-washed bungalow-style cottages—one is a three-bedroom that sleeps six—overlook 16 acres of palm trees and views of Mount St. Helena. There are also 24 lodge rooms, three "view" rooms, and two other houses on-site for larger groups. There are bike rentals and a bocce court, but best of all, there's a gorgeous Olympic-sized mineral pool. It's an easy walk to downtown shopping and dining. The spa offers a quirky treatment: a volcanic-ash mud bath. It turns out that the grounds are full of volcanic ash, a holdover from the eruption thousands of years ago of nearby Mount Konocti.

Roman Spa (www.romanspahotsprings.com, 707-942-4441, 800-914-8957, 1300 Washington Street, Calistoga, CA 94515; $–$$$). Lushly landscaped grounds surround this older but well-tended, 60-room motel-type resort. Half of the units have kitchenettes. There's an outdoor mineral pool and whirlpool plus a large indoor whirlpool and sauna.

Up Valley Inn & Hot Springs (www.upvalleyinn.com, 707-942-9400, 1865 Lincoln Avenue, Calistoga, CA 94515; $$–$$$). This motel offers 55 rooms, a hot mineral-water swimming pool, a hot mineral-water whirlpool, a sauna, and a steam room. The complimentary breakfast includes hot entrées such as eggs and sausage.

Avenue, Calistoga, CA 94515). Here's a cozy and casual spot for the morning brew, with plenty of seating inside and out. There is a full array of freshly baked breakfast goods such as scones, bagels, and muffins. Salads, sandwiches, and smoothies are also available for lunch.

Checkers (www.checkersnapavalley .com, 707-942-9300, 1414 Lincoln Avenue, Calistoga, CA 94515). If you like pizza with panache, check out Checkers. The interior is festive, with abstract art, polished pine, and black tile. There are traditional pies of sausage and pepperoni, of course, but there's also Thai pizza, topped with marinated chicken, cilantro, and peanuts.

✪ **Solbar** (www.solage.aubergeresorts .com, 707-226-0850, 755 Silverado Trail, Calistoga, CA 94515; $$$$; cuisine: California, American). This restaurant at Solage Calistoga (see entry under *Lodging*) is driven by the seasons of Northern California, with an eye to fresh, local produce. The four-course tasting menu

at dinner can include sautéed halibut with fennel crema and charred Spanish octopus with beluga lentils. On certain days, the restaurant also features a comfort-food favorite—fried chicken. The decor is contemporary and bright, with an oversized fireplace to give the sleek design plenty of warmth. There's also outside dining, which is a treat.

A STREET SCENE IN DOWNTOWN CALISTOGA TIM FISH

✴ Entertainment

On a warm evening, try the patio bar at **Calistoga Inn Restaurant & Brewery** (www.calistogainn.com/brewery.html, 707-942-4101, 1250 Lincoln Avenue, Calistoga, CA 94515).

✴ Selective Shopping

A Man's Supply (707-942-2280, 1343 Lincoln Avenue, Calistoga, CA 94515). This store features cigars and rugged and casual wear for men.

Calistoga Wine Stop (707-942-5556, 800-648-4521, 1458 Lincoln Avenue, Calistoga, CA 94515). Housed in an 1866 Central Pacific railroad car in the oldest railroad depot in California, this shop has a solid lineup of current Napa and Sonoma wines. Prices are average.

Casa Design (707-942-2228, 1419 Lincoln Avenue, Calistoga, CA 94515). The shop offers custom furniture, linens, mirrors, and original artwork.

Chateau Ste. Shirts (707-942-5039; 1355 Lincoln Avenue, Calistoga, CA 94515). This merchant has stylish swimwear and sportswear and even sells the Ugg line of shoes.

Copperfield's Books (707-942-1616, 1330 Lincoln Avenue, Calistoga, CA 94515). This is the only bookstore in town, and it carries candles and calendars, and sponsors readings and book signings.

✪ **Enoteca Wine Shop** (www.enoteca wineshop.com, 707-942-1117, 1348-B Lincoln Avenue, Calistoga, CA 94515). Here you'll find great selection and a savvy staff to help you shop in a store that, surprisingly, resembles a cave. This shop specializes in local, small-production wines as well as Old World wines.

✎ ✿ **Sharpsteen Museum** (www .sharpsteenmuseum.org, 707-341-2443, 1311 Washington Street, Calistoga, CA 94515; admission: donation appreciated; daily 11–4). If you want a quick lesson in early Napa life, this quaint museum is the place to go. Ben and Bernice Sharpsteen created the museum almost as a hobby after Ben retired from being a producer for Walt Disney and the couple moved to Calistoga. Before long, it became a community project, and today it's run by volunteers. The first section of this museum is devoted to the Sharpsteens themselves, and a miniature model of early Calistoga follows.

✪ **Zenobia** (707-942-1050, 1410 Lincoln Avenue, Calistoga, CA 94515). This store, a whimsical space, sells candles, cards, clothing, and inspirational wall hangings.

✴ Special Events

✎ **Napa County Fair** (www.napacounty fair.org, 707-942-5111, fairgrounds at 1435 N. Oak Street, Calistoga, CA 94515). Every July, the fair offers down-home fun, but with a twist of chic Napa style that includes social gatherings and wine tastings. There are the usual rides, animals, produce, and music, plus wine, wine, wine.

OPPOSITE: SO MANY OPTIONS, SO LITTLE TIME
TIM FISH

WINEGROWERS DRY CREEK VALLEY

A. RAFANELLI →

HEALDSBURG

← LAMBERT BRIDGE

← PASTERICK

QUIVIRA →

← EVERETT RIDGE

RAYMOND BURR VNYRDS. →

← ALDERBROOK

MICHEL SCHLUMBERGER →

← ARMIDA

GÖPFRICH VINEYARDS →

PRESTON VINEYARDS →

← MILL CREEK VINEYARDS

← PEZZI KING VINEYARDS

AMPHORA →

← DE LA MONTANYA

HEALDSBURG

"**R**ustic chic" is the phrase that comes to mind when we think of Healdsburg, a Sonoma County town where Range Rovers and BMWs cohabitate. It's the hub of three premier wine regions—the Dry Creek, Russian River, and Alexander valleys.

Healdsburg has attracted upscale hotels like Les Mars and Hotel Healdsburg, with their respective restaurants, Chalkboard and Dry Creek Kitchen. But despite the flurry of top-rate chefs, and celebrity sightings of Martha Stewart and Bob Dylan, Healdsburg continues to have a charming small-town feel. The fall harvest is a ritual that seems to ground everyone; it brings out the earthy farmer in vintners who endeavor to make peace with Mother Nature yet again. The prayer is always the same: *Please, oh please, let the grapes ripen before the rains come.*

✳ To See and Do

GALLERIES AND MUSEUMS ✒ ✤ **Erickson Fine Art Gallery** (707-431-7073, 324 Healdsburg Avenue, Healdsburg, CA 95448). This attractive gallery is just off the square in downtown Healdsburg. It has a fine collection of serious art with only a smattering of frivolous landscapes.

✒ ✤ **Healdsburg Museum** (707-431-3325, 221 Matheson Street, Healdsburg, CA 95448; Wednesday–Sunday, 11–4). This museum is devoted to early Healdsburg and northern Sonoma County history, including Indian artifacts and 15,000 photographs.

WATER SPORTS ✒ **River's Edge** (707-433-7247, www.riversedgekayakandcanoe.com, 1 Healdsburg Avenue, Healdsburg, CA 95448). This outfit offers two-day, full-day, and half-day trips down the Russian River. Because the Pacific Ocean is chilly and the surf is a bit rugged, the Russian River is a good alternative for a leisurely day on the water. During the hot summer, riverside beaches are popular with families who enjoy swimming in the refreshing water while canoes glide past. Canoes and kayaks can be rented near Healdsburg or Guerneville for a leisurely trip, with stops where you can relax or swim along the way. Don't be surprised if you spot a few nude sunbathers. The county doesn't condone it, but the freewheeling '60s still live in West County.

Lake Sonoma (www.lakesonoma.com, 707-433-4533, 3333 Skaggs Springs Road, Geyserville, CA 95441; near Dry Creek Road). Forty miles of trails wind through the 3,600 acres of redwood groves and oak woodlands surrounding Sonoma's man-made lake. A visitor center is located at the base of the dam. Other activities include camping, boating, swimming, and visiting a fish hatchery.

✳ Wineries

Let your palate roam through Wine Country. Whether you're a novice or an old pro, there's plenty to learn from bellying up to the bar. There are countless wineries to choose from in Healdsburg and just up the road in Geyserville.

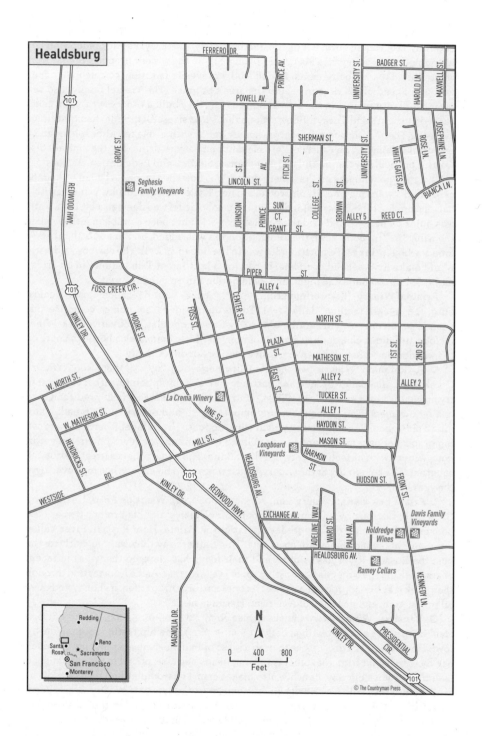

Healdsburg

FERRERO DR.
PRINCE AV.
POWELL AV.
UNIVERSITY ST.
BADGER ST.
MAXWELL ST.
HAROLD LN.
JOSEPHINE LN.
ROSE LN.
WHITE GATES AV.
SHERMAN ST.
UNIVERSITY ST.
BIANCA LN.
GROVE ST.
Seghesio Family Vineyards
LINCOLN ST.
ST.
AV.
FITCH ST.
COLLEGE ST.
BROWN ST.
UNIVERSITY ST.
JOHNSON
PRINCE
SUN CT.
GRANT ST.
ALLEY 5
REED CT.
REDWOOD HWY.
FOSS CREEK CIR.
PIPER ST.
ALLEY 4
MOORE ST.
FOSS ST.
CENTER ST.
NORTH ST.
KINLEY DR.
PLAZA ST.
EAST ST.
1ST ST.
2ND ST.
MATHESON ST.
W. NORTH ST.
ALLEY 2
ALLEY 2
La Crema Winery
VINE ST.
TUCKER ST.
W. MATHESON ST.
ALLEY 1
HENDRICKS ST.
HAYDON ST.
MILL ST.
MASON ST.
RD.
Longboard Vineyards
HARMON ST.
Davis Family Vineyards
WESTSIDE
HEALDSBURG AV.
HUDSON ST.
FRONT ST.
KINLEY DR.
REDWOOD HWY.
EXCHANGE AV.
ADELINE WAY
WARD ST.
PALM AV.
Holdredge Wines
HEALDSBURG AV.
Ramey Cellars
KENNEDY LN.
MAGNOLIA DR.
PRESIDENTIAL CIR.
KINLEY DR.

Redding
Santa Rosa
Reno
Sacramento
San Francisco
Monterey

N

0   400   800
Feet

© The Countryman Press

HEALDSBURG

✪ **Alexander Valley Vineyards** (www.avvwine.com, 707-433-7209, 800-888-7209, 8644 Highway 128, Healdsburg, CA 95448; tastings daily 10–5). Cyrus Alexander, who lent his name to this valley, has his gravesite on a hill on the winery property not far from where his 1840s adobe remains. A visit to the gravesite is fitting, to celebrate a man who was ahead of his time in seeing the area's promise. The Wetzel family also saw promise, planting vines in the early 1960s; in 1975, they built a winery with a cool cellar carved into a hill and a gravity-flow system that's less stressful to wine than traditional systems. The tasting room is a large, homey space with a relaxed atmosphere and a beautiful fireplace. The cabernets are elegant and easy to drink, but the zins are also worthy, particularly the playful trio Temptation, Sin Zin, and Redemption. As the story goes, a 1979 poker game on the winery property is how the zin mania began. When the card sharks were playing, Hank Wetzel's sister, Katie Wetzel Murphy, came in with a barrel sample of the latest zinfandel, but the alcohol level was deemed a bit high. Katie was quick on her feet and said the alcohol level wouldn't pose a problem if they called the wine Sin Zin. Soon after, the Redemption Zin was added, and in 2004, thanks to a lone cowboy in Texas, Temptation Zin was in the lineup as well. The cowboy said a trio would make his weekend complete: he'd drink a bottling of Temptation Zin on Friday night, Sin Zin on Saturday night, and Redemption Zin on Sunday night.

Armida Winery (www.armida.com, 707-433-2222, 2201 Westside Road, Healdsburg, CA 95448; tastings daily 11–5). Three unique geodesic domes comprise this winery, which occupies the border of the Dry Creek and Russian River valleys. Wines include zinfandel, chardonnay, and pinot noir, all nicely done. Buy a bottle to share on the wooden deck that offers an expansive view of Sonoma County.

✪ **A. Rafanelli Winery** (www.arafanelliwinery.com, 707-433-1385, 4685 W. Dry Creek Road, Healdsburg, CA 95448; tastings and tours by appointment). If you want to try one of the best zinfandels in Wine Country, a trip to this small, folksy redwood barn is a requirement. The wines are nearly impossible to find otherwise. Rafanelli epitomizes old-school Sonoma County: good wine, no fuss. The Rafanellis have been growing grapes for generations and began making wine in 1974, believing their vineyards, not a winery with hi-tech gadgets, did the talking. The winery makes great merlot and cabernet. The hospitality at the winery, which was once a bit snooty, has improved over the years.

✪ **Arista** (www.aristawinery.com, 707-473-0606, 7015 Westside Road, Healdsburg, CA 95448; tastings by appointment). Mark McWilliams and his brother Ben are the bookends overseeing the day-to-day operations at Arista. Here Russian River Valley pinot noir and chardonnay are class acts. The vintners say they want to cultivate the best the Russian River has to offer, and their focus has elevated the wines in recent years. Visiting the winery's new tasting room is a rare treat. Aside from tasting through their rock star lineup, you get a peek at its one-acre organic garden, its honey and olive oil production, and its brood of American Heritage hens.

✪ **Banshee Wines** (www.bansheewines.com, 707-395-0915, 325 Center Street, Healdsburg, CA 95448; tastings daily 11 a.m.–7 p.m.). The hip tasting room in downtown Healdsburg is a great place to grab a glass of Banshee's heady pinot noir. A touch earthy with bright fruit, this pinot is turning heads because, priced in the $30 range, it over delivers in a big way. Banshee also makes smart chardonnay and rosé.

✪ **Bella Vineyards** (www.bellawinery.com, 707-473-9171, 9711 W. Dry Creek Road, Healdsburg, CA 95448; tastings daily 11–4:30). Situated at the far end of a country road, Bella isn't the sort of winery you stumble onto, but it's well worth the trek. Scott and Lynn Adams are a passionate young couple who decided to live the dream and started Bella. The focus is zinfandel and syrah, mostly from 80- or 100-year-old vines, and the wines are supple yet full of character. While you're tasting, be sure to check out the wine cave.

Chalk Hill Estate (www.chalkhill .com, 707-657-4837, 10300 Chalk Hill Road, Healdsburg, CA 95448; tastings daily 10–4 by appointment). The white soil gives the Chalk Hill area its name—even though it's really volcanic ash, not chalk. Fred Furth and his former wife, Peggy, established this winery well off the beaten path in 1980 and hired a series of talented winemakers. In June 2010, they sold the winery to William Foley, the chairman of two Florida financial companies, with the intent of keeping it family owned. White wines thrive in the area, and chardonnay is the winery's specialty; it ranges from average to excellent. The sauvignon blanc is consistently a beauty. Be sure to try their estate red—which is a California Bordeaux blend.

A PEEK AT THE HIP TASTING ROOM OF BANSHEE WINES

✪ **Copain Wines** (www.copainwines .com, 707-836-8822, 7800 Eastside Road, Healdsburg, CA 95448; tastings by appointment). Founder and winemaker Wells Guthrie produces syrahs, chardonnays, and pinot noir, and they are not to be missed. Guthrie is taken by French winemaking and apprenticed for two years with the revered Michel Chapoutier in France's Rhone Valley. His winemaking philosophy is to make wines that are firmly rooted in California but have a European sensibility: his goal is to create elegant, nuanced wines.

✪ **Davis Family Vineyards** (www.davisfamilyvineyards.com, 707-433-3858, tasting room: 52 Front Street, Healdsburg, CA 95448; tastings Thursday–Monday 11–5 or by appointment). When you drink his wines, you can almost taste the passion Guy Davis has for winemaking. He produces a little of everything, but he seems particularly apt at pinot noir made from Russian River Valley grapes. The winery isn't fancy, but that's the charm. Best of all, you get to taste the wines right in the barrel room, and the staff is laid-back and friendly.

✪ **Dry Creek Vineyard** (www.drycreekvineyard.com, 707-433-1000, 800-864-9463, 3770 Lambert Bridge Road, Healdsburg, CA 95448; tastings daily 10:30–5). Dry Creek Valley, we've always imagined, is what Napa Valley used to be: small, quiet, and unaffected by it all. It was a land of prunes and pears when Dave Stare, a former railroad engineer, arrived. Designed after the small country wineries of France, Dry Creek has always reminded us of a simple country chapel. It only adds to the pleasure that Dry

Creek's wines are consistently fine, often exceptional, as you'll discover in the tasting room. The atmosphere is laid-back, and the staff is chatty. Dry Creek has made its name with fumé blanc, a crisp wine that dominates the winery's production. The chenin blanc is so fruity and distinctive that we prefer it over many chardonnays. As for reds, the zinfandel is always one of the best, and the cabernet sauvignon has fine character and can be exceptional in a good vintage. The picnic area, shaded mostly by tall trees, is one of the best in Wine Country.

Ferrari-Carano Vineyards and Winery (www.ferrari-carano.com, 707-433-6700, 800-831-0381, 8761 Dry Creek Road, Healdsburg, CA 95448; tastings daily 10–5). Ferrari-Carano seems to be on every restaurant wine list in America. The chardonnay is its flagship—a big, lush, complex wine. The fumé blanc is also impressive in its own right, while the cabernet sauvignon and merlot are both solid efforts. Situated in northern Dry Creek Valley, Ferrari-Carano makes a bold statement. Villa Fiore, the winery's visitor center, is an extravagant Mediterranean palace surrounded by brushy lawns, flowers (more than 18,000 tulips bloom every spring), and vineyards. The tasting room has a faux marble floor and a mahogany and black-granite tasting bar. Visitors descend the limestone staircase to what is possibly the most opulent underground cellar in Wine Country.

Field Stone Winery & Vineyards (www.fieldstonewinery.com, 707-433-7266, 800-54-GRAPE, 10075 Highway 128, Healdsburg, CA 95448; tastings daily 10–5). Cozy

VILLA FIORE AT FERRARI-CARANO IS WELL KNOWN FOR ITS STRIKING GARDENS TIM FISH

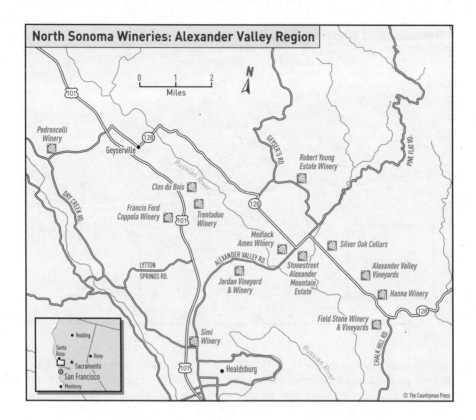

inside an Alexander Valley knoll, this winery takes its name from the rugged stone that decorates the facade. Open the wide wooden door and amble past the oak barrels to the tasting room—and you've pretty much taken the tour. A house specialty is petite sirah from circa-1894 vines. It's a ripe bruiser. The cabernet sauvignon is also recommended. The picnic grounds are superb.

Foppiano Vineyards (www.foppiano.com, 707-433-7272, 12707 Old Redwood Highway, Healdsburg, CA 95448; tastings daily 11–5). Five generations of Foppianos have tended vines here. John Foppiano arrived from Genoa in 1896 and planted a vineyard. Wine was sold in bulk and, later, in jugs. The family began moving into premium wine in the 1970s. The winery is unabashedly utilitarian, and the tasting room is in an unassuming wood cottage. The self-guided vineyard tour is worth a few minutes. Foppiano's star is its beefy petite sirah made from old vines.

Fritz Underground Winery (www.fritzwinery.com, 707-894-3389, 800-418-9463, 24691 Dutcher Creek Road, Cloverdale, CA 95425; tastings daily 10:30–4:30). This winery, in the farthest reaches of northern Sonoma wine country, is built like a bunker into the side of a hill. Well off the road and hidden amid the scrub trees, Fritz blends into the countryside. Fritz takes zinfandel quite seriously, and it relies on gnarly old vines to make a burly yet graceful zin. Pinot noir, chardonnay, and sauvignon blanc, too, are generally fine examples; try the melon, a white that's easy to quaff.

Gary Farrell Winery (www.garyfarrellwinery.com, 707-473-2909, 10701 Westside Road, Healdsburg, CA 95448; tastings by appointment). While Gary Farrell has moved on to boutique winemaking with his Aylsian brand in Forestville, this winery is still

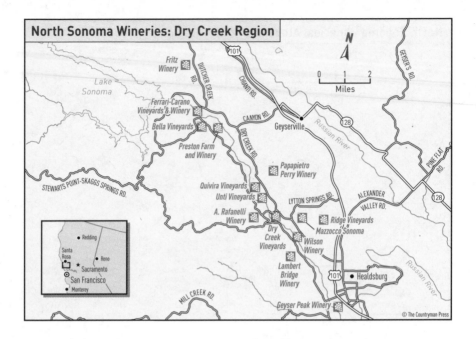

making great pinot noir. The Farrell style, which you can still taste on the palate, is elegant, complex, and fruit-forward. The winery has a knack for pinot noir, chardonnay, and zinfandel. Situated like a mission-style chapel on a hill above the Russian River, the tasting room offers wide and glorious views of the surrounding landscape.

Geyser Peak Winery (www.geyserpeakwinery.com, 707-857-2500, 800-255-WINE, 2306 Magnolia Drive, Healdsburg, CA 95448; tastings daily 10–5). This winery went through a golden era in the 1990s, but production has expanded, and in recent vintages the wines have been good but not up to the old standards. Founded in 1880 by Augustus Quitzow, the winery is a complex of buildings both old and new. The main, ivy-covered building has a commanding view of Alexander Valley. In the tasting room, the staff pours selections from Geyser Peak's large repertoire. Don't miss the shiraz and cabernet sauvignon.

✪ **Hanna Winery** (www.hannawinery.com, 707-431-4310 ext 116, tasting room: 9280 Highway 128, Healdsburg, CA 95448; tastings daily 10–4). Noted cardiac surgeon Elias Hanna went into the wine business in 1985. Because the winery is well off the tourist path, Hanna opened a tasting room in the heart of its Alexander Valley vineyard. The building—a Frank Lloyd Wright–style pagoda—makes for a striking image, set among the rolling hills. Hanna owns prime vineyard space around Sonoma County, and the best wines to date are its bright sauvignon blanc, its sleek pinot noir, and a solid chardonnay.

✪ **Holdredge Wines** (www.holdredge.com, 707-431-1424, 51 Front Street, Healdsburg, CA 95448; tastings Friday–Monday 11–4:30). What started as a hobby for John Holdredge turned into a second job. A Santa Rosa attorney by day, he's a winemaker, grape grower, and wine salesman during what's left of his 24 hours. Wife Carri at first indulged him and then joined the winery when he launched it in 2001. Tasting is a low-key affair amid the barrels in the winery, a historic old redwood barn on the outskirts of Healdsburg. Pinot noir is the main focus, but Holdredge also makes a little zinfandel and syrah, and stylistically the wines are concentrated, lush, and complex.

✪ **J Vineyards & Winery** (www.jwine.com, 888-594-6326, 11447 Old Redwood Highway, Healdsburg, CA 95448; tastings daily 11–5). The large tasting room is a stylish bar with angular concrete walls and bold modern art, and the winery produces a steely Brut as well as first-rate still wines such as pinot noir, chardonnay, and pinot gris (sometimes known as pinot grigio). Wine and food pairing at most wineries is a cracker with a smear of something, but J does it right. By appointment only and at an additional cost, the tour takes place in the reserve room, also called the Bubble Room, where you begin with a glass of bubbly and move on to a progressive food and wine pairing, ending with a decadent dessert and dessert wine. Visitors tour the winery along a concrete balcony overlooking the entire plant, where the *méthode champenoise,* the French technique of making sparkling wine, is detailed.

✪ **Jordan Vineyard & Winery** (www.jordanwinery.com, 707-431-5250, 800-654-1213, 1474 Alexander Valley Road, Healdsburg, CA 95448; tastings and tours by appointment). This spectacular French-style chateau rose from a former prune orchard in the mid-1970s to become one of Sonoma County's premier wineries. Covered in ivy, the chateau seems like a grand classic, but inside it's a state-of-the-art winery. The forest of towering wood tanks in its aging room is an impressive sight. Jordan's cabernet sauvignon is elegant and ready to drink on release—one reason it's such a popular wine in restaurants. One tour explores the lush gardens and vineyards, 18 acres of olive trees, and the winemaking facility.

✪ **La Crema Winery** (www.lacrema .com, 707-431-9400, tasting room: 235 Healdsburg Avenue, Healdsburg, CA 95448; tastings daily 10:30–5:30). La Crema has a long history in Sonoma County, and the winery is currently making some of its best wines to date. Pinot noir and chardonnay dominate the lineup. Both are typical plush and fruit-forward wines, and while prices have been creeping up in recent vintages, the cost-versus-quality ratio remains good. Part of Jackson Family Wines, La Crema runs this smart-looking tasting room just off the Healdsburg Plaza, easy to access for most travelers. But for those who want to experience the source of La Crema's bottlings, the winery itself is in Windsor, not far from its expansive tasting room. The three-story property at 3575 Slusser Road in Windsor has historic roots. The 200-acre Saralee's Vineyard was named after the late Saralee Kunde, one of the finest growers in Sonoma County. In her

AT THE LA CREMA TASTING ROOM, THE STRONG SUIT IS PINOT NOIR AND CHARDONNAY honor, this upscale tasting room is a hub for wine education, as well as for food and wine pairing.

Lambert Bridge Winery (www.lambertbridge.com, 707-431-9600, 800-975-0555, 4085 W. Dry Creek Road, Healdsburg, CA 95448; tastings daily 10:30–4:30). "Quaint" is a woefully abused word, but we can't think of a better way to describe Lambert Bridge. Open since 1975, Lambert Bridge has maintained a low profile. This romantic little winery, with redwood siding and a porch shaded by wisteria, is a comfortable fit among the oaks and vines covering the hillsides overlooking Dry Creek. Inside, it's a comfortable space done in rich, dark wood. Merlot and chardonnay are specialties. There's a delightful picnic area out front, making this one of the best wineries around for a casual lunch.

Landmark Vineyards at Hop Kiln Estate (www.landmarkwine.com, 707-433-6491, 6050 Westside Road, Healdsburg, CA 95448; tastings daily 10–4:45). This winery began life as an ode to beer, not wine. Hops were a major crop along Sonoma County's Russian River at the turn of the twentieth century. This is one of the few remnants from that era. Built in 1905, the unusual stone barn is topped with three pyramid towers. Landmark Vineyards now serves its wines, pinot noir and chardonnay, in this historic tasting room. It offers an array of local cheeses and charcuterie to complement your tasting, so you have the option to build your own picnic on the premises.

✪ **Leo Steen Wines** (www.leosteenwines.com, 707-433-3097, 53 Front Street, Healdsburg, CA 95448; tastings Friday–Monday, 1–4). The son of a chef, Leo Steen Hansen said he finds great joy in helping others "taste" the synergy between food and wine. The winemaker from Denmark is particularly gifted with chenin blanc, a rare bird among varietals. He also produces small-scale Rhone varietals, including grenache and syrah, but at his tasting room, don't miss the tangy quench of his spot-on chenin blancs.

✪ **Longboard Vineyards** (www.longboardvineyards.com, 707-433-3473, 5 Fitch Street, Healdsburg, CA 95448; tastings daily 11–6). A surfer tried and true, Oded Shakked named his winery after his surfboard of choice. In his mind, both surfing and winemaking require balance, harmony, and a respect for nature. A beach bum born near Tel Aviv, Shakked studied winemaking in California, and for many years he made bubbly at J Wine Co., before launching his own winery a few years back. The tasting room, inside a warehouse near downtown, is a hangout for surfers and wine drinkers alike. Merlot and cabernet are the specialties, but Shakked also makes a tasty syrah and sauvignon blanc.

✪ **Macrostie** (www.macrostiewinery.com, 707-473-9303, 4605 Westside Road, Healdsburg, CA 95448; tastings daily). This is a house of pinot noir and chardonnay, and the winery consistently proves itself as a benchmark for these varietals. Vintner Steve MacRostie has been at this for decades and he's proven he's worth his mettle. A visit to the winery will give you a glimpse at its small-lot winemaking, as well as treating you to a range of tastings. Check the winery's website for tasting options.

Mazzocco Sonoma (www.mazzocco.com, 707-433-3399, 800-501-8466, 1400 Lytton Springs Road, Healdsburg, CA 95448; tastings daily 11–5). This winery is hardly a visual treat, but it occupies prime zinfandel land. Founded by Tom Mazzocco in 1984, the winery has weathered ups and downs, but one constant has remained: great zinfandel—big and spicy, yet carrying itself with considerable finesse. The cabernet sauvignon, sauvignon blanc, petite sirah, and chardonnay also have charm.

✪ **Medlock Ames** (www.medlockames.com, 707-431-8845, 3487 Alexander Valley Road, Healdsburg, CA 95448; tastings daily 10–5). Medlock Ames's tasting room offers a full slate of wines and a glimpse of its earthy roots, with homemade preserves, pickles, and organic produce lining the walls. Certified organic, Medlock Ames has sustainable farming practices, using solar power and electric and biodiesel vehicles, deploying weed-eating sheep, and growing blocks of vegetables that they sell to local chefs. The vintners produce cabernet, pinot noir, merlot, red blends, rosé, chardonnay, and sauvignon blanc. There's not a bad wine in the lot, but the sauvignon blanc is particularly good. The winery is located at its Bell Mountain Ranch site, where a tour takes you through vineyards, olive groves, and the winery itself.

Mill Creek Vineyards (www.millcreekwinery.com, 707-431-2121, 1401 Westside Road, Healdsburg, CA 95448; tastings daily 10–5). It's hard to miss this tasting room, a redwood barn with a waterwheel. The Kreck family has been growing grapes since 1965 and bottled their first wine with the 1974 vintage. Mill Creek helped pioneer merlot but is not among the masters. Sauvignon blanc is the winery's best effort, and it's a delightful companion for a picnic on the winery's deck. Other wines include cabernet, zinfandel, and chardonnay.

Papapietro Perry Winery (www.papapietro-perry.com, 707-433-0422, 877-GO-PINOT, 4791 Dry Creek Road, Healdsburg, CA 95448; tastings daily 11–4:30). The winery name may be a little hard to pronounce, but you'll have no trouble drinking the wines. Ben Papapietro and Bruce Perry were bitten by the bug way back in the 1970s, when they used to help out with the harvest at Williams Selyem Winery. After making their own homemade wine for years, they started the winery in 1998. Zinfandel and pinot noir are their passions, and these wines are ripe and richly structured. The winery and tasting room are located just off Dry Creek Road, amid a rural complex of small producers.

✪ **Preston Farm & Winery** (www.prestonfarmandwinery.com, 707-433-3372, 800-305-9707, 9282 W. Dry Creek Road, Healdsburg, CA 95448; tastings daily 11–4:30). On the northern edge of Dry Creek Valley, this out-of-the-way winery has been quietly redefining itself in recent years. Lou and Susan Preston began as growers in 1973, specializing in grapes cherished by old Italian farmers: zinfandel and sauvignon blanc. A winery followed two years later, and Preston made its name with zinfandel and sauvignon blanc. However, Rhone varietals have taken on importance in recent years. The tasting room of this grand California barn was expanded a few years back, and there's a plush lawn for picnicking just off the tasting room porch. An olive oil and bread fanatic, Lou Preston has his own bakery on the property, and olive trees are scattered around the site.

✪ **Quivira Vineyards** (www.quivirawine.com, 707-431-8333, 800-292-8339, 4900 W. Dry Creek Road, Healdsburg, CA 95448; tastings daily 11–4). Quivira was a wealthy kingdom of legend that explorers believed was hidden in what is now Sonoma County. Although the name belongs to antiquity, this Quivira is a modern winery inside and out, and Quivira's zinfandel, sauvignon blanc, and Rhone varietals are worth checking out.

✪ **Ramey Wine Cellars** (www.rameywine.com, 707-433-0870, 25 Healdsburg Avenue, Healdsburg, CA 95448; tastings by appointment). Vintner David Ramey has an adventuresome spirit and the determination to make the highest-quality wine through a series of ongoing experiments. He embraces wines of unique character and believes you have to take a risk if you want to reach for great bottlings. Making "safe" wine, he says, is not the point.

✪ **Ridge Vineyards** (www.ridgewine.com, 707-433-7721, 650 Lytton Springs Road, Healdsburg, CA 95448; tastings daily 11–4). This Sonoma County outpost of the popular Santa Cruz Mountain producer was once exclusively a destination for zinfandel lovers, but now the winery has become part of the attraction. Environmentally friendly, it has a smooth, contemporary construction that was achieved with recycled lumber and straw bale–insulated walls. Solar panels produce much of the winery's energy. Ridge produces most of its zinfandels on the property, and there's a range offered for tasting. As you sip the Lytton Springs bottling, be sure to gaze out the window at the thick, century-year-old vines that produced it.

Rochioli Vineyards & Winery (www.rochioliwinery.com, 707-433-2305, 6192 Westside Road, Healdsburg, CA 95448; tastings daily 11–4). The pinot noir vineyards of Rochioli are the envy of all winemakers. The top pinots in the business—Gary Farrell, Williams Selyem, and, of course, Rochioli (pronounced row-key-OH-lee)—begin here. Three generations of Rochiolis have been growing grapes along the Russian River. They stay close to the land, and because of that, they make great wine. In the modest tasting room, which looks out across vineyards toward the river, every wine is a winner. The chardonnay has a ripe apple taste with crisp acidity, and the sauvignon blanc is flowery and complex.

✪ **Rodney Strong Vineyards** (www.rodneystrong.com, 707-431-1533, 800-678-4763, 11455 Old Redwood Highway, Healdsburg, CA 95448; tastings daily 10–5). A dramatic pyramid of concrete and wood, this winery has weathered many incarnations and owners over the years, but it seems to be coming into its own again. The wines are reliable and frequently superb, with cabernet sauvignon, chardonnay, and pinot noir among the standouts. Balconies outside the tasting room overlook the tanks and oak barrels, so a tour may be academic.

✪ **Seghesio Family Vineyards** (www.seghesio.com, 707-433-3579, 700 Grove Street, Healdsburg, CA 95448; tastings daily 10–5). The winery, now owned by Crimson Wine Group, dates back to 1895, with four generations of Seghesios following the lead of the founder, Italian immigrant Edoardo Seghesio. The winery continues to feel like a family-owned venture, with several Seghesios still working in key posts. The winery

SEGHESIO WINERY'S OLD-VINE ZIN

produces many Italian-style varieties such as sangiovese, barbera, pinot grigio, and arneis, but it's best known for its supple yet intense zinfandel. The Tuscan-style tasting room is shaded by tall trees, and it's absolutely striking.

○ **Silver Oak Cellars** (www.silveroak.com, 707-942-7082, 7300 Highway 128, Healdsburg Avenue, Healdsburg, CA 95448; tastings by appointment). This winery celebrates Alexander Valley cabernet sauvignon, with a sister property in Oakville that pays homage to Napa Valley cab. Here the tasting room, which overlooks the winery's prime cabernet vineyards, sits right next to an iconic water tower. Just 10 minutes east of downtown Healdsburg, Silver Oak offers an interesting food-and-wine-pairing experience.

Simi Winery (www.simiwinery.com, 707-433-6981, 800-746-4880, 16275 Healdsburg Avenue, Healdsburg, CA 95448; tastings daily 10–5). If we had to choose only one winery to visit—akin to limiting yourself to one glass of champagne on New Year's Eve—that would be a tough call, but we'd vote for Simi, an alluring combination of history and hi-tech gadgetry. You never feel you're being herded through a factory, even though the winery is hardly small. The staff knows wine but doesn't lord it over you. And best of all: the wines are first-rate. Simi gives one of the best tours, offering peeks at everything from the oak-barrel aging room to the bottling line. The tasting room is a cordial spot. Try the sauvignon blanc, the chardonnay (always delightful), and the impressive cabernet sauvignons.

○ **Stonestreet Alexander Mountain Estate** (wwwstonestreetwines.com, 800-355-8008, 7111 Highway 128, Healdsburg, CA 95448; tastings daily 11–4:30). The winery makes a tasty cabernet sauvignon, chardonnay, and Legacy Meritage Red. But its views of the Mayacamas Mountains also make it worth a visit, especially when you have a picnic on the patio. There are specialty tastings and even a private tasting with a tour of the property, combined with lunch and pours of single-vineyard wines. For those who can't make it to the winery, the Stonestreet Tasting Room on the Healdsburg Plaza (337 Healdsburg Avenue) is a smart alternative. It's a crisp, clean, modern space with plenty to pour, but keep your eye on the cab and the chardonnay.

○ **Unti Vineyards** (www.untivineyards.com, 707-433-5590, 4202 Dry Creek Road, Healdsburg, CA 95448; tastings daily 10–4 by appointment). One of the charms of driving through the back roads of Sonoma County is discovering a small winery such as Unti that sells most of its wine out the door. The Unti family began growing grapes in 1990 and started making wine in 1997. The tasting room is basic, so Unti lets the wine do the talking, and the wines are intense and authentic. The zinfandel is elegant in the classic Dry Creek Valley style, and the grenache and barbera are full of personality. This place is a gem.

Wilson Winery (www.wilsonwinery.com, 707-433-4355, 800-433-4602, 1960 Dry Creek Road, Healdsburg, CA 95448; tastings daily 11–5). The Wilson family owns more than 220 acres of prime Dry Creek hillside vineyards, and that's part of the key to the winery's success. Wilson makes a wide range of wines but zinfandel is its strong suit, as you might expect, because that's Dry Creek's specialty. The zins here are powerful and peppery. The winery is in an old tin barn, a local landmark, and the tasting room in the back side of the barn offers a soothing view of the surrounding vineyards.

GEYSERVILLE

Clos du Bois (www.closdubois.com, 707-857-3100, 800-222-3189, 19410 Geyserville Avenue, Geyserville, CA 95441; tastings daily 10–4:30). Clos du Bois, one of Sonoma's largest and most prominent wineries, seems to do everything well and a few things superbly. It may not produce big flashy wines, but its offerings are seldom disappointing—which is surprising, considering the larger roster of wines that range from values to collectibles. Vineyards are key to this success; the winery has access to some 1,000 prime acres in Alexander and Dry Creek valleys. The Calcaire chardonnay is a lush, Burgundian, fruit-driven wine with minimal butter and oak, although we often prefer the straightforward character of the regular chardonnay. The cabernet sauvignons and merlots are generally impressive. The tasting room is a friendly spot, and the staff is knowledgeable, but they never roll their eyes at novice questions.

De Lorimier Winery (www.delorimier winery.com, 707-857-2000, 800-546-7718, 2001 Highway 128, Geyserville, CA 95441; tastings daily 10:30–5). Set amid a sea of vines in the north end of Alexander Valley, this winery—a modern barn with brown shingles—is well off the beaten path. It dates to 1986, when surgeon Alfred de Lorimier decided to make wine with the

AT HIS WINERY, FAMED DIRECTOR FRANCIS FORD COPPOLA HAS CREATED A MUSEUM FOR HIS MOVIE MEMORABILIA, INCLUDING THIS CAR FROM *TUCKER* TIM FISH

grapes he'd been growing for years. The biggest successes are sauvignon blanc. De Lorimier's latest focus is on Bordeaux blends and single-vineyard cabernet sauvignon. The winery is owned by the Wilson Family (of Wilson Winery), which also owns Matrix, Mazzocco Vineyards, and Jackson Keys in Mendocino.

✪ **Francis Ford Coppola Winery** (www.francisfordcoppolawinery.com, 707-857-1471, 877-590-3329, 300 Via Archimedes, Geyserville, CA 95441; tastings daily 11–5:30). This dramatic chalet, inspired by the old hop kilns that once spread across the Russian River Valley, was once Chateau Souverain but is now home to Francis Ford Coppola's winery. Coppola is experimenting with a family-oriented approach: "a wine wonderland." He's created a resort-style wine experience for the entire family, with a pool near the tasting room, bocce courts, a movie gallery, and more. Coppola, the Academy Award–winning director best known for the films *The Godfather* trilogy and *Apocalypse Now,* said, "When we began to develop the idea for this winery, we thought it should be like a resort, basically a wine wonderland, a park of pleasure where people of all ages can enjoy the best things in life." No age discrimination here. Check out the live music on Sundays and the zucchini fries at Rustic, the winery's full-service restaurant. The winery makes a full slate of wines, the Diamond Series and the Director's Cut brands being two of the best.

Pedroncelli Winery (www.pedroncelli.com, 707-857-3531, 800-836-3894, 1220 Canyon Road, Geyserville, CA 95441; tastings daily 10–4:30). One of Sonoma County's oldest wineries—its origins date to 1904—Pedroncelli is also an old reliable. The winery and tasting room are agreeable but not elaborate. The wines are solid, although modestly scaled, and the prices are fair. Two generations of Pedroncellis tend the place. Try the cabernet sauvignon, sauvignon blanc, and zinfandel—all nicely done.

✪ **Robert Young Estate Winery** (www.ryew.com, 707-431-4811, 4960 Red Winery Road, Geyserville, CA 95441; tastings daily 10–4:30). Back in the early 1960s, many people thought Robert Young was crazy for planting a 14-acre cabernet vineyard in an old prune orchard, but he did it anyway and helped revive Alexander Valley as a wine region. These days, the Young family has 300 acres of vines, and after watching wineries such as Chateau St. Jean win medals with their grapes, they started making their own wine in 1997. The winery, appropriately, is in an old prune barn, and the tasting room is little more than a simple counter, but the chardonnay and cabernet are wonderful examples of how some places are uniquely suited to grape growing.

✪ **Trentadue Winery** (www.trentadue.com, 707-433-3104, 888-332-3032, 19170 Geyserville Avenue, Geyserville, CA 95441; tastings daily 10–5). Trentadue makes Arnold Schwarzenegger wines: massive, muscular reds that won't be taken lightly. The Trentadue family has been making wine since 1969, favoring hearty classic Tuscan varietals such as carignane and sangiovese. After a spotty history, wine quality here took a leap in the 1990s. The tasting room is packed with gifts and picnic supplies, which you can put to fine use on the trellis-covered picnic patio. A fun feature is the tractor-powered gondola tour of the property. You can even taste wines along the way.

❋ Lodging

✪ **Belle de Jour Inn** (www.belledejourinn .com, 707-431-9777, 16276 Healdsburg Avenue, Healdsburg, CA 95448; $$$– $$$$). A peaceful B&B inn on the northern outskirts of Healdsburg, Belle de Jour is set on a tranquil 6-acre hilltop with lovely views of rolling hills and distant mountains. The Italianate main farmhouse, built around 1873, is where the innkeepers live and prepare scrumptious breakfasts. The five guest suites, decorated with French country–inspired furniture, are set behind the main house. The inn is centrally located for touring Napa and Sonoma, and the Hearns are superb hosts.

✪ **Camellia Inn** (www.camelliainn .com, 707-433-8182, 800-727-8182, 211 North Street, Healdsburg, CA 95448; $$–$$$). This 1869 Italianate Victorian home entered the turn of the twentieth century as Healdsburg's first hospital. It's now a magnificent inn with nine guest rooms and still has many of its original and unique architectural details, including the twin marble fireplaces in the double parlor. On a quiet residential street just two blocks from the plaza, the inn is named for the 50 or so varieties of camellias that grace its gardens. A full breakfast buffet is served in the dining room, dominated by a mahogany fireplace mantel. The innkeepers also offer a spa on-site with several massage possibilities. Additionally, a few off-site lodging options are available.

Dry Creek Inn Best Western (www .drycreekinn.com, 707-433-0300, 800-222-5784, 198 Dry Creek Road, Healdsburg, CA 95448; $–$$$). This motel is distinguished by its outstanding location for wine touring. There is upgraded motel decor throughout, and a spectacular view of Dry Creek Valley is the payoff in many rooms. The 163 rooms are equipped with refrigerators and coffeemakers, and a continental breakfast is included—great for families. This property underwent a $1 million renovation in 2014. It's well situated for a day of wine tasting followed by dining downtown on the plaza. The downside: The inn fronts busy Highway 101, but the road quiets considerably at night.

Duchamp Hotel (www.duchamphotel .com, 707-431-1300, 800-431-9341, 421 Foss Street, Healdsburg, CA 95448; $$$–$$$$). Tucked just two blocks from Healdsburg Plaza, the Duchamp offers six private stand-alone one-story suites that each overlook a full-sized pool. The suites are sleek, each with a minimalistic European design sensibility, including California king beds, private patios, Aveda toiletries, and large spa-style bathrooms. You'll feel like you've got the property to yourself, as staff is only on-site during select hours (check-in, breakfast service). It's a perfect option for couples or small groups looking for a contemporary option to the plentiful number of traditional bed & breakfasts that are located in the region. The closest thing to antiques you'll find is

Boutique winemaking at its best.

The Healdsburg Shed (www.healdsburgshed.com)

Francis Ford Coppola Winery (www.francisfordcoppolawinery.com)

Honor Mansion (www.honormansion.com)

Arista (www.aristawinery.com); Holdredge Wines (www.holdredge.com); Davis Family Vineyards (www.davisfamilyvineyards.com); Medlock Ames (www.medlockames.com); Leo Steen Wines (www.leosteenwines.com); Ramey Wine Cellars (www.rameywinecellars.com)

Valette (www.valettehealdsburg.com)

Journeymen Meat Co. (www.journeymanmeat.com)

Jimtown Store (www.jimtown.com)

h2hotel (www.h2hotel.com)

Barndiva (www.barndiva.com); known as a hip restaurant with late-night appeal, you can order exotic drinks from the bar until 11 p.m.

Downtown Bakery & Creamery (www.downtownbakery.net) and Costeaux French Bakery (www.costeaux.com).

Seghesio (www.seghesio.com)

that each suite is named after a famous artist, including Warhol, Picasso, and Miro.

Grape Leaf Inn (www.grapeleafinn.com, 707-433-8140, 539 Johnson Street, Healdsburg, CA 95448; $$$–$$$$). The 13 elegant guest rooms in this 1900 Queen Anne Victorian are furnished with armoires and warm oak accents, and all are named for grape varietals. The inn's quiet porch is perfect for unwinding after a day of wine touring. A full country breakfast is served in the dining room. Wine is served nightly, and the inn is within walking distance of Healdsburg's historic downtown plaza.

Haydon Street Inn (www.haydon.com, 707-433-5228, 321 Haydon Street, Healdsburg, CA 95448; $$–$$$). In a quiet residential area and surrounded by trees, this Queen Anne Victorian inn has nine charming guest rooms, all with hardwood floors, antiques, down comforters, and private baths. An additional cottage on the site has three guest rooms, including a full suite. A generous breakfast buffet is crafted by owner John, a retired chef, and served in the dining room. The inn is a short walk to Healdsburg's plaza.

Healdsburg Inn on the Plaza (www.healdsburginn.com, 707-433-6991, 800-431-8663, 112 Matheson Street, Healdsburg, CA 95448; $$$$). Right on Healdsburg's delightful downtown plaza, this 12-room inn has a solarium and a roof garden, the common area where guests take breakfast and afternoon refreshments.

✪ **Honor Mansion** (www.honormansion.com, 707-433-4277, 800-554-4667, 891 Grove Street, Healdsburg, CA 95448; $$$–$$$$). Honor Mansion has—appropriately—won its share of honors. It was named one of the most romantic inns by American Historic Inns. Built in 1883, this Victorian mansion is named after Dr. Herbert Honor, whose family owned the property for more than 100 years. The Fowlers bought the inn in 1994 and remodeled the entire building—and these innkeepers will spoil you outright, from mints on your pillow to scrumptious afternoon appetizers. There's a breakfast buffet, and you'll want to check out the inn's Honor Mansion Cookbook. Most of the guest rooms and suites feature queen- and king-sized beds, fireplaces, comfy sitting areas, and great views, and many have spa tubs; a couple have claw-foot tubs. The inn is near the Healdsburg Plaza and a short drive from many wineries in the area.

○ **Hotel Healdsburg** (www.hotel healdsburg.com, 707-431-2800, 800-889-7188, 25 Matheson Street, Healdsburg, CA 95448; $$$–$$$$). This contemporary, three-story hotel is right on the main square of Healdsburg. The hotel is modern in decor but remains warm and inviting, with a stone fireplace in the lobby and—for those who like to people-watch—a screened-in porch. Hotel Healdsburg has 55 rooms, all designed to pamper: oversized bathrooms done in Italian glass mosaic tile, 6-foot soaking tubs, private balconies, and down comforters. In addition, a complimentary gourmet breakfast with smoked salmon and made-to-order eggs is served in the lounge. Right off the lobby is Dry Creek Kitchen, a restaurant owned by star chef Charlie Palmer—best known for his Aureole restaurants in New York and Las Vegas. Showcasing American cuisine and wine from Sonoma County, the restaurant serves lunch and dinner (see entry under *Restaurants*). The hotel's location on the downtown square can be a drawback for guests who are sensitive to noise.

○ **h2hotel** (www.h2hotel.com, 707-922-5251, 219 Healdsburg Avenue, Healdsburg, CA 95448; $$–$$$). Conveniently located near the town square, this "green" hotel describes its 36 guest rooms as "eco-chic." The furnishings are spare but aesthetically pleasing and intended to soothe: you'll find organic cotton linens and robes, bamboo floors, and ergonomic chairs. All rooms feature a private balcony or patio. Another draw is the hotel's ever-popular Spoonbar restaurant, which serves Mediterranean eats, inventive cocktails, and wines that are international in scope, yet accent the local grapes.

○ **Les Mars** (www.hotellesmars.com, 707-433-4211, 27 North Street Healdsburg, CA 95448; $$$–$$$$). Les Mars feels like a European hotel on American turf. Its front lobby is elegant, with seventeenth- and eighteenth-century antiques, warm wood, and soft colors. It offers Old World luxury and twenty-first-century technology in its 16 rooms—such as entertainment amenities housed within a Louis XV armoire. Les Mars is one of the most decadent hotels in Wine Country, particularly for the palate. The restaurant is Chalkboard, which replaced the upscale Cyrus, and is decidedly low key in comparison. But it has good farm-to-table eats, drawing from its 3-acre farm at Chalk Hill Estate Winery (see listing under *Restaurants*).

○ **Madrona Manor** (www.madrona manor.com, 707-433-4231, 800-258-4003, 1001 Westside Road, Healdsburg, CA 95448; $$$–$$$$). This country inn and restaurant is the grande dame of Sonoma County. With its mansard roof, expansive porch, and surrounding lush gardens, this three-story Victorian built in 1881 is a majestic sight amid a glade of trees. Large and ornate antiques decorate most of the mansion's formal guest

HONOR MANSION IS A SOPHISTICATED BED & BREAKFAST ON A QUIET HEALDSBURG STREET TIM FISH

rooms. There are 22 rooms and suites on the property. Well off the main road, Madrona Manor guarantees an unhurried stay and a return to the slower pace of the home's Victorian heyday. Buffet breakfast is included. The restaurant is also first-rate (see *Where to Eat*).

✷ Where to Eat

✪ **Barndiva** (www.barndiva.com, 707-431-0100, 231 Center Street, Healdsburg, CA 95448; $$$$; cuisine: California). In Wine Country, Barndiva is known as a hip restaurant with late-night appeal where you can order exotic drinks from the bar until 11 p.m. It's also known for celebrating all things local, searching out the best local produce from local farmers, ranchers, and vintners, etc. A safe bet is the crispy duck leg confit. Whether you opt for lunch, an early dinner, or a nightcap, you won't be disappointed. The food is tasty, the drinks are festive, and although the waitstaff may be young, they're dedicated. What's more, the decor is charming. The restaurant is rustic-chic, a cedar barn with a

14-foot ceiling and a sleek mahogany bar. The wine list is sophisticated and fairly priced, with more than 150 bottles and about 10 specialty cocktails at the going rate. The menu follows suit. Good picks include fish and duck entrées. Tip: On a warm summer's night, the back patio is perfect.

Brass Rabbit (www.thebrassrabbit healdsburg.com, 707-473-8580, 109 Plaza Street, Healdsburg, CA 95448; $$$$; cuisine: California). The restaurant, formerly Bistro Ralph, sports a shiny tin tile roof, block cutout pendant lights, oak tables, and a chef's counter/bar overlooking a six-foot Argentinian-style wood-burning grill complete with a rotisserie and plancha. Expect elegant cooking, too, because executive chef Shane McAnelly also runs the kitchen of Chalkboard Restaurant a few blocks away. Yet this is more casual dining, offering staples like Kurobuta pork schnitzel with sauerkraut, a hefty cheeseburger with truffle aioli, and a standout Spanish octopus roasted with chickpeas, peppers, almond, harissa, and an indulgent bit of pork belly. Of course, there is rabbit, sourced from Marin's own Devil's

THE DRINK MENU AT BARNDIVA FEATURES THE EXOTIC

Gulch Ranch and hopping through in the form of rillettes or the must-order rabbit pot pie studded with bacon, mushroom, turnip, carrots, and divine truffle rabbit gravy under buttery puff pastry. For sipping, the California wine list covers the usual suspects plus some special gems like Cobb and Cirq, while cocktails take a whimsical supper-club theme for signatures like the Vesper of Mayfair vodka, gin, Kina L'Aero d'Or, and blue cheese–stuffed olives.

✪ **Bravas Bar de Tapas** (www.stark restaurants.com, 707-433-7700, 420 Center Street, Healdsburg, CA 95448; $$–$$$; cuisine: Spanish). You don't need a passport to feel like you've traveled to Spain, with chef Mark Stark's inventive twist on tapas. Something wholly unique here is the Ham and Cheese Bar, offering up a variety of Spanish as well as local cheeses and the thinly sliced Ibérico ham. As for drink, Bravas will satisfy wine lovers as well as the late-night crowd with highlights that include local and Spanish wines, sangria, and Spanish-inspired cocktails. The restaurant itself is housed in a charming cottage, intimate yet sleek and hip. Best of all, all year-round you can enjoy your meal indoors or out, and Bravas offers patio dining at its best, with whimsical lighting.

✪ **Chalkboard** (www.chalkboard healdsburg.com, 707 473-8030; 29 North Street, Healdsburg, CA 95448; $$; cuisine: California). This casual spot has a farm-to-table focus, drawing produce and herbs from its 3-acre farm at Chalk Hill Estate Vineyards & Winery. Chalkboard is creative and delivers an excellent range of small plates that play well in today's economy. Replacing the upscale Cyrus, Chalkboard is decidedly more low key. Rustic wooden tables replace linens, and as for the windows, there are no longer those fussy Austrian shades. Naturally, in this casual setting, there's no place for Cyrus's champagne, caviar, and cheese carts, and we must admit we miss the decadence.

But Chalkboard won't disappoint those looking for a casual setting and tasty food. The restaurant is owned by Bill Foley, the executive who owns Chalk Hill, Sebastiani, and other wineries; and David Fink, whose holdings include the L'Auberge Carmel hotel and Aubergine restaurant in Carmel.

Costeaux French Bakery (www .costeaux.com, 707-433-1913, 417 Healdsburg Avenue, CA 95448; open daily). This is a bright and breezy place to enjoy coffee and Parisian treats throughout the day. Its signature is bread, ranging from rustic sourdough rolls to multigrain bread to sweet French loaves. It also serves breakfast and lunch, with a full range of options from breakfast pastries to soups, salads, and sandwiches, as well as tasty desserts like French Fruit Tart and Triple Chocolate Mousse.

✪ **Dry Creek Kitchen** (www.dry creekkitchen.com, 707-431-0330, 317 Healdsburg Avenue, Healdsburg, CA 95448; $$$; cuisine: California). Given chef-owner Charlie Palmer's track record with his ever-expanding restaurant empire, it's not surprising that Dry Creek Kitchen raised the culinary bar in Sonoma County. Palmer, who moved his family to Sonoma more than a decade ago, divides his time between Wine Country and his restaurants in New York and Las Vegas. The decor is contemporary, with big columns that sweep dramatically toward the ceiling, and subtle colors: cream with pear-green trim. It's comfortable, clean, and simple. The menu follows the seasons and features local products almost exclusively: meat, seafood, produce, artisan cheeses, and, of course, wine. Palmer never gets in the way of these fine ingredients, and yet he somehow finds a way to give them an intriguing twist. The wine list is extensive and has a particularly good offering of pinot noirs and zinfandels, and although prices are generally high, there's no corkage fee for guests who bring in their own first two bottles of Sonoma County wine.

TREATS GALORE AT DOWNTOWN BAKERY & CREAMERY

✪ 🍴 **Downtown Bakery & Creamery**
(www.downtownbakery.net, 707-431-2719, 308A Center Street, Healdsburg, CA 95448). There are fabulous desserts here, but it doesn't look like much as you walk in. What's the secret? The Chez Panisse connection. Owner Kathleen Stewart is a veteran of that famed Berkeley kitchen. Tortes and cakes are ungodly delicious, as are the sticky buns, the monster Fig Newton–like cookies, the galettes, and the blueberry scones. Don't miss the famous donut muffins, which were once featured on the Food Network's *The Best Thing I Ever Ate*. Breakfast should include pancakes. Chef Kathleen Stewart tested countless recipes when she was writing an article for *Fine Cooking* magazine, and the rejects got tossed on Stewart's back patio, a feast for the pigeons, which, it turns out, weren't picky. The pancakes now served at the bakery made the final cut. Breakfast is available Friday through Monday, and sandwiches, such as turkey on focaccia with homemade mayonnaise, are available for lunch. They also have great coffee and ice cream. Enjoy your goodies in their indoor seating or in the plaza across the street.

✪ **Dry Creek General Store** (www.drycreekgeneralstore1881.com, 707-433-4171, 3495 Dry Creek Road, Healdsburg, CA 95448). A few years back, Gina Gallo of Gallo of Sonoma Winery purchased this rural gathering spot, a landmark of Sonoma's rustic heritage. Keep your eye out for fancy trappings such as a wine rack and gourmet goodies amid the rustic charm. Drop into this charming country store for a delicious deli sandwich, and in the summer on Thursday nights, don't miss the General's Store BBQ, starting at 6:30 p.m.

Flying Goat Coffee Roastery (707-433-9081, 324 Center Street, Healdsburg, CA 95448; 707-433-8003, 419 Center Street, Healdsburg, CA 95448). Here's a stylish spot for a cup of java. Have a muffin while you smell the roaster at work.

✪ **Healdsburg Bar & Grill** (www .healdsburgbarandgrill.com, 707-433-3333, 245 Healdsburg Avenue, Healdsburg, CA 95448; $$; cuisine: California). Nick Peyton and Douglas Keane opened this highbrow burger joint. With their credentials on the restaurant scene, it's no surprise that the burger—freshly ground All Natural Meyer Beef on a Toasted Costeaux Bakery Sourdough Bun—is a hit. Other appealing concoctions include the fries; get them with chipotle salt or truffle oil and Parmigiano-Reggiano.

✪ ✿ **Healdsburg Shed** (www.healdsburg shed.com, 707-431-7433, 25 North Street, Healdsburg, CA 95448; open Wednesday–Monday 8–9, 8–6 Tuesday). Here farmers and foodies find common ground, and there's so much to explore. Shed Café is central to the space, which also includes a garden shop, a market, and even a fermentation bar, among other things. Owners Cindy Daniel and husband Doug Lipton say the idea behind the venture is to celebrate the growers and the land where they toil. Inside this hulk of a building, the feel is of a lively village. The café serves breakfast and lunch with its focus on veggie-inspired dishes. Then you have the fermentation bar, where you can sip wine and beer on tap. And for those attempting a green thumb, there's the garden shop, where you can find plenty of tools and, yes, organic garden seeds. What makes this place especially fun are the workshops and events where like-minded foodies and growers can commingle.

✪ **Jimtown Store** (www.jimtown.com, 707-433-1212, 6706 Highway 128, Healdsburg, CA 95448). An Alexander Valley landmark for a century, this former general store and gas depot, which had been abandoned for years, was resuscitated in 1991 with a touch of gourmet chic. Today, Carrie Brown's Jimtown Store remains quaint yet sophisticated, drawing national attention along the way. Sandwiches are first-rate, and the aisles include old-fashioned candy, old-fashioned sodas, baked goods, antiques, toys, and memorabilia. Enjoy wine sold by the glass or bottle as you browse.

✪ **Journeyman Meat Co.** (www .journeymanmeat.com, 404 Center Street, 707-395-MEAT, Healdsburg, CA 95448; $$). If you're looking for little Italy in Sonoma County, you've found it here. This is an artisan shop, and the meat is cut, cured, and crafted just 20 miles away. Here you'll find a curated butcher counter and tasty offerings from a wood-fired oven. The locals and savvy travelers gather here to grab hearty fare like a Bacon Burger or a Pizza Bianco. Of course, not to be missed on the menu are the Wine & Salumi Flights. The shop showcases the Journeyman and San Lorenzo wines, produced by Pete and Cathy Seghesio's family, as well as other brands. The decor is upscale modern, with irreverent touches. The doorknob, for instance, is an oversized cleaver.

✪ **Madrona Manor** (www.madrona manor.com, 707-433-4231, 800-258-4003, 1001 Westside Road, Healdsburg, CA 95448; $$$$; cuisine: California, French). It's a shame to approach this 1881 Victorian in the dark. Rising three stories to a steep mansard roof, this inn is a majestic sight set in a quiet glade, amid lush gardens (see listing under *Lodging*). The dining rooms, which used to be as stark and formal as a starched white shirt, now have warmer but still elegant tones. The service is very attentive, and Madrona Manor has one of the best wine cellars around, particularly if you like newer "blue chip" wines. The location is the main reason for coming to the manor. The food is dependably good, if rather uninspired, and evening there overall should be an enjoyable one. Perhaps the experience simply pales next to all the competition in Healdsburg.

Oakville Grocery (www.oakville grocery.com, 707-433-3200, 124 Matheson Street, Healdsburg, CA 95448). Napa Valley invaded Sonoma with this satellite of the successful upscale grocery.

Who needs a designated driver when you can sip on the town square? There are tasting rooms aplenty, some old and some new. Here are the latest: La Crema, 235 Healdsburg Avenue, www.lacrema.com, 707-431-9400; Thumbprint Cellars, 102 Matheson Street, www.thumbprintcellar.com, 707-433-2397.

Bear Republic Brewing Co. (345 Healdsburg Avenue, www.bearrepublic.com, 707-433-BEER). This brewery may be Healdsburg's hottest nightspot, featuring food, live music, and some excellent handcrafted beers. The Scottish-style Red Rocket Ale is a specialty, and they also make a yummy Hefeweizen (pronounced HEF-ay-vite-zen), a light German brew perfect for a warm summer day. The atmosphere is lively, and from your table or the bar, you can watch brewing at work. As for the food, stick with the basic pub fare—burgers, etc.—and you won't go wrong.

Goodies include duck pâté, cold cuts, cheese, olives, fresh produce, and artisan breads. Order a sandwich or pizza or a

BE SURE TO TRY CHEF DUSTIN VALETTE'S "TRUST ME" MENU. YOU WON'T REGRET IT

rotisserie chicken. There's even wine available by the glass. Take the food with you or eat on the patio. During the summer months of June to August, Oakville Grocery serves paella for Tuesday night's music on the plaza. Paella is a Spanish saffron-flavored dish containing rice, meat, seafood, and vegetables.

✪ **SingleThread Farm** (www.single threadfarms.com, 707-723-4646, 131 North Street, Healdsburg, CA 95448; $$$$; cuisine: Japanese). Wine Country—and much of the country at large—has never seen anything so magnificent as this contemporary shrine to kaiseki, a traditional multicourse Japanese dinner. Chef Kyle Connaughton is so dedicated to his culinary art that he changes his series of courses daily to reflect the 72 five-day microseason agricultural cycles guided by the ancient Japanese farmers' almanac. It's such an immersion into the architecture of ingredients, in fact, that menus aren't presented until the end of the meal, because the chef wants you to "feel" the food more than just eat it. It's special, indeed, just to get the spectacular produce. The chef's wife, Katina Connaughton, runs a five-acre farm nearby plus a 3,000-square-foot garden on the restaurant's rooftop. Fish, naturally, comes straight from Japan. The result is an array of luxurious dishes like black cod fukkura-san (cooked donabe-style, in an earthenware pot) kissed with leeks, brassicas, and chamomile broth, or Guinea hen dobin mushi in a roulade with matsutake mushroom broth, pickled Tokyo turnip, and curls of miso-cured squash. Such food ($295 per person) deserves a jaw-dropping setting, and the 55-seat space delivers with its open kitchen, where you can watch chefs hunched over handmade pottery plates arranging food with tweezers. Wine and sake augment such rare, unusual pairings ($185–$355 per person) that the guidance from the sommelier is much appreciated.

Taqueria El Sombrero (www.el sombrerohbg.com, 707-433-3818, 245 Center Street, Healdsburg, CA 95448). Ignore the atmosphere and relish the food just off the plaza. The restaurant uses whole beans, not canned refrieds, and grilled meat.

❍ Valette (www.valettehealdsburg .com, 707-473-0946, 344 Center Street, Healdsburg, CA 95448; $$$$). Dustin Valette opened his restaurant just across the square from Charlie Palmer's Dry Creek Kitchen, where he was executive chef for six years. Valette is particularly gifted with beef, and this is a restaurant that caters to the carnivore. Dishes include cocoa nib-crusted Liberty duck breast, local Duroc pork trio, and charred Wagyu New York steak. But what's most appealing to many is chef Valette's "Trust Me" Tasting Menu. It comes with a minimum of four courses. Why wouldn't guests trust chef Valette? He's a regular at his own restaurant, cooking most nights, and he makes a point of greeting guests in the house. Valette's has an impressive wine list that showcases California vintners, while also including imports. It also has a nice mix of wines by the glass. This is one of the best dining experiences in Wine Country; the food is delicious, the service is attentive, and chef Valette's in the kitchen.

❍ Willi's Seafood and Raw Bar (www .starkrestaurants.com, 707-433-9191, 403

Healdsburg Avenue, Healdsburg, CA 95448; $$–$$$$; cuisine: seafood, eclectic). We love the energy of this place. You just want to pull up a chair or a barstool and hang out. There's a hip, industrial feel to the joint, and the best seats are the private booths on the upper level. The menu is composed entirely of small plates, with seafood and Latino spices playing a strong role. The flavors are bold, and sometimes a dish goes overboard with too many ingredients, but we're generally won over. Plates range from fresh shellfish, cevich, tartars, and New England–style sandwich rolls to skewers. The wine list is quite small, but the prices are fair and there's a decent selection by the glass.

✳ Entertainment

Bear Republic Brewing Co. (707-433-BEER, 345 Healdsburg Avenue, Healdsburg, CA 95448). This brewery makes excellent handcrafted beers, and has music occasionally during the summer.

Raven Film Center (707-522-0330, 415 Center Street, Healdsburg, CA 95448). The main Raven Theater is easily the finest movie house in Wine Country, but sadly, the downtown Healdsburg theater seldom shows films these days. Four smaller theaters were added behind the

HEALDSBURG PLAZA RETAINS A SMALL-TOWN CHARM

original theater, and they show first-run movies and the occasional art film. Wine and beer are served, along with sandwiches and other snacks.

Raven Performing Arts Theater (www.raventheater.org, 707-433-6335, 115 North Street, Healdsburg, CA 95448). This venue stages musical acts—everything from rap to Los Lobos, Taj Mahal, and comic Will Durst—as well as dance and theatrical performances. Check the website for current offerings.

River Rock Casino (www.riverrock casino.com, 3250 Highway 128, Geyserville, CA 95441). This tribal-owned casino has slot machines featuring classics like video poker, and it offers everything from penny slots to $100 pulls. Just be sure not to gamble away your wine budget.

✳ Selective Shopping

Copperfield's Books (707-433-9270, 106 Matheson Street, Healdsburg, CA 95448). This store provides locals and tourists alike with thousands of titles to choose from.

Clutch (www.clutchhealdsburg.com, 707-433-8189, 307 Healdsburg Avenue, Healdsburg, CA 95448). This shop features men's and women's accessories.

Fideaux (707-433-9935, 43 North Street, Healdsburg, CA 95448). The shop caters to cats and dogs with whimsical items that include wine-barrel doghouses and breed-specific clocks.

Levin & Co. (707-433-1118, 306 Center Street, Healdsburg, CA 95448). This

BEST DAY IN SONOMA COUNTY

Our tour of Sonoma County finds its base in Healdsburg. Here we set you up with a 24-hour itinerary, featuring wine tasting, a massage and swim, dinner at the most reputable place in Sonoma County, and a nightcap fit for a diva.

1. Naturally, we begin with a scrumptious breakfast to get ourselves percolating with caffeine: **Downtown Bakery & Creamery** (Healdsburg; www.downtownbakery.net). Tortes and cakes are ungodly delicious, as are the sticky buns, the monster Fig Newton–like cookies, and the blueberry scones. **Costeaux French Bakery** (Healdsburg; www.costeaux.com) is another great option for discerning palates who are fans of French bread, among other assorted treats. Here you'll find great breakfast and lunch fare.

2. Next up, wine tasting, of course. Here are two great options:

Seghesio (Healdsburg; www.seghesio.com). The winery produces many Italian-style varieties such as sangiovese, barbera, pinot grigio, and arneis, but it's known for its supple yet intense zinfandel.

Francis Ford Coppola Winery (Geyserville; www.francisfordcoppolawinery.com). A resort-style wine experience for the entire family, with a pool near the tasting room, bocce courts, a movie gallery, and more.

3. Lunch at a place that stocks both gourmet food and memorabilia: **Jimtown Store** (Healdsburg; www.jimtown.com). An Alexander Valley landmark for a century, this former general store and gas depot was resuscitated in 1991 with a touch of gourmet chic. Today, Carrie Brown's Jimtown Store remains quaint yet sophisticated, having drawn national attention along the way. The sandwiches are first-rate, and the aisles are full of old-fashioned candy, toys, and memorabilia.

4. Unwind. Have a massage and swim at the **Spa at Hotel Healdsburg** (Healdsburg; www.hotelhealdsburg.com). There's an understated sophistication to this spa, which is secluded deep inside this downtown hotel. Treatments range from pedicures to facials to hot stone massages and detoxifying seaweed wraps. Guests have access to a whirlpool tub and pool.

5. Ready for dinner? **Madrona Manor** (Healdsburg; www.madronamanor.com) is the grande dame of Sonoma County with its mansard roof, expansive porch, and surrounding lush gardens. The restaurant here is top-rate, but if you're up for a bit of driving, Forestville's **Farmhouse Inn** (www.farmhouseinn.com) trumps. With its Michelin-starred chef and master sommelier, it's the savvy pick.

6. Go for a nightcap at **Barndiva** (Healdsburg; www.barndiva.com), where you can order exotic cocktails until 11 p.m. in a rustic-chic cedar barn. The drinks and the decor charm.

7. End the day at **Honor Mansion** (Healdsburg; www.honormansion.com), named one of the most romantic inns by American Historic Inns. Tomorrow you'll enjoy a full gourmet breakfast, with complimentary mimosas.

lively shop caters to the book and music lover, specializing in the classics and high-quality fiction.

Plaza Gourmet (707-433-7116, 108 Matheson Street, Healdsburg, CA 95448). This store could outfit Martha Stewart's kitchen. It has a wide range of kitchenware, tableware, books, and candles.

Saint Dizier Home (707-473-0980, 259 Center Street, Healdsburg, CA 95448). This store features Ralph Lauren Collection furnishings, with some Henredon furniture in stock.

Susan Graf Limited (707-433-6495, 100 Matheson Street, Healdsburg, CA 95448). The establishment carries upscale men's and women's clothing, with lines such as Kate Spade and Delman.

SPA HEAVEN

A Simple Touch (www.asimpletouchspa.com, 707-433-6856, 239C Center Street, Healdsburg, CA 95448). An intimate spot just off the Healdsburg Plaza, the lobby welcomes you with warm tones, and a bit of Tuscany. With a large tub room, one couples room, and two treatment rooms, A Simple Touch offers individual care. The mud baths are fango style—a light and warm chocolate-milk-like blend of mineral water and powdered mud. There are champagne baths as well as herbal facials, Swedish deep-tissue massage, sports massage, and hot rocks massage.

Spa at Hotel Healdsburg (www.hotelhealdsburg.com, 707-433-4747, 327 Healdsburg Avenue, Healdsburg, CA 95448) There's an understated sophistication to this spa, which is secluded deep inside this downtown hotel. There are six treatment rooms, and the decor blends soothing colors with plantation shutters and pecan wood floors. Guests have access to a whirlpool tub and pool. Treatments range from pedicures and facials to hot stone massages and wine-and-honey wraps.

✲ Special Events

Barrel Tasting along the Wine Road (www.wineroad.com, 707-433-4335, Russian River Wine Road, countryside surrounding Healdsburg, CA). Typically the first spring event of the wine season (over two weekends in March), barrel tasting helps lift wine lovers out of the winter doldrums. Besides, everyone loves a sneak preview of wine that hasn't been bottled yet. Approximately 100 wineries pour samples.

Healdsburg Plaza Tuesday Concert Series (707-433-6935, downtown Healdsburg, CA 95448). Held June through August, this series offers an eclectic array of music and livens up Tuesday afternoons from 6 to 8 p.m. on this lovely plaza.

Rodney Strong Concert Series (800-514-3849, 11455 Old Redwood Highway, Healdsburg, CA 95448). There's a summer-long series of concerts on this winery's lawn.

OPPOSITE: MISSION SAN FRANCISCO SOLANO IS A HISTORIC TREASURE

CITY OF SONOMA

The old world–style Sonoma Plaza is the heart of a family-friendly downtown, and buildings like the fading but still regal Sebastiani Theatre, circa 1933, speak of a less complicated time. The central plaza is arguably the most charming of all town squares in Wine Country. It's an 8-acre park with two ponds, populated with ducks and geese, a play structure, and a rose garden. Surrounding the Sonoma Plaza are a number of historic buildings. Shops, galleries, coffeehouses, and tasting rooms line the streets adjacent to the square.

On a historical note, the Bear Flag Monument is the place where the Bear Flag was raised in 1846, proclaiming the end of Mexican rule of the state. The monument has a backdrop of lush greenery, and there are plenty of kids roaming the grounds, with mothers sipping lattes not far behind. There is a laid-back, lazy-Sunday-afternoon feel to the square at all times, which is particularly appealing to tourists who come to Wine Country to revive themselves, to take a hiatus from their cell phones, to be unreachable, off the grid. The oldest city in the area, Sonoma also has many of the oldest buildings, including adobes like the simple but majestic Mission San Francisco Solano.

Sonoma has a great lineup of wineries, including Buena Vista Winery, revered for its place in history, and Benziger Family Winery, held in high esteem for being an eco-pioneer.

✳ To See

ART GALLERY ✪ **Lisa Kristine Gallery** (www.lisakristine.com, 707-938-3860, 452 First Street E., Sonoma, CA 95476). The photographer Lisa Kristine has been recognized by the United Nations for capturing striking images of indigenous peoples. This gallery on the Sonoma Plaza takes you a world away, giving a glimpse of other cultures. "Each image is made with reverence for the subject," Kristine says. "In order for me to photograph a person in the unaffected environment of self, there must be a trust between us. Without this, a stirring image cannot be created." While traveling the world with her camera, she has run out of food and water and contracted diseases, but she's taken it all in stride. Why? It began when, as a child, she was fascinated by her mother's anthropology books. Kristine goes to the ends of the earth to get her amazing shots because she's "fascinated by people everywhere."

TIGERS GUARDIAN PHOTOGRAPHED BY LISA KRISTINE OF LISA KRISTINE GALLERY IN SONOMA

HISTORIC BUILDINGS ✪ ⚔ **Mission San Francisco Solano** (707-938-9560, Parks

& Recreation Department, 114 E. Spain Street, Sonoma, CA 95476). The Sonoma mission was the last to be established, and the mission system was dissolved in 1833. It became a center of religion and culture under General Mariano Vallejo's rule, but it was sold by the Catholic Church in 1881. Used over the years as a blacksmith's shop and hay barn, the mission was nearly lost until the state intervened in 1906; restoration began three years later.

HIGH PLATEAU PHOTOGRAPHED BY LISA KRISTINE OF LISA KRISTINE GALLERY IN SONOMA

 General Vallejo Home (707-939-9559, Parks & Recreation Department, Third Street and W. Spain Street, Sonoma, CA 95476, 0.5 mile west of Sonoma Plaza). General Mariano Vallejo may have been the most powerful man in Northern California in the 1850s, but he had a sense of poetry about him when he named his house Lachryma Montis. Latin for "tears of the mountain," the name was derived from a mountain spring on the property. Vallejo's home, finished in 1852, reflects his embrace of North American culture. Instead of an adobe house, he built a two-story Gothic Victorian. The house was prefabricated—designed and built on the East Coast and shipped around Cape Horn. Vallejo and his family lived in the house for 35 years; the state bought the property in 1933.

 Sebastiani Theatre (707-996-2020, 476 First Street E., Sonoma, CA 95476). This is a delightful old restored theater showing first-run films.

✳ To Do

BIKING **Sonoma Valley Cyclery** (707-935-3377, 20091 Broadway, Sonoma, CA 95476). This shop helps you slow your pace and explore Wine Country by bicycle.

 Sonoma Valley Bike Tours (www.sonomavalleybiketours.com). Riding a bicycle built for two is a romantic way to see the sights.

BIPLANE TOURS **Vintage Aircraft** (707-938-2444, www.vintageaircraft.com, Sonoma Valley Airport, 23982 Arnold Drive, Sonoma, CA 95476). Red Baron, move over. These scenic tours of Napa Valley and Sonoma County are in vintage biplanes that have been meticulously restored. Aerobatic flights are also available, offering loops, rolls, and "kamikaze" flights. Not for the faint of heart.

GOLF **Sonoma Golf Club** (707-996-0300, 707-939-4100, www.sonomagolfclub.com, 17700 Arnold Drive, Sonoma, CA 95476). This is a private course—an individual can play only if he or she is a guest at Fairmont Sonoma Mission Inn. It offers 18 championship holes, par 72; a driving range; a putting green; and a restaurant. Moderate to expensive.

PARKS **Jack London State Historic Park** (707-938-5216, 2400 London Ranch Road, Glen Ellen, CA 95442; off Arnold Drive). Writer Jack London fell in love with the Valley of the Moon and began buying land there in 1905. By the time he died in 1916, he was immersed in the innovative projects of his Beauty Ranch. Visitors can traverse these 800 acres, seeing the remains of the Londons' Wolf House mansion, hiking 7 miles of trails, and taking in a scenic three-and-a-half-mile climb with breathtaking views of the Valley of the Moon.

Sugarloaf Ridge State Park (707-833-5712, 2605 Adobe Canyon Road, Kenwood, CA 95452; 7 miles east of Santa Rosa on Highway 12, north on Adobe Canyon Road). This 2,500-acre park offers 47 developed campsites, an observatory, 25 miles of nature trails, hiking, horseback-riding trails, and exhibitions. Trailers up to 27 feet long and campers up to 23 feet long are permitted.

✐ ✪ **TrainTown** (www.traintown.com, 707-938-3912, 20264 Broadway, Sonoma, CA 95476; 1 mile south of Sonoma Plaza). Take a 20-minute ride on a scale-model steam train around 10 acres of beautifully landscaped park, through a 140-foot tunnel, over bridges, and past historic replica structures. Also offered: a petting zoo, exhibitions, and amusement rides. TrainTown is open daily June to September, and Friday to Sunday the rest of the year. Admission: general admission and parking is free; amusement rides additional.

SEBASTIANI THEATRE GIVES THE HEALDSBURG PLAZA OLD-WORLD CHARM

SPAS ✪ **Fairmont Sonoma Mission Inn & Spa** (www.fairmont.com/sonoma, 707-938-9000, 866-540-4499, 100 Boyes Boulevard, Sonoma, CA 95476). Who's that lounging in the mineral pool? Billy Crystal? The waters at this Wine Country favorite for the rich and famous have made this site a destination since Native Americans first considered it a healing ground. It's also Wine Country's most expensive spa. The inn has recently tapped into a new source of mineral water, and the soft and lightly green liquid warms the pool and Jacuzzi. The spa house is a stylish combo of mission and art deco, and the pool area is in a peaceful grove of trees. The array of treatments is mind-boggling, from Swedish and sports massage to seaweed body wraps, hair and foot care, waxing, color analysis, and nearly a dozen different facials. There's also a fitness center.

❊ Wineries

✪ **Anaba** (www.anabawines.com, 707-996-4188, 60 Bonneau Road, Sonoma, CA 95476; tastings daily 10:30–5:30). The wines here are crafted from Rhone and Burgundian grape varietals; the pinot noirs and chardonnays are their most exciting offerings. The tasting room in this Carneros perch is also charming, a restored 100-year-old farmhouse. There's a tasting bar inside, or guests can sit on the patio overlooking the vineyards. Guests are welcome to bring a picnic for that patio. For the curious, the name

"Anaba" is derived from anabatic winds, which glider pilots rely on for flight. The winery celebrates these winds as a "gift of nature," ushering in cool air to slow the ripening process down so the vines can produce robust flavors in the grapes.

Arrowood Vineyards & Winery (www.arrowoodvineyards.com, 707-935-2600, 800-938-5170, 14347 Sonoma Highway, Glen Ellen, CA 95442; tastings daily 10–4:30). Richard Arrowood was one of the first high-profile winemakers in Sonoma County. After toiling at a number of wineries over the years, Arrowood and his wife, Alis, opened this winery in 1986, and the wines are among the best in California. The visitor center features a dramatic two-story limestone fireplace and views of the vineyard. The varietals most revered here are chardonnay, rich and complex, cabernet sauvignon, and Malbec. Arrowood has changed hands a number of times and is now owned by JFWines. Vintner Arrowood no longer produces his namesake brand, having turned his attention to boutique winemaking with Amapola Creek.

Benziger Family Winery (www.benziger.com, 707-935-4076, 888-490-2739, 1883 London Ranch Road, Glen Ellen, CA 95442; tastings daily 10–5). If this winery seems familiar, there's a reason. Millions know this spot along the gentle slope of Sonoma Mountain as Glen Ellen Winery, the king of the $5 bottle of vino. From a run-down grape ranch purchased from a naked hippie doctor in 1981, the Benziger clan built a multimillion-dollar Goliath. They eventually sold the Glen Ellen brand but kept the ranch, which dates to 1860, and now concentrate on their premium Benziger label. The Benzigers may have downsized, but the winery grounds are more beautiful than ever and are now entirely biodynamic; Benziger is at the forefront of California's "true wine" movement. Past an old farmhouse and down the hill is the wooden ranch barn that serves as aging cellar and tasting room. The Benziger Tribute is a Bordeaux-style wine and was selected by *Wine and Spirits Magazine* in 2009 as the best cab blend in America. Cabernet sauvignons can be a knockout in a good vintage, and the citrusy sauvignon blanc is usually a winner.

B. R. Cohn Winery (www.brcohn.com, 707-938-4064, 800-330-4064, 15000 Sonoma Highway, Glen Ellen, CA 95442; tastings daily 10–5). Manager for the Doobie Brothers and other rock bands, Bruce Cohn began a second career in wine when he bought Olive Hill Ranch in 1974. Cohn sold his grapes until 1984, when he bottled his first cabernet sauvignon. Ripe and concentrated, it was an immediate hit. Subsequent vintages have fared similarly, but the chardonnay and merlot are more routine. The tasting room has a handsome mahogany bar and marble fireplace and sits on a knoll covered with olive trees. Cohn, now retired, led the renaissance of premium California olive oil production decades ago, and the property's olive groves are stellar.

Buena Vista Winery (www.buenavistawinery.com, 800-926-1266, 18000 Old Winery Road, Sonoma, CA 95476; tastings daily 10–5). This is where it all began: California's oldest premium winery. Buena Vista is where Agoston Haraszthy, known as the Father of California Wine, started his experiments

TRAIN TOWN HOLDS GREAT ALLURE FOR KIDS TIM FISH

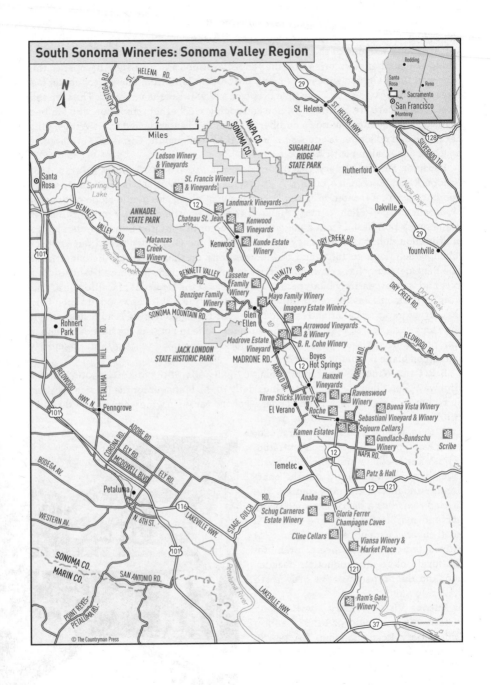

South Sonoma Wineries: Sonoma Valley Region

N

0   2   4
Miles

HELENA RD.
CALISTOGA RD.
ST. HELENA RD.
29
St. Helena
ST. HELENA HWY.

Redding
Santa Rosa
Reno
Sacramento
San Francisco
Monterey

128
SILVERADO TR.

NAPA CO.
SONOMA CO.

SUGARLOAF RIDGE STATE PARK

Rutherford

Napa River

Ledson Winery & Vineyards

St. Francis Winery & Vineyards

Santa Rosa

Spring Lake

BENNETT VALLEY RD.

ANNADEL STATE PARK

Landmark Vineyards

Chateau St. Jean

Kenwood Vineyards

Oakville

29

Matanzas Creek Winery

Kenwood

Kunde Estate Winery

DRY CREEK RD.

Yountville

101

Matanzas Creek

BENNETT VALLEY RD.

Lasseter Family Winery

TRINITY RD.

DRY CREEK RD.

Dry Creek

Benziger Family Winery

Mayo Family Winery

Imagery Estate Winery

SONOMA MOUNTAIN RD.

Glen Ellen

Arrowood Vineyards & Winery

REDWOOD RD.

Rohnert Park

REDWOOD HWY. N.

PETALUMA HILL RD.

JACK LONDON STATE HISTORIC PARK

Madrove Estate Vineyard

MADRONE RD.

B. R. Cohn Winery

Boyes Hot Springs

12

MORRBOM RD.

Hanzell Vineyards

Ravenswood Winery

Buena Vista Winery

Penngrove

CORONA RD.
ELY RD.
McDOWELL BLVD.
ELY RD.
ADOBE RD.

Three Sticks Winery

El Verano

Roche

Sebastiani Vineyard & Winery

Sojourn Cellars

Kamen Estates

Gundlach-Bundschu Winery

Scribe

NAPA RD.

12

BODEGA AV.

Petaluma

Temelec

Patz & Hall

12   121

WESTERN AV.

116

N. 6TH ST.

LAKEVILLE HWY.

STAGE GULCH RD.

Anaba

Schug Carneros Estate Winery

Gloria Ferrer Champagne Caves

101

Cline Cellars

Viansa Winery & Market Place

SONOMA CO.
MARIN CO.

SAN ANTONIO RD.

Petaluma River

121

POINT REYES-PETALUMA RD.

LAKEVILLE HWY.

Ram's Gate Winery

37

© The Countryman Press

in 1857. Although others had made wine in Sonoma before this, they had used only the coarse mission-variety grapes brought north by Spanish missionaries for Mass wine. Haraszthy was the first to believe that the noble grapes of Bordeaux and Burgundy could thrive in California. Visitors to Buena Vista stroll down a gentle, quarter-mile path, past thick blackberry bushes and tall eucalyptus trees, to the tasting room set inside the thick stone Press House, built in 1863. The wine is made a few miles away. Buena Vista's reputation has varied widely over time, but the wines have improved significantly in recent years.

BUENA VISTA IS CALIFORNIA'S OLDEST PREMIUM WINERY TIM FISH

○ **Chateau St. Jean** (www.chateaustjean.com, 707-257-5784, 8555 Sonoma Highway, Kenwood, CA 95452; tastings daily 10–5 at visitor center, daily 10–4:30 by reservation). Surrounded by luxuriant lawns and tall trees, with Sugarloaf Ridge in the distance, Chateau St. Jean—a modern version of a medieval French castle—is a visual treat. Opening in 1973, Chateau St. Jean drew immediate acclaim for its white wines, particularly the Robert Young Vineyard chardonnay, a luscious and oaky beauty that helped set the standard for chardonnay. Ironically, its red wines are now drawing attention. Its cabernet sauvignons and merlots are lush and well structured. There's a spacious visitor center behind the chateau. Buy a bottle of the riesling, chardonnay, or sauvignon blanc to pour with a picnic; the winery has one of Sonoma's best picnic grounds.

Cline Cellars (www.clinecellars.com, 707-940-4030, 800-546-2070, 24737 Arnold Drive, Sonoma, CA 95476; tastings daily 10–6). Cline was Rhone before Rhone was popular. Fred Cline got started in the East Bay in 1982, preferring unsung Rhone-style grapes such as carignan and mourvèdre. Cline then took up shop in Sonoma's Carneros District in 1991. The tasting room is housed in an 1850s farmhouse with a wraparound porch; the pleasant grounds have duck ponds and rose gardens. Nearby, viognier and syrah grapes are grown in the Carneros District, and pinot noir grapes are from the Petaluma Gap AVA. The winery also has had great success with zinfandel.

○ **Gloria Ferrer Caves & Vineyards** (www.gloriaferrer.com, 707-933-1917, 23555 Carneros Highway/Highway 121, Sonoma, CA 95476; tastings daily 10–5). If you've had the pleasure of paying a mere $10 for Cordon Negro, the simple but tasty little sparkling wine in the ink-black bottle, then you already know the people behind Gloria Ferrer. Freixenet of Spain is the world's largest producer of sparkling wine, and it was drawn to the great promise of California. Gloria Ferrer, named for the wife of Freixenet's president, makes consistently good bubbly at fair prices. It also makes admirable still wines: merlot, syrah, pinot, and chardonnay. The Carneros location places Gloria

Ferrer away from the high-traffic areas. Sitting dramatically on the gentle slope of a hill, the winery, done in warm tones of brown and red, is a bit of Barcelona. Gloria Ferrer's tour has great appeal, particularly tours of the caves carved from the hillside where the sparkling wine ages. This is one of the area's most romantic places to sit and sip some bubbly.

Gundlach-Bundschu Winery (www.gunbun.com, 707-938-5277, 2000 Denmark Street, Sonoma, CA 95476; tastings daily 11–4:30 November–April, 11–5:30 May–October). Passionate about wine and the Sonoma Valley, Jim Bundschu doesn't take himself too seriously. At a wine auction a few years back, he dressed as Batman, and his winery's humorous posters are classic. He even hijacked the Napa Valley Wine Train and—gasp!—handed out samples of Sonoma Valley wine. Behind all this frivolity is great wine and rich history. Since 1858, six generations have tended the winery's home vineyard, Rhinefarm—but wine wasn't bottled from Prohibition until Jim restored the original stone winery in the early 1970s. Located down a winding road, it's worth the trek. Take time to tour the winery's 10,000-square-foot cave.

Hanzell Vineyards (www.hanzell.com, 707-996-3860, 18596 Lomita Avenue, Sonoma, CA 95476; tastings and tours by appointment). The original boutique winery, Hanzell has greatly influenced California winemaking. The late ambassador James Zellerbach, who founded the winery in 1956, patterned it after the chateaux of Burgundy. The winery, with its dark wood and pitched roof, was modeled after Clos de Vougeot, and Hanzell was the first winemaker in California to barrel-ferment chardonnay and to use French oak barrels for aging. The winery went through a few rough years, but the pinot noir and chardonnay are now up to the old standards.

Imagery Estate Winery (www.imagerywinery.com, 707-935-4500, 877-550-4278, 14335 Highway 12, Glen Ellen, CA 95442; tastings Monday–Friday 10–4:30, Saturday and Sunday 10–5:30). Art and single-vineyard wines are the focus of this energetic winery run by the Benziger family. The artist collection series features boldly designed labels and offbeat varietals such as tempranillo and sangiovese, while the vineyard collection features distinctive cabernets, merlots, and other grapes from one unique place. The wines are sold almost exclusively at the winery, so you know you'll be able to taste a wine you'd never be able to buy back home.

Kamen Estate Wines (www.kamenwines.com, 707-938-7292, 111-B E. Napa Street, Sonoma, CA 95476; tastings daily noon–5:40; from 11 Friday–Sunday). Robert Kamen, the vintner who grew up in a city housing project in the Bronx and earned a PhD, is known for screenplays that have become major motion pictures, like *A Walk in the Clouds* and *The Karate Kid* series. Kamen's "bottled screenplays" are wines, especially his cabernet sauvignons, which also have star power. Kamen came to Sonoma to celebrate selling his first screenplay and came across a 280-acre property, a swath of Mt. Veeder with a view of the San Francisco Bay. He fell in love with it, and a week later, he owned it. Here, mountain-grown cabernet thrives at 1,100 to 1,400 feet, and that's his focus, although he also produces syrah and sauvignon blanc. From this perch Kamen keeps an eye on his vines while he continues to write. His other screenplays include *Taps*; *The Professional*; *The Transporter* series; *Lethal Weapon III*; *Taken*; and *Taken II*.

🍇 **Kenwood Vineyards** (www.kenwoodvineyards.com, 707-282-4228, 9592 Sonoma Highway, Kenwood, CA 95452; tastings daily 10–5). Don't let Kenwood Vineyards fool you. The tasting room might be in a rustic little barn, but behind the simple charm is a savvy winery, one of Sonoma County's largest. There's a homey and relaxed tasting room with wines that will please everyone in your group. Built by the Pagani brothers in 1906, the winery doesn't really have a specialty. Whites or reds, they have success with both. There's no better wine with fresh oysters than Kenwood's lemony sauvignon blanc. Try Kenwood's cabernet sauvignons, particularly the expensive but outstanding Artist Series—big wines with great aging potential.

Kunde Estate Winery (www.kunde.com, 707-833-5501, 9825 Sonoma Highway, Kenwood, CA 95452; tastings daily 10:30–5). Since 1904, five generations of Kundes have grown grapes. Stopping production during World War II, the clan began making wine again in the late 1980s. The Kundes have 2,000 acres of vineyards, and they know the personality of each varietal grape and put that to use. The strengths are chardonnay, typically elegant and creamy, and a muscular zinfandel made from 100-year-old vines. The winery is housed in a stylish white barn. In the hillside beyond, the Kundes have carved out a $5 million cave to age their wine. Visitors to the tasting room can watch the winery in action through picture windows.

Landmark Vineyards (www.landmarkwine.com, 707-833-0053, 101 Adobe Canyon Road, Kenwood, CA 95452; tastings daily 10–5). This attractive mission-style winery, in the shadow of Sugarloaf Ridge, is a house of chardonnay. Landmark began in Windsor in 1974, but suburban squeeze forced a move south in 1989, when Damaris Deere Ford assumed control. The menu includes two impressive chardonnays and a pinot noir. The tasting room is an appealing space, with a cathedral ceiling, fireplace, and granite bar. The cloistered courtyard looks onto the eastern slopes.

Ledson Winery and Vineyards (www.ledson.com, 707-537-3810, 7335 Sonoma Highway, Kenwood, CA 95452; tastings daily 10–5). From the road, this winery looks a bit like Wayne Manor from the 1960s *Batman* TV show. Originally designed as the Ledson family home, the 16,000-square-foot gothic "castle" turns heads on Sonoma Highway. Make your way up the long drive and through the vines, enter through the portico, and

LANDMARK VINEYARDS, IN THE SHADOW OF SUGAR LOAF RIDGE, IS A HOUSE OF CHARDONNAY TIM FISH

you'll see that the interior is just as extravagant as the outside. The wines are good but not great, with sauvignon blanc and chardonnay generally leading the pack.

Madrone Estate (www.valleyofthemoonwinery.com, 707-939-4500, 777 Madrone Road, Glen Ellen, CA 95442; tastings daily 10–5). A few years back the winery was run-down, and the wines had a nasty reputation. Just about the only thing left from the old days is the winery's original 110-year-old foundation. The new tasting room is sleek and modern, and so is the winery's bottle design, a stark yet dramatic etched bottle. But what about the wines? They're good and getting better, particularly the zinfandel and syrah. Valley of the Moon is its second label.

Mayo Family Winery (www.mayofamilywinery.com, 707-938-9401, 13101 Arnold Drive, Glen Ellen, CA 95442; tastings daily 10:30–6:30). Owner Henry Mayo had a career in real estate, but in 1990 he decided to forsake his business for grapes. It all began with a property in Kenwood he transformed into Laurel Hill Vineyards. By 1993, the Mayo family was bottling wine. The tasting room opened in July 2003, a more accessible location than the main winery nearby in the hills. Mayo produces more than a dozen varietals, but zinfandel and pinot steal the limelight. Mayo also operates a Reserve Tasting room in Kenwood.

✪ **Patz & Hall** (www.patzhall.com, 707-265-7700, tasting room: 21200 Eighth Street E., Sonoma, CA 95476; tastings daily by appointment). One of the true stars of California wine, Patz & Hall specializes in chardonnay and pinot noir. The winery harvests grapes from top vineyards around Northern California—such as Hyde and Pisoni—and the wines aren't cheap, but they're astounding for their plush and rich flavors and deep aromas. The winery's tasting room is called Sonoma House, where wine-and-food pairings are also offered.

✪ **Ram's Gate Winery** (www.ramsgatewinery.com, 707-721-8700, 28700 Arnold Drive, Sonoma, CA 95476; tastings Thursday–Monday from 11 by appointment). Here the pinot noir and the chardonnay from the Carneros are standouts. The winery is also a great place to sip and gaze, with nearly 360-degree views reaching down to the wetlands and the San Francisco Bay. The winery has a weathered farmstead and old barn feel to it, while the inside is urban chic. The tasting room is in a redwood-sided room with a 30-foot ceiling, with touches of marble and steel. There are plenty of tasting options here, but one of the best is to take a basket of food through the vineyard to the pond for a picnic. Ram's Gate Winery is owned by Jeff O'Neill, a third-generation vintner who owns O'Neill Vintners and the wine brand Xtant in the Napa Valley.

✪ **Ravenswood Winery** (www.ravenswoodwinery.com, 707-933-2332, 888-669-4679, 18701 Gehricke Road, Sonoma, CA 95476; tastings daily 10–4:30). Zin lovers have long been wise to Ravenswood, an unassuming stone winery built into the side of a hill—and the location fits the label: a classic image of a circle of ravens. The old tasting room is a busy spot but made soothing by a crackling fire. If you're lucky, Ravenswood will pour one of its top zinfandels. A sure way to sample the good stuff is to visit in the late winter and spring, when the zins are still in the barrel. Ravenswood's tour typically includes a walk through the vineyard and a barrel tasting. Because the winery is small, the tour is brief, but guides are detailed in their discussion of Ravenswood's natural approach to winemaking.

Roche Winery Tasting Room (www.rochewinery.com, 707-935-7115, 800-825-9475, 122 W. Spain Street, Sonoma, CA 95476; tastings daily 11–7:30). This quaint tasting room is in a 1940s Craftsman-style building right off the historic Sonoma Plaza. Here they have an indoor tasting bar and an outdoor one. House specialties include chardonnay and pinot noir, but syrah and merlot also deserve a taste. Joe and Genevieve Roche, both physicians, decided to live the dream, and they brought their family to Sonoma Valley, where they reared both vines and children.

Schug Carneros Estate Winery (www.schugwinery.com, 707-939-9363, 800-966-9365, 602 Bonneau Road, Sonoma, CA 95476; tastings daily 10–5). Nestled against a windswept hill on the western edge of Carneros is a little bit of Germany. Architecturally, Schug's winery would be more at home along the Rhine, where the winemaker was raised. His wines, too, reflect his European heritage. The late Walter Schug established his impressive credentials at Joseph Phelps, where he was winemaker from 1973 to 1983. The current wines, poured in a cozy tasting room, are distinctive and more European in style than those produced by most California wineries.

✪ **Scribe Winery** (www.scribewinery.com, 707-939-1858, 2100 Denmark Street, Sonoma, CA 95476; tastings daily). This winery earned its cult status by reeling in celebrities like Amy Schumer to partake in some afternoon sipping. Chardonnay, riesling, dry rosé, and lean pinot noir are specialties here and it makes perfect sense; the vintners are brilliant at drawing in foodies who are searching for the ultimate crisp match. Check out the winery's website and you'll see the winery's strategy in play—a host of food-centric events at its historic hacienda appealing to daytrippers and, yes, celebrities.

✪ **Sebastiani Vineyards & Winery** (www.sebastiani.com, 707- 933-3200, 800-888-5532, 389 Fourth Street E., Sonoma, CA 95476; tastings daily 10–5). For many people, Sebastiani is another way to spell "Sonoma." It's the epitome of the county's wine tradition: an unpretentious family winery—big, old, and Italian. Once among Sonoma County's largest wineries, Sebastiani trimmed production considerably a few years back to focus on quality. It remains one of Sonoma's most popular tourist attractions. The winery dates to 1896, when Samuele Sebastiani crushed his first grapes—zinfandel, to be precise. The press he used is still on display in the tasting room. Samuele's son August, a man with an affinity for bib overalls and stout, simple wines, built the winery's reputation on inexpensive jug wines. Since his death in 1980, the family has concentrated on premium wines. Visitors can taste Sebastiani's wide range of wines. Try the Sonoma County cabernet sauvignon and merlot, delightful wines and excellent bargains.

Sojourn Cellars (www.sojourncellars.com, 707-938-7212, 141 E. Napa Street, Sonoma, CA 95476; tastings daily 10–5 by appointment). The partners behind this venture—Craig Haserot and Erich Bradley—met on a tennis court. Isn't that where most business ventures begin? When they realized they both wanted to make handcrafted wine, they figured they both won the match. They say their winemaking style is decidedly New World with Old World sensibilities. The focus here is on pinot noir, with about a half a dozen bottlings released each year, while the cabernet is limited to a few. They are making noise with both varietals, so check them out.

St. Francis Winery and Vineyard (www.stfranciswinery.com, 707-538-9463, 888-675-9463, 100 Pythian Road, Kenwood, CA 95452; tastings daily 10–5). Merlot is the current popular flavor, and St. Francis makes two of the best, a regular and a reserve. Both are gorgeous and full bodied, with enough muscle to age a few years. Another success story for St. Francis is its chardonnay, done in a lean and fruity style. Its old-vine zinfandel packs a punch with its brilliant fruit. The wines can all be sampled at the lovely mission-style visitor center located near the winery.

✪ **Three Sticks Wines** (www.threestickswines.com, 707-996-3328, 143 W. Spain Street, Sonoma, CA 95476; tastings by appointment). Don Van Staaveren is the revered winemaker behind this brand, and he's best known for helping to craft the Chateau St. Jean's 1996 Cinq Cépages, which was named *Wine Spectator*'s number one wine in 1999. To Van Staaveren's credit, Three Sticks also makes a great lineup of wines: pinot noir, chardonnay, cabernet sauvignon, and cabernet franc. Van Staaveren's winemaking strategy seems to be working. The winemaker said he hasn't crushed a grape deliberately since 1990. Instead he lets the ripe grapes do their magic. Head poobah, vintner

Bill Price, is well known as an investor of savvy wineries like Chateau St. Jean, Kosta Browne, and Kistler Vineyards, among others. The Durell Vineyard is in the spotlight at Three Sticks, although the winery sources from other growers in the region as well.

Viansa Sonoma Winery and Marketplace (www.viansa.com, 707-935-4726, 800-995-4740, 25200 Arnold Drive, Sonoma, CA 95476; tastings daily 10–5). This tribute to Tuscany is situated high atop a knoll in the Carneros District. Done in warm shades with a terra-cotta tile roof and Italian opera music in the background, Viansa is one of Wine Country's most festive spots. Even the stainless-steel wine tanks are adorned with colorful faux marble frescoes. The marketplace offers sumptuous picnic fare, plus a picnic area with a dramatic view. Viansa is concentrating increasingly—and with considerable success—on Italian-style wines such as barbera and nebbiolo, as well as blends that recall a hearty Chianti.

WINE COLLECTIVES These tasting rooms offer a broad range of boutique wines—labels made in such small quantities that they typically aren't found in retail shops. Enjoy these rare offerings.

Cornerstone Sonoma (707-933-3010, www.cornerstonesonoma.com, 23570 Arnold Drive/Highway 121, Sonoma, CA 95476). A one-stop shop for tasting some of Sonoma County's best wines. The lineup includes Keating, Meadowcroft, and Tricycle. There's even a craft distillery, Prohibition Spirits, where you can sip the hard stuff. The collective is a rare find because it's also an eye-catching hub of interesting shops such as Artefact Design & Salvage and several plots of gardens and rotating art installations (and the interesting test gardens cultivated by *Sunset* magazine).

✳ Lodging

✪ **Beltane Ranch** (www.beltaneranch .com, 707-833-4233, 11775 Sonoma Highway, Glen Ellen, CA 95442; $$$). This former bunkhouse was built in 1890 and has been everything from a turkey farm to a historic farmhouse with ties to the Underground Railroad. The ranch was even rumored to be a brothel, but now it's a quiet and unpretentious B&B with five rooms and a private cottage that underwent renovation in 2017. It sits on 1,600 acres of land, amid vineyards and olive trees. (The inn even raises its own grass-fed beef, makes its own Beltane Ranch Olive Oil, and produces a sauvignon blanc that was well received by *Wine Spectator*.) A full breakfast, featuring the inn's own produce and farm-raised eggs, is served in the wood-paneled dining room or on the wraparound veranda. An added bonus is the remarkable hiking trail on the property, which takes you past vineyards.

Bungalows 313 (www.bungalows313 .com, 707-996-8091, 313 First Street E.,

Sonoma, CA 95476; $$$–$$$$). Located just a half block from the Sonoma Plaza, this inn is near the best restaurants, shops, and historical sites, but it is also hidden in a secluded compound. There's a lovely little garden with a stone fountain, perfect for relaxing in a chair with a good book. There are six bungalows in all, each with a kitchenette, a distinct personality, and modern furnishings. Dolce bungalow and Vita bungalow both have two-story lofts, and each looks out over a private garden.

✪ **The Cottage Inn & Spa** (www .cottageinnandspa.com, 707-996-0719, 310 First Street E., Sonoma, CA 95476; $$$–$$$$). Not far from the downtown plaza, this inn is a quiet oasis. A Mediterranean-style courtyard is enclosed by a high stucco wall and features a fountain and whirlpool. Many have private entrances or patios; some have fireplaces and whirlpool baths. Freshly baked goodies are delivered each morning, allowing guests a private continental breakfast.

El Dorado Hotel (www.eldorado sonoma.com, 707-996-3030,

Lisa Kristine (www.lisakristine.com)
Olea Hotel (www.oleahotel.com)
Ram's Gate Winery (www.ramsgatewinery.com)
MacArthur Place (www.macarthurplace.com)
The Inn at Ramekins (www.ramekins.com)
Mission San Francisco Solano (www.missiontour.org/sonoma)
Café La Haye (www.cafelahaye.com) and Maya (www.mayarestaurant.com).
Sebastiani Vineyards & Winery (www.sebastiani.com)
Gloria Ferrer Caves & Vineyards (www.gloriaferrer.com)
Hopmonk Tavern (www.hopmonk.com)
ScribeWinery (www.scribewinery.com)
Sigh (www.sighsonoma.com)

800-289-3031, 405 First Street W., Sonoma, CA 95476; $$$). The El Dorado is a special hotel. Restored to its original elegance, it has 27 rooms, all with private baths. The hotel offers four street-level bungalows for easy entry and are handicapped-accessible. The lobby restaurant, El Dorado Kitchen, serves California cuisine.

El Pueblo Inn (www.elpuebloinn.com, 707-996-3651, 896 W. Napa Street, Sonoma, CA 95476; $$). A mere 15-minute walk west of the historic Sonoma Plaza, El Pueblo Inn offers all the necessities for those seeking to escape to Wine Country without breaking the bank. The family-owned hotel offers simple, tastefully designed rooms with all the amenities, including free WiFi and in-room refrigerators that can store plenty of bottles of wine (or beer from the nearby Sonoma Springs Brewing Co., located about one block away). Opt for the larger California Rooms, with private patios. They're the most spacious rooms on the property, and many of them include fireplaces. Colorful, well-tended gardens surround a rare perk found in the world of accommodations: a 24-hour pool and hot tub. All stays include a continental breakfast, which features freshly squeezed juices and locally sourced ingredients.

✪ **Fairmont Sonoma Mission Inn & Spa** (www.fairmont.com/sonoma, 707-938-9000, 866-540-4499, 100 Boyes Boulevard, Sonoma, CA 95476; $$$$). Sonoma County's premier hotel, and part of the prestigious Fairmont chain, was built on a site once considered a sacred healing ground by Native Americans. By the turn of the twentieth century, the area had become a getaway for well-heeled San Franciscans, who came to the Sonoma hotel to "take the waters." The spa is among the most luxurious in Wine Country. Guests of the resort have privileges at the Sonoma Golf Club. The 13-acre grounds also include Santé, the inn's upscale fine dining restaurant; it has received a Michelin Star, but sadly the food is not quite up to the price tag. If there's a drawback to the Sonoma Mission Inn, it's the location. Although convenient to wineries and historic sites of Sonoma Valley, it's located along a hectic and well-developed thoroughfare. The grounds, however, remain peaceful. Tom Cruise, Billy Crystal, and Sylvester Stallone have all stayed here.

✪ **Gaige House Inn + Ryokan** (www.thegaigehouse.com, 707-935-0237, 800-935-0237, 13540 Arnold Drive, Glen Ellen, CA 95442; $$$–$$$$). This exceptional inn is a sanctuary off the beaten path. A Queen Anne Italianate built in the 1890s, it has 23 guest rooms, all elegantly done in modern tones. "Ryokan" reflects the experience inspired by

FIND SERENITY IN A ZEN SUITE AT GAIGE HOUSE INN

traditional Japanese inns. At the back of the property are eight Zen suites in sleek Asian design, some overlooking Calabazas Creek. A breakfast buffet is served daily and included in the rate. The pool is in a lovely setting, and Swedish and hot stone massages are offered. It's in an ideal location for wine touring and Sonoma dining.

✪ **Inn at Ramekins** (www.ramekins .com, 707-933-0450, 450 W. Spain Street, Sonoma, CA 95476; $$$–$$$$). This has to rate as one of the most food-savvy B&Bs of all. The six guest rooms are on the second floor of Ramekins Sonoma Valley Culinary School, well within reach of delectable aromas. A continental breakfast is served daily. It also offers in-house wine tasting as well as at several local wineries. Ramekins is also just a few blocks from the historic Sonoma Plaza.

An Inn 2 Remember (www.aninn2 remember.com, 707-938-2909, 800-382-7895, 171 W. Spain Street, Sonoma, CA 95476; $$–$$$). This inn is decorated throughout with French vintage furniture and decor. Each of the seven guest rooms (three in the main house and four in the adjacent cottage) has a private bath, air-conditioning, and a ceiling fan. Five rooms have private decks and entrances. Three rooms have gas fireplaces, and three are equipped with large whirlpool tubs. A light in-room breakfast is included. This is a charming inn, reasonably priced and in an excellent location for strolling to all of Sonoma's

finest. A selection of bicycles is available to guests.

✪ **Kenwood Inn and Spa** (www .kenwoodinn.com, 707-833-1293, 800-353-6966, 10400 Sonoma Highway, Kenwood, CA 95452; $$$$). This intimate resort looks like a small Tuscan village in a grove of oak trees. The inn includes 29 rooms situated around three courtyards on the 2.5-acre property. At the heart of the compound are the pool, gardens, and spa facility. A breakfast buffet is included. Traffic along Highway 12 quiets dramatically at night.

Ledson Hotel (www.ledsonhotel .com, 707-996-9779, 480 First Street E., Sonoma, CA 95476; $$$$). This luxury two-story hotel is situated on the charming Sonoma Plaza. Six individually decorated rooms are on the upper floor. The Zina Lounge on the ground floor offers wine tastings with food pairings. The heart of Wine Country appears to be shifting from Sonoma Valley to Healdsburg and St. Helena, making retail shops on Sonoma Plaza less vibrant than in years past, but this hotel is still a lovely place to stay. The wine list offers more than 30 selections, with a natural emphasis on Sonoma County, including Ledson's Harmony Collection. The occasional live music is a plus.

Lodge at Sonoma Renaissance Resort and Spa (www.marriott.com, 707-935-6600, 866-263-0758, 1325 Broadway, Sonoma, CA 95476; $$$$). One of the largest hotels in Sonoma Valley, this 182-room lodge is part of the Renaissance/Marriott family of hotels. The 9-acre complex features a main lodge and 18 cottages. The lodge is elegantly designed in classic California-mission style. The courtyard is impressive, with its towering Canary Island date palms. The spa features private cabanas and a mineral-water pool. There are two fire pits located on the upper pool decks where you can sit and sip cocktails at night with blankets provided for guests. Be sure to check out Carneros Bistro and Bar, the lodge's restaurant, a handsome space that features fresh pastas; wood-fired pizzas; and steaks, seafood, and other treats from the rotisserie.

○ **MacArthur Place** (www.macarthur place.com, 707-938-2929, 800-722-1866, 29 E. MacArthur Street, Sonoma, CA 95476; $$$$). MacArthur Place is Wine Country living at its most luxurious. Sixty-four rooms and suites are set in a private 7-acre compound lush with gardens and sculptures. The property was once a working vineyard and ranch, and the original house—a grand Victorian built in the 1850s—includes 10 rooms. Twenty-nine deluxe suites were added, and each includes a wood-burning fireplace, a king-sized bed, a whirlpool tub, and a TV with a DVD player with six-speaker sound. Guests of the resort can enjoy a complimentary wine-and-cheese reception nightly. The property's historic barn is home to a conference center as well as a cocktail bar and the valley's premier steakhouse, Saddles.

○ **Olea Hotel** (www.oleahotel.com, 707-996-5131, 5131 Warm Springs Road, Glen Ellen, CA 95442; $$–$$$). This is a tranquil spot that includes guest rooms in the main Hillside building, as well as some private cottages in the garden area. The hotel offers a hot tub and spa treatments, but best of all it serves up decadent dishes, with an executive chef preparing two-course breakfasts. One lip-smacking example is a first course of a fruit smoothie shooter and seasonal fruit, with a second course of a poached farm egg on a cheesy-grits fritter and wilted mustard greens, with creole butter emulsion and Hobbs bacon. This is serious caloric fun.

Sonoma Valley Inn, Best Western (www.sonomavalleyinn.com, 707-938-9200, 800-334-5784, 550 Second Street

ONCE A WORKING VINEYARD AND RANCH, MACARTHUR PLACE IS NOW A LUXURIOUS INN AND SPA TIM FISH

W., Sonoma, CA 95476; $$–$$$). "An intimate hotel" may be the best way to describe this exceptional lodge just a block from Sonoma Plaza. Rooms and furnishings are well above average, and many are equipped with kitchenettes, wet bars, whirlpools, and fireplaces. Most of the rooms open onto a lovely courtyard. It's ideal for families visiting the valley. Complimentary continental breakfast is included.

BASQUE BOULANGERIE CAFE WILL DELIGHT FRANCOPHILES

✳ Where to Eat

♻ **Basque Boulangerie Cafe** (www.basque boulangerie.com, 707-935-7687, 460 First Street E., Sonoma, CA 95476). More than a bakery, this stylish storefront has a deli, a coffee bar, and even some wine selections. Popular sandwiches include chicken salad and prosciutto and Brie. For some reason, however, it has yet to master the classic croissant.

🍴 **Café Citti** (www.cafecitti.com, 707-833-2690, 9049 Sonoma Highway, Kenwood, CA 95452; $$; cuisine: Italian). A trattoria in the strictest Italian sense— casual atmosphere with hearty wine and yummy, inexpensive pasta—Café Citti is a pleasure. There's a menu, but most people rely on the chalkboard on the wall. Customers order from the counter, cafeteria style. Lunch includes sandwiches: sweet Italian sausage and the usual cold deli fare. Pasta is mix and match; choose penne, linguine, and the like, and pair it with your sauce (marinara or Bolognese, to name a couple) of choice. Other offerings include a zesty Caesar salad and homemade focaccia, plus a luxurious risotto with mushrooms and garlic and a traditional Italian herb-roasted chicken that is to die for. For dessert, don't miss the crème brûlée or the tiramisu. For those traveling with kids, this is a perfect place to stop.

♻ **Cafe la Haye** (www.cafelahaye .com, 707-935-5994, 140 E. Napa Street, Sonoma, CA 95476; $$$; cuisine: California). Café la Haye is classy yet simple in its sophistication. More important, the food stands up to the best in Wine Country. If you're looking for a great meal on the Sonoma town square, this is the spot. Entrées include a changing daily risotto, along with a crusted pork chop with ricotta dumplings and mustard cream. The wine list complements the menu, and it's well focused, with a good selection of wines from Sonoma County and Napa Valley. As for the decor, the restaurant is tiny but seems spacious, with high wooden rafters and an upper level of seating—yet it still manages to feel cozy.

Carneros Bistro (www.marriott.com, 707-931-2042, 1325 Broadway, Sonoma, CA 95476; $$$; cuisine: Wine Country bistro). Carneros aspires to be a serious dining destination, and it nearly pulls it off. The food is good and the service shows promise. The restaurant is part of the Lodge at Sonoma, a 182-room complex owned by Marriott Hotels. Carneros is the wine-growing region at the southern base of Napa Valley and Sonoma County, and the restaurant emphasizes wines produced from Sonoma County's 18 appellations. The portions are big, and so are the flavors. Prices on the wine list are set at the going rate, and it's a good selection that emphasizes wines of the region. The room itself has a large and airy atmosphere, with an open kitchen and cathedral ceiling, but there's something rather generic about the place.

Della Santina's (www.dellasantinas.com, 707-935-0576, 133 E. Napa Street, Sonoma, CA 95476; $$; cuisine: Italian). Ah, the mighty aromas that escape from this café! Don't overlook this Italian trattoria just off bustling Sonoma Plaza. The food is as authentic and unfussy as the best from Mama's kitchen. In summer, the intimate dining room gives way to a glorious garden patio, shady and green. The warm din of the kitchen mingles with Puccini and Verdi. Appetizers include a Caesar salad that's a vibrant cut above the usual, and the antipasto plate is everything it should be: fat with prosciutto and olives. Pastas are first-rate, and the roasted meats—particularly chicken, pork, and duck—are a specialty, yet quality varies. At one meal the chicken is dry and flavorless, but at the next, it's tender and heavenly. The wine list is modest but well suited to the food.

✪ **El Dorado Kitchen** (www.eldorado sonoma.com, 707-996-3220, 800-289-3031, 405 First Street W., Sonoma, CA 95476; $$$; cuisine: California). Seasonal produce is at its best here, with earthy yet sophisticated dishes served at this upscale restaurant in the El Dorado Hotel (see entry under *Lodging*) right on Sonoma Plaza. Ingredients are sourced from local purveyors, in alignment with its ecofriendly philosophy. While fresh produce guides the menu, don't expect every dish to be light. Rich dishes stream out of the kitchen in equal measure. Good examples are the fettucine carbonara and the seafood paella. This is one of the few restaurants on the square that welcomes large parties that can gather around a 21-foot-long table created from a single wood plank, once part of a Vermont bridge. There's also an outdoor courtyard for those who prefer to eat in a garden-like setting. This restaurant has it all—a charming setting, delicious food, and impeccable service.

✪ **The Girl & the Fig** (www.thegirland thefig.com, 707-938-3634, 110 W. Spain Street, Sonoma, CA 95476; $$$; cuisine: French country). The Girl & the Fig has its fans, even though the food and service are maddeningly inconsistent. Certainly, the restaurant is both appealing and convenient in its location on Sonoma Plaza, adjacent to the lobby of the Sonoma Hotel, and with its tall, broad, wood-framed windows and light, mustard-colored walls, it's a pretty stop to spend a couple of hours. The whole place feels breezy. The menu offers plenty of comfort, ranging from a salami and Brie sandwich and sirloin burger to duck confit with butter beans and butternut squash. Be sure to sample something from the cheese cart. The wine list is refreshing, even daring, and fairly priced. It focuses on California-produced, Rhone-style wines, with an emphasis on California syrahs. Few will complain that it's limited in scope, because there's plenty to choose from, and Rhone-style wines are food friendly.

✪ **Glen Ellen Inn** (www.glenelleninn .com, 707-996-6409, 13670 Arnold Drive, Glen Ellen, CA 95442; $$$; cuisine: California fusion). Glen Ellen Inn is not the quaint little dining room we once loved, but owners Chris and Karen Bertrand have added some sophistication to its small-town charm—and in this quiet corner of the world, Chris holds his own with Wine Country's finest chefs. The

CAFÉ LA HAYE IS SPACIOUS YET COZY, AND THE FOOD STANDS UP TO THE BEST IN WINE COUNTRY

Bertrands have continually expanded their restaurant over the years, adding an oyster grill, martini bar, and a collection of cottages in recent years. The food certainly hasn't suffered from the expansion. As for service, it's still first-rate, and the wine list specializes in the best Sonoma Valley wines, including a smart list of wines by the glass. Bertrand, schooled at Fifth Avenue Grill in Manhattan, cooks with a French accent, relying on fresh, local ingredients. The salads are exceptional. Specialties include luscious seafood and just about anything Bertrand does with filet mignon and salmon. For dessert, give in to the ever-popular Glen Ellen Inn sundae or the s'mores.

Harvest Moon Café (www.harvest mooncafesonoma.com, 707-933-8160, 487 First Street W., Sonoma, CA 95476; $$$; cuisine: California). This café on the Sonoma Plaza is a cozy retreat with sidewalk seating as well as a patio out back. Inside, rich warm colors and great aromas make you feel like you're dining at a friend's house. Harvest Moon offers comfort food at its best, with dishes such as the rib eye steak and specialty pastas. Tasty lighter fare includes the sautéed Hawaiian yellowtail. Entrées change daily. The wine list has a good showing of local wines with a strong sampling of imports.

Maya (www.mayarestaurant.com, 707-935-3500, 101 E. Napa Street, Sonoma, CA 95476; $$–$$$; cuisine: Mexican, Yucatan style). This place is fun, plain and simple. The atmosphere is festive, with warm wood accents, colorful Mexican decor and artifacts, and a bar stacked as high as a Mayan temple with upscale tequilas. The food is not your typical Mexican cuisine, and it's generally quite appealing. It takes its inspiration from the Mayan region in southern Mexico, but the kitchen also offers its own take on dishes such as hanger steak and a mixed grill of steak, prawns, and chicken served with tortillas. Signature dishes include pork roasted in banana leaves. The wine list is limited, but there's a creative offering of drinks such as margaritas, sangria, and specialty tequilas.

○ **Saddles** (www.macarthurplace.com, 707-933-3191, 29 E. MacArthur Street, Sonoma, CA 95476; $$–$$$; cuisine: steak and seafood). If you want to order up a 10-ounce martini and a steak on the side, this is the place to go. Saddles is located in the MacArthur Place resort (see *Lodging*). In Wine Country, a good steakhouse is a rare find, and the prime-cut meats here are outstanding—but don't expect to be wowed by the service. The western theme, a bit overdone, carries throughout the restaurant: cowboy boots, hats, and branding irons. The steaks are good, but oh, that price tag! The wine list has a solid selection of newer, mostly California wines. Prices are reasonable. A plus: those great martini offerings!

Salt & Stone (www.saltstonekenwood .com, 707-833-6326, 9900 Highway 12, Kenwood, CA 95452; $$$; cuisine: American). The decor of this chic farmhouse, in gray and ivory tones, is welcoming, and the mirrors on the walls make it feel expansive. The food is top-rate here across the board. Some outstanding dishes include oysters, steamed mussels, coq au vin, and the lava cake. But of all the desserts, the bread pudding is by far the most impressive, moist and delicious with a dollop of caramel. The wine list is weighted to the region's tastiest wines, with some imports in the mix. The service is smart and courteous. The owners are chef David and Diane LaMonica, the former owners of Mendocino's acclaimed Café Beaujolais, so it's not surprising that this restaurant is all the talk.

○ **Sante-Fairmont Sonoma Mission Inn** (www.santediningroom.com, 707-939-2407, 100 Boyes Boulevard, Sonoma, CA 95476; $$$$, prix fixe: $149, with additional wine pairing of $99, a la carte menu also available; cuisine: California with French influences). Santé is a handsome, mission-style dining room, with dark wood beams, iron chandeliers, and wooden floors—but it's never a good sign when the best thing you can say about a restaurant refers to its decor. The food doesn't live up to the price, although that isn't unusual at many hotel restaurants. The menu promises rich and deeply flavored dishes but the result is too often ill-conceived and boring. The wine list is one of the best in Sonoma County, although it comes at a premium. If you're a hotel guest and prefer to eat in rather than out, this is a comfortable spot, but if you have the energy, there are far better places to dine nearby.

Sunflower Caffe (www.sonoma sunflower.com, 707-996-6645, 421 First Street W., Sonoma, CA 95476). This rustic-style café is housed in an adobe building constructed in the 1830s. It has a lovely garden patio with a wine bar, Mediterranean-influenced food, and an art gallery.

Yeti Restaurant (www.yeticuisine .com, 707-996-9930, 14301 Arnold Drive, Suite 19, Glen Ellen, CA 95442; $–$$; cuisine: Indian). Arguably the best Indian restaurant in all of Wine Country, Yeti is a rare find. The food is as authentic and tasty as you'd find in New York City and the service is just as smart. The naan is particularly good, and the curries are rich and complex. There are simply no misses on the menu. The decor takes you to India, and dining here is a relaxed affair.

✳ Entertainment

⊙ Sigh (www.sighsonoma.com, 707-996-2444, 120 W. Napa Street, Sonoma, CA 95476; tastings daily). This is a trendsetter, the first bar to build its business around bubbles—sparkling wine and champagne—in Northern California, and it has a cult following. According to its website, the bar is named after "the sound of the cork escaping from a bottle of champagne, which should mimic the sigh of a contented woman." The bar has reeled in rave reviews and bubbly fanatics are taken by the decor, Sigh's expansive marble bar, its shades of cream and light pink, and its fluffy pillows. For those looking for something out of the ordinary, at Sigh it's possible to purchase a saber, a cavalry sword with a curved blade. For the uninitiated, a saber is used to open a bottle of champagne in ceremonial occasions; the technique is known as "sabrage." Sigh is available for private parties, and in addition to bubbles, it serves still wine and beer by the glass, flight, or bottle. The wine list is serious and includes stellar picks, whether from large producers like Dom Perignon or from local favorites like Iron Horse Vineyards and Gloria Ferrer.

⊙ Hopmonk Tavern (www.hopmonk .com, 707-935-9100, 691 Broadway, Sonoma, CA 95476). There are great artisan brews here, along with live music and tasty gourmet pub food. Dean Biersch has found a second beer haven with Hopmonk Tavern after selling his share of the Gordon Biersch Brewery & Restaurant Group. He moved to Sonoma in 2000 and immersed himself in the great brewing of the North Bay. Hopmonk Tavern is a great stage for these tasty brews, which include Hopmonk IPA, Lagunitas Little Sumpin Sumpin, and Moonlight Bombay by Boat.

Murphy's Irish Pub (707-935-0660, 464 First Street E., Sonoma, CA 95476). This pub in Sonoma Valley is small but cozy, and it offers a great selection of imported ales.

✳ Selective Shopping

Artifax Art-to-Wear Clothing (707-996-9494, 450-C First Street E., Sonoma, CA 95476). This shop is a true sensory experience. Expect interesting women's clothing and accessories.

The Candlestick (707-933-0700, 38 W. Spain Street, Sonoma, CA 95476). This store offers clever specialty candles, oil lamps, and even whimsical nightlights.

Chico's (707-933-0100, 29 E. Napa Street, Sonoma, CA 95476). This store offers chic women's clothing and accessories.

Chocolate Cow (www.chocolate cowsonoma.com, 707-935-3564, 452 First Street E., Sonoma, CA 95476). These folks are "udderly" cow crazy—the black-and-white heifer image is everywhere, from T-shirts to stuffed animals. The place also stocks candy, chocolates, fudge, and ice cream.

Global Heart Fair Trade (707-939-2847, www.globalheartfairtrade.com, 423 First Street W., Sonoma, CA 95476). This establishment is a great find. Vowing fair-trading practices, Global Heart is replete with pieces made by artists who live in developing countries. It has an interesting mix of clothing, jewelry, toys, games, and even musical instruments.

Harvest Home Stores (707-933-9044, 20820 Broadway, Sonoma, CA 95476). The shop has lovely custom furniture, sofas, and leather chairs.

Olive Press (707-939-8900, www.the olivepress.com, 24724 Highway 121 at Jacuzzi Family Winery, Sonoma, CA 95476). Had your fill of wine tasting? Perhaps it's time to branch out. This smart den makes and sells olive oils that rival Italy's best. Enjoy a complimentary taste.

Readers' Books (707-939-1779, 130 E. Napa Street, Sonoma, CA 95476). Although perhaps not the City Lights of Sonoma County, this bookstore has the reputation of being urbane and literary. Expect great classics and fiction, an expansive cookbook section, and myriad books for children.

Sonoma Cheese Factory (www .sonomacheesefactory.com, 707-996-1931, 2 W. Spain Street, Sonoma, CA 95476). The Viviani family began making cheese in Sonoma in 1931. Although it's a "factory" in name only (the cheese is now made elsewhere), this supermarket-sized gourmet deli has much appeal, with made-to-order gourmet sandwiches, gift items, and Sonoma Valley wines. There's a coffee and gelato bar, and tasty samples abound. Shady Sonoma Plaza is nearby.

Sonoma Home (707-939-6900, 497 First Street W., Sonoma, CA 95476). Here you'll find great ideas for home decor and the garden, from furniture and books to pillows.

🐾 **Three Dog Bakery** (www.threedog .com, 707-933-9780, 526 Broadway, Sonoma, CA 95476). This bakery (for dogs) offers goodies made without salt and refined sugar; treats are sweetened with applesauce or honey. They have snacks for your kitty, too. Ninety percent of the customers are, surprisingly, tourists who stop in because they're homesick for their pooches. FYI: The hands-down favorite dog treat is the carrot cake.

Tiddle E. Winks (707-939-6933 or 707-93-WOWEE, 115 E. Napa Street, Sonoma, CA 95476). The shop is full of fun retro items. Owner Heidi Geffen says she rounds up her old toys, tins, and pendants by doing her version of time travel—boarding a Pan Am flight back to the 1950s.

Vella Cheese Company (www.vella cheese.com, 707-938-3232, 800-848-0505, 315 Second Street E., Sonoma, CA 95476). The dry jack is to die for. This is a Sonoma classic that dates to 1931 and is worth a visit.

BODEGA BAY
& WEST COUNTY

BODEGA BAY & WEST COUNTY

Bodega Bay is best known as the backdrop of Alfred Hitchcock's thriller *The Birds*. The filming began in 1961, and for three months the cameras rolled in this foggy coastal town. Tippy Hedren shared the screen with hundreds of avian costars, both mechanical and live.

One of the most dramatic scenes of the film takes place at the 145-year-old Potter Schoolhouse behind St. Teresa's Church. The building, five miles south of Bodega Bay, is still standing, one of the town's most popular tourist attractions. Fans of the Hitchcock film often stop by for a photo out front. It's a private home now, but it's occasionally open for private tours.

Once you secure a snapshot, be sure to sample some clam chowder on the piers and, by all means, don't leave town without catching a glimpse of Bodega Head, with the thrashing waters of the Pacific Ocean below. The beauty of Bodega Bay is in its calm: the fishing boats in the quiet waters, the docks, and, yes, the birds. Wine lovers have plenty to choose from in West County, from big wineries like Korbel to the smaller boutiques like Merry Edwards. Prime your palate for a great tasting tour. Good eats are plentiful in Bodega Bay and West County. There's great seafood—including some of the best clam chowder on the West Coast. The town of Sebastopol offers the best shopping in West County, and it's worth spending time (and money) here, even though it's a pretzel of a town, with plenty of twists and turns.

Sonoma County's 62-mile coastline has a rustic beauty scarcely changed from the days when the Miwok and Pomo Indians were the only inhabitants of the area. Visitors flock to the Sonoma coast to enjoy some of the most spectacular views in all of California. The rugged cliffs, continually battered by the wild Pacific Ocean, afford a setting of breathtaking beauty. Thanks to the foresight of those who fought to preserve public access to the coast, there are many points from which to view the ocean along Highway 1. Particularly popular is the stretch between Bodega Bay and Jenner, where several beaches offer a variety of topography and vistas for hiking, picnicking, wetsuit diving, surfing, or just relaxing.

Whatever your activity, it's important to remember at all times that the Pacific Ocean can be dangerous. Every year, deaths are caused by unpredictable waves and the strong undertow. Be cautious.

Bodega Bay harbor offers protection from the rough Pacific surf and serves

FEATURED IN HITCHCOCK'S *THE BIRDS*, THE POTTER SCHOOLHOUSE IS STILL A POPULAR TOURIST STOP EVEN THOUGH IT'S A PRIVATE HOME NOW

as the homeport for many commercial fishing boats. After gaining fame as the setting of Alfred Hitchcock's *The Birds,* the town of Bodega Bay has now become a well-known stopover and destination spot for California residents and visitors alike. Sport fishing, harbor cruises, and whale-watching trips can be arranged from Porto Bodega Marina, off Highway 1 on Bay Flat Road. The gentle beaches on the west side of the harbor afford a perfect spot for windsurfing or sea kayaking.

✳ To See

GALLERIES **Bodega Landmark Studio** (www.artbodega.com, 707-876-3477, 17255 Bodega Highway, Bodega, CA 94923). West County artists are the specialty here, with a focus on oils, watercolors, ceramics, blown glass, fine art photography, and jewelry.

Ren Brown Collection (www.renbrown .com, 707-875-2922, 1781 Highway 1, Bodega Bay, CA 94923). Modern Japanese prints are the focus of this gallery, and famous Japanese artists exhibiting here include Shinoda Toko and Tanaka Ryohei.

HISTORIC SITE ✿ **Fort Ross** (www .fortross.org, 707-847-3286, 19005 Coast Highway 1, Jenner, CA 95450). A quick history quiz: who were Sonoma's first settlers (besides the Indians, of course)? If

THERE ARE DRAMATIC WAVES ON THE BODEGA HEAD

you said the Spanish, you're wrong. It was actually the Russians, who established Fort Ross, which predated the Sonoma Mission by 11 years. The Russian-American Trading Company, a firm controlled largely by the Imperial Russian government, came to California to escape the cruel winters of Alaska and to hunt for valuable sea otters. Its workers landed south in Bodega Bay, which they called Rumiantsev, and explored to the north. On a windy bluff overlooking the Pacific, they built their fort and community, now the centerpiece of Fort Ross State Historic Park.

✳ To Do

BEACHES Here are some of the beaches along the coast, listed from north to south. For detailed information, call the Sonoma County Tourism Program (800-576-6662). Some of the beaches have a day-use fee.

✿ **Bodega Headlands** (707-875-3483, at the end of Bay Flat Road and Westside Road, off Highway 1, Bodega Bay, CA 94923). Originally part of the Sierra Nevadas,

COOLING OFF ON THE COAST

The Sonoma coast is Wine Country's busiest recreational spot. Whatever water sport you prefer—scuba diving, abalone diving, surfboarding, kayaking—there's plenty to do on the coast. The water temperatures range from 40 to 55 degrees, making a full wetsuit a minimum requirement, with many divers preferring drysuits for added comfort. Diving is a year-round activity, as long as the sea is calm. Divers must respect the power of the ocean.

Abalone can be harvested from April to December (excluding July). Scuba equipment is not allowed while hunting these succulent creatures, and there's a limit of four abalone per person. You'll also need a license to harvest them.

the headlands stretch like a curved arm out to the sea. For 40 million years, they have ridden the Pacific Plate northward, out of step with the land on the other side of the San Andreas Fault. The cliffs of the headlands provide a spectacular vista of the Pacific coast, with the best spots to watch for whales in the winter and early spring. It's not a bad idea to bring binoculars and a jacket. Also of interest at the headlands is the **Bodega Marine Lab** (www.bml.ucdavis.edu, 707-875-2211, 2099 Westside Road, Bodega Bay, CA 94923), open to the public on Friday from 2 to 4 p.m. It's educational, and kids will love it.

✎ **Doran Regional Park** (707-875-3540, 201 Doran Beach Road, off Highway 1, south of Bodega Bay, CA 94923). This is a popular family spot because of its level, sandy beach and overnight camping facilities. An annual sand castle competition is held every August.

Salt Point State Park (707-847-3221, 800-444-7275, 25050 Highway 1, Jenner, CA 95450, north of Timber Cove). Here you'll find 4,114 acres along 5 miles of shore, offering picnicking, horseback riding, fishing, skin diving, and hiking. More than 20 miles of trails wind through tall forests, windswept headlands, a stunted pygmy forest, and grassy valleys along the San Andreas

A DOCK IN BODEGA BAY THAT CAPTURES THE BEAUTY OF THIS QUAINT FISHING VILLAGE

TIDEPOOLING

The Sonoma coastline is as productive as a tropical rain forest. When the tide goes out twice daily, living things from the sea—starfish, snails, and sea anemones, among others—take refuge in the rocks.

Be patient and discover the magic. A hermit crab may creep out of its turban shell; a sea anemone's green tentacles may entwine a mussel. Track the sculpins as they scurry through the water, and keep an eye out for starfish playing dead. These oases of sea life are full of old-timers. Starfish may be 10 years old and snails may be 20 to 30 years old.

Remember: Please don't remove anything from the pools; even an empty shell might be a hermit crab's mobile home. Tidepoolers are advised to wear waterproof boots for the best exploration. Be cautious. Crabs pinch, octopuses bite, and sea urchin spines are prickly. Also, beware of sleeper waves—those unexpectedly large waves that sneak up and sweep away beachcombers.

For additional insight into the world of the tidepool, visit the Bodega Marine Laboratory (www.bml.ucdavis.edu, 707-875-2211, 2099 Westside Road, Bodega Bay, CA 94923). The laboratory is open to the public on Friday from 2 to 4 p.m.

Where are the best places to tidepool? Nearly any rocky place along Sonoma Coast State Beach, which stretches between Bodega Bay and Jenner. The Bodega Marine Lab recommends two: try the north end of Salmon Beach, which is accessible from any Highway 1 pulloff north of the Salmon Creek Bridge. Shell Beach, a few miles south of Jenner on Highway 1, is more remote, requiring a trip down steep stairs, but it's worth it.

Fault. Camping is available. Adjacent to the park is Kruse Rhododendron State Reserve. In May and June, the brilliant pink blossoms of native rhododendrons brighten the forest along the path.

Goat Rock Beach (707-875-3483, off Highway 1, south of Jenner). Named for the huge beach rock that bears a resemblance to the hunched back of a grazing goat, the beach extends from the sandbars along the mouth of the Russian River, where sea lions and their young exit the waters of the river at certain times of the year. They're fun to watch, but please don't disturb them.

Sonoma Coast State Beach (707-875-3483, Salmon Creek, Bodega Bay, CA 94923). This is actually a chain of many beaches along 18 miles of coastline, from Goat Rock to Bodega Head. Each has its own personality and invites different activities, whether it's tidepooling or a serious game of volleyball. Wildflowers brighten the cliffs in the spring. The coast is always cool in the summer, offering an escape from inland heat.

Bodega Dunes (707-875-3483; 3095 Highway 1, Bodega Bay, CA 94923). Here you'll find a boardwalk and 5 miles of trails through the dunes. No dogs are allowed on the beach, trails, or dunes because of endangered western snowy plover in these areas, but dogs are allowed in the campground, which has 98 sites for tents and RVs up to 31 feet long.

WATER SPORTS **Bodega Bay Surf Shack** (www.bodegabaysurf.com, 707-875-3944, 1400 Highway 1, Bodega Bay, CA 94923). Here you'll find instruction and tips, and rentals and sales, including kayaks.

Bodega Bay Kayak (www.bodegabaykayak.com, 707-875-8899, 1580 Eastshore Drive, Bodega Bay, CA 94923). Offers rentals, sales, and tours at $75 per person.

Seals Watersports (www.sealswatersports.com, 707-542-3100, 2112 Armory Drive, Santa Rosa, CA 95401). Offers diving courses, rentals, equipment sales, and diving trips.

WHALE WATCHING

One of the great attractions in California is the opportunity to watch gray whales in their annual round-trip migration between summer feeding grounds in the Bering Sea and their breeding and birthing waters off Baja California. From late May to October, the gray whales feed in the cold Pacific waters to build up fat for their 12,000-mile pilgrimage. Then, beginning in late November, they head south, passing close enough to shore to navigate by sight as well as to avoid killer whales in the deeper waters. Their return usually starts in late February and lasts until early June.

Point Reyes Lighthouse (415-464-5100) at the tip of the Point Reyes National Seashore in Marin County—about a 1.5-hour drive from Santa Rosa—offers one of the best vantage points in the state for whale watching. The lighthouse is open from 10 to 4:30 Friday through Monday, but parking is limited and extremely crowded on weekends. Shuttle bus service is offered during peak whale-watching season. Call ahead to check on visibility, because the lighthouse sits on the windiest and rainiest spot on the entire Pacific Coast and can close unexpectedly due to weather conditions.

Sonoma County offers good whale-watching sites, including Gualala Point, Stillwater Cove, Fort Ross, and Bodega Head. On a clear day, you'll have plenty of company to share sightings—everyone bundled against the sea breezes, toting binoculars and picnic lunches, and ready to spend several hours searching for the telltale white spouts shooting above the blue Pacific waters.

For a close-up view, reserve a place on a whale-watching boat out of Bodega Bay. Remember that it's typically 15 degrees colder on the water, so wear plenty of warm clothes. Law prohibits boaters from harassing whales, but the large mammals have little fear of man and often approach boats at sea. All boats leave from Porto Bodega Marina on Bay Flat Road, off Highway 1. The boating season is January through April, and boats run if the weather permits it. Contact **Bodega Bay Sport Fishing Center (707-875-3344, 1410 Bay Flat Road, Bodega Bay, CA 94923)** or **The Boathouse (707-875-3495, 1445 Highway 1, Bodega Bay, CA 94923).**

✳ Wineries

⊙ **The Barlow** (www.thebarlow.net, 707-824-5600, 6770 McKinley Street, Sebastopol, CA 95472). The Barlow has become the pulse of Sebastopol, a food, wine, and art mecca that is definitely worth a stop. This urban-chic village, once the Barlow Apple Center, has reinvented itself. It's now a 12-acre property with buildings that resemble metal Oakland lofts. They have high ceilings and metal roll-up storefronts, but there's also a splash of Wine Country in the mix with fire pits and a bocce ball court. This is a big draw for millennials, 88 million strong, the largest segment of the population, and one tenants definitely want to court. A sampling of some hotshot tenants that will interest those passionate about food and drink

THE BARLOW IS A PEDESTRIAN-FRIENDLY VILLAGE DEDICATED TO FOOD, WINE, AND ART   TIM FISH

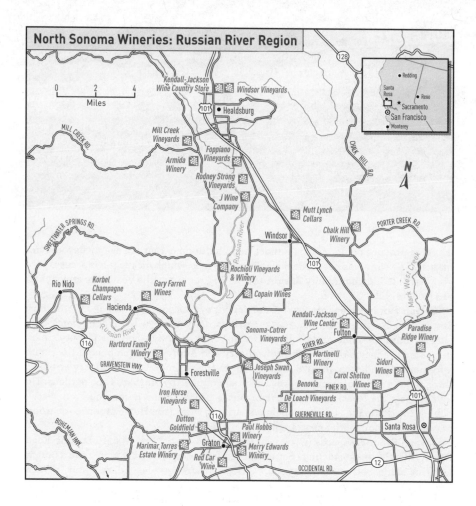

North Sonoma Wineries: Russian River Region

include Kosta Browne Winery (www.kostabrowne.com, not open to the public); Zazu Kitchen & Farm (www.zazukitchen.com); MacPhail Wines (www.macphailwine.com); Wind Gap Wines (www.windgapwines.com); Marimar Estate Vineyards & Winery (www.marimarestate.com); Spirit Works Distillery (www.spiritworksdistillery.com); and Woodfour Brewing Company (www.woodfourbrewing.com).

Dutton-Goldfield (www.duttongoldfield.com, 707-823-3887, 3100 Gravenstein Highway N., Sebastopol, CA 95472; tastings daily 10–4:30). This winery has a magic touch with cool-climate pinot noir and chardonnay from the Russian River Valley, and zin lovers are particularly fond of its sassy zinfandel. Here's the back story of the partners behind this brand: Steve Dutton is a fifth-generation farmer who began working with his father, the late Warren Dutton, when he was five years old. Meanwhile, Dan Goldfield began his career in research chemistry but realized a life in the lab was not his calling when he tasted 1969 Burgundies. The duo has been making outstanding wine since the late 1990s.

❍ **Hartford Family Winery** (www.hartfordwines.com, 707-887-8030, 800-588-0234, 8075 Martinelli Road, Forestville, CA 95436; tastings daily 10–4:30). If you've ever dreamed of retiring to some grand estate in wine country, Hartford is the sort of place you might have in mind. Hidden amid the lush canyons of West County, this stately

Osmosis Day Spa Sanctuary (www.osmosis.com, 707-823-8231, 209 Bohemian Highway, Freestone, CA 95472). A truly unique experience, Osmosis is the only place in the Western world that offers Japanese-style enzyme baths. The baths are similar to mud baths in only one way: you're covered from neck to toe. In this case, though, it's not mud but a sawdust-like mix of fragrant cedar, rice bran, and more than 600 active enzymes. The concoction ferments and generates gentle and natural heat. Guests don kimonos and begin their treatment in a Japanese sitting room, sipping enzyme tea as they gaze through shoji doors into the Japanese garden. Baths can be taken solo or with a friend. The treatment concludes with a shower and a 30-minute blanket wrap or Swedish massage. An enzyme bath with a 75-minute massage runs from $229 to $249. ✪

mansion produces pinot noir, zinfandel, and chardonnay that are deeply flavored and intense. The winery is part of Jackson Family Wines, which means it has access to top vineyards in Sonoma County. Inside, the tasting room has the venerable atmosphere of a private club.

✪ **Iron Horse Vineyards** (www.ironhorsevineyards.com, 707-887-1507, 9786 Ross Station Road, Sebastopol, CA 95472; tastings daily 10–4:30 by appointment). This winery, amid the undulating hills of Green Valley is one of Sonoma County's most respected producers of sparkling wine. Barry and Audrey Sterling bought the estate, a former railroad stop, in 1976. Elegant in its sheer simplicity, the winery stretches throughout a series of wooden barns and is surrounded by vineyards and gardens. The tour reveals the classic *méthode champenoise* process used in making French-style bubbly. In addition to its line of opulent sparkling wine, Iron Horse produces chardonnay and pinot noir, both fine examples.

Joseph Swan Vineyards (www.swanwinery.com, 707-573-3747, 2916 Laguna Road, Forestville, CA 95436; tastings Saturday–Sunday 11–4:30). Hardly more than a bungalow, this modest structure contradicts Joseph Swan's near-legendary status in Wine Country. Beginning in 1969, Swan was a pioneer of zinfandel, crafting heroically ripe and long-lived wines. Pinot noir became Swan's star in the 1980s. Swan died in 1989, and son-in-law Rod Berglund is now winemaker. Although the zins are no longer legendary, they remain fine and authentic creations.

✪ **Korbel Champagne Cellars** (www.korbel.com, 707-824-7000, 707-824-7316, 13250 River Road, Guerneville, CA 95446; tastings daily 10–4:30). As you drive through the gorgeous redwood forests of the Russian River area, you'll see this century-old, ivy-covered stone wine cellar rising nobly from a hillside. Korbel is one of Wine Country's most popular destinations, offering romance, history, and beauty. To avoid the crowds in summer, arrive early in the morning or late in the afternoon. The half-hour tour is great fun. The Korbel brothers from Czechoslovakia came to Guerneville for the trees, which were perfect for cigar boxes. When the trees were cleared, they planted grapes and made wine using *méthode champenoise*, the traditional French method of making champagne. You'll poke your nose in large wood aging tanks and learn the mystery of the riddling room, where sediment is slowly tapped from each bottle. The tasting room is one of the friendliest around, and any or all of the winery's dependable sparklers are on offer. During the summer, Korbel's prized antique garden is also available for touring.

Marimar Estate (www.marimarestate.com, 707-823-4365, 11400 Graton Road, Sebastopol, CA 95472; tastings daily 11–5). Marimar Torres's family in Spain has been making wine for generations, so when she came to Sonoma County in the mid-1970s, she was beginning her own wine legacy. In 1992, she built this Catalan farmhouse-inspired winery amid the isolated, rolling hills of West Sonoma County and planted 60 acres of pinot noir and chardonnay vineyards. The wines reflect a European passion for refinement and elegant complexity. The tasting room hardly seems like one. It's more like you've stopped in for a glass of wine at a neighbor's place down the road. Offerings include a Tapas and Wine Pairing for $55, which includes five different wines and four tapas. Drop-ins are welcome, but reservations are greatly appreciated.

✪ **Martinelli Winery** (www.martinelliwinery.com, 707-525-0570, 800-346-1627, 3360 River Road, Windsor, CA 95492; tastings daily 10–5). This historic hop barn painted a vivid red is home to a prized zinfandel called Jackass Hill. The wine comes from the steepest hillside vineyards in Sonoma County, planted in 1905. Like many old-vine zins, it grabs your taste buds like a two-horse team. The winery also makes a tasty chardonnay and pinot noir, and they're all lush and complex. This is a family winery, through and through, growing out of four generations of Martinellis farming.

✪ **Merry Edwards Winery** (www.merryedwards.com, 707-823-7466, 888-388-9050, 2959 Gravenstein Highway N., Sebastopol, CA 95472; tastings daily 9:30–4:30). Merry Edwards is best known for producing cult pinot noirs, jammy, full-bodied beauties from the Russian River Valley. But Edwards is also making noise with a striking sauvignon blanc. In addition, she dabbles in chardonnay and sparkling wine on a less regular basis. Edwards is well respected as one of California's first female winemakers, drawing plenty of attention in the early 1970s for her determination to show she had the muscle to make wine along with the guys. She ultimately decided to be her own boss, founding her winery in 1997. Edwards and her crew are proponents of sustainability, and among the concoctions you might see in her vineyards are organic mushroom composts.

🐾 **Mutt Lynch** (www.muttlynchwinery.com, 707-687-5089, 9050 Windsor Road, Windsor, CA 95492; tastings Wednesday–Saturday 11–4 by appointment). This winery claims to be the most dog-friendly in wine country, with brands like mbf (man's best friend) Zinfandel and Unleashed Chardonnay. It also offers a Yappy Hour with appetizers for humans and snacks for dogs. Check its website for the latest events. As *Dog Fancy* magazine puts it, "With the exception of Paris, you'd be hard pressed to find a more canine-inclusive place to sip wine in Sonoma County." The vintners use the money earned at dog-friendly events to benefit local animal-rescue organizations.

Paul Hobbs Winery (www.paulhobbswinery.com, 707-824-9879, 3355 Gravenstein Highway N., Sebastopol, CA 95472; tastings by appointment). The wine here is off-the-charts good, but the winemaker is one of the most controversial in all of Wine Country. Environmentalists complain he's pushing the limits of the law and have amassed in protest. Meanwhile, Hobbs maintains he's not sidestepping regulations, and that he's just doing his best to make top-notch wines. To his credit, an article in *Forbes* magazine coined Hobbs the "Steve Jobs of wine," because he's a "quality fanatic." He makes a winning lineup—pinot noir, chardonnay, cabernet sauvignon, and syrah. Hobbs has said if he weren't a winemaker, he might enjoy being a watchmaker or a surgeon, because he likes things that require a "high degree of detail or complexity."

✪ **Red Car Wine** (www.redcarwine.com, 707-829-8500, 8400 Graton Road, Sebastopol, CA 95472; tastings daily 10–5). Red Car has a great lineup of varietals, with pinot, syrah, and chardonnay stealing the limelight. The winery offers three labels: Box Car, Trolley, and Red Car, ranging roughly from $25 to $70. The winery also gets points for creativity, with the name Red Car a tribute to the electric trolley cars that ran throughout Los Angeles from the late nineteenth century through the early 1960s. The tasting room on Graton is unfussy, with tasty pours available. It's a fun place to stop in on the way to the coast. Here's the back story: Red Car was founded by Carroll Kemp and

Mark Estrin with a Hollywood connection—Carroll as producer, Mark as screenwriter. They began their venture with 50 cases of syrah from a single ton of grapes.

✪ **Ron Rubin Winery** (www.ronrubinwinery.com, 707-887-8130, 5220 Ross Road, Sebastopol, CA 95472; tastings by appointment). Vintner Ron Rubin calls himself "the beverage guy," because he's also the owner of the esteemed Republic of Tea. He says both wine and tea have a great deal in common, like blending sessions, although with tea they're called "cuppings." Rubin's background in tea makes him a gifted and inventive vintner. Here the standouts are the unoaked chardonnay, the rosé, and the old-vine zinfandel.

Sonoma-Cutrer Vineyards (www.sonomacutrer.com, 707-237-3489, 877-797-3489, 4401 Slusser Road, Windsor, CA 95492; tastings and tours 10–4 by appointment). Harvest is called "crush," yet crush is a crude way to describe the way Sonoma-Cutrer makes chardonnay. Pampering is more like it. Grapes arrive in small boxes and are then chilled to 40 degrees in a specially designed cooling tunnel. Then they are hand-sorted and, left in whole clusters, put through a gentle membrane press. A tour reveals the entire process as well as an underground aging cellar. Once the leader in California chardonnay, Sonoma-Cutrer now has keen competition. Brice Cutrer Jones, a jet fighter pilot in the Vietnam War, founded the winery in 1981 and built an ultramodern facility that blends into the hills. (Sonoma-Cutrer also has two world-class croquet courts.) The winery is owned by conglomerate Brown-Forman, which owns well-known consumer brands such as Jack Daniel's and Canadian Mist.

✳ Lodging

Applewood Inn (www.applewoodinn .com, 707-869-9093, 800-555-8509, 13555 Highway 116, Guerneville, CA 95446; $$$–$$$$). This mission-style inn hidden in a stand of redwoods is one of Sonoma County's finest. It's romantic and formal yet familiar, like a wealthy grandmother's house. The site was originally an apple orchard and now harbors a circa-1922 mansion with nine rooms and Piccola Casa, a matching house added in 1995, with seven rooms. Three suites and another building were added in 1999. The common area is centered on a huge double-sided stone fireplace. Meals are served in the inn's freestanding restaurant, Applewood Restaurant, which specializes in Mediterranean cuisine.

Bodega Bay Lodge and Spa (www .bodegabaylodge.com, 707-875-3525, 888-875-2250, 103 Highway 1, Bodega Bay, CA 94923; $$$–$$$$). This wood-shingled seaside lodge—well appointed and intimate—is sheltered from coastal winds but close enough for the sound of the surf. All rooms have ocean or bay views and private balconies, and many feature fireplaces, vaulted ceilings, spa baths, refrigerators, wet bars, and coffeemakers. Even the pool and whirlpool offer breathtaking views. The Drakes Sonoma County Kitchen restaurant is expensive, but it's one of the best on the Sonoma coast.

Bodega Coast Inn (707-875-2217, www .bodegacoastinn.com, 521 Highway 1, Bodega Bay, CA 94923; $$–$$$). Once a Holiday Inn, this inn has 45 attractively appointed rooms and suites, with balconies offering lovely views of Bodega Bay harbor. A few rooms have fireplaces, whirlpool tubs, and vaulted ceilings. Some rooms have two-person whirlpools.

Bodega Harbor Inn (707-875-3594, www.bodegaharborinn.com, 1345 Bodega Avenue at Highway 1, Bodega Bay, CA 94923; $). This hotel offers 14 rooms, 2 suites, cottages, and vacation homes. Some rooms have bay views, decks, fireplaces, and kitchens. It's a bit funky but comfortable.

Fairfield Inn & Suites (www.wine countryhi.com, 707-829-6677, 1101 Gravenstein Highway S., Sebastopol, CA 95472; $–$$$). This pleasant, 82-room

OUR TOP OVERALL PICKS FOR BODEGA BAY AND WEST COUNTY

The Farmhouse Inn & Spa (www.farmhouseinn.com)
The Barlow (www.thebarlow.net)
Inn at Occidental (www.innatoccidental.com) and Osmosis (www.osmosis.com)
Zazu Kitchen & Farm (www.zazukitchen.com)
Iron Horse (www.ironhorsevineyards.com) and Korbel Champagne Cellars (www.korbel.com)
Tides Wharf Fish Market
Sonoma Coast State Beach
Underwood Bar & Bistro (www.underwoodgraton.com)
Mom's Apple Pie (www.momsapplepieusa.com)
Merry Edwards (www.merryedwards.com)

inn is just one of two hotels Sebastopol offers. Included are a pool, spa, fitness center, and continental breakfast. Each room has a refrigerator, a coffeemaker, and complimentary Wi-Fi.

✪ ⚲ **Farmhouse Inn & Spa** (www.farmhouseinn.com, 707-887-3300, 800-464-6642, 7871 River Road, Forestville, CA 95436; $$$–$$$$). Built as a farmhouse in 1878, this inn later became a horse ranch and later still, a roadhouse lodge. Today, not only is it one of the most stylish inns in Sonoma County, but it's also home to one of the finest restaurants in Wine Country. The interior of the main house sets a distinct New England tone, with a long, Shaker-style dining room where a rich breakfast feast is spread. The savvy inn has built its reputation as an extraordinary spot for weddings and conferences. The innkeeper and staff are exceptionally friendly.

✪ **Inn at Occidental** (www.innatoccidental.com, 707-874-1047, 800-522-6324, 3657 Church Street, Occidental, CA 95465; $$$–$$$$). Perched on a hill overlooking the quiet village of Occidental, this comfortable, three-story Victorian inn is a jewel, one of Wine Country's best. It is well off the beaten path and delightfully so. Guarded by fruit trees and a lush courtyard garden with a fountain, the inn was built in 1876. The Wolsborns are exceptional hosts, offering wine, cheese, and homemade cookies

by the living room hearth each evening. A superb gourmet breakfast is served in the dining room or on the porch.

THE FARMHOUSE INN IS A QUAINT RETREAT THAT HAS ONE OF THE FINEST RESTAURANTS IN WINE COUNTRY

TYPICAL BREAKFAST FARE FOR GUESTS OF THE INN AT OCCIDENTAL COURTESY OF THE INN AT OCCIDENTAL

The Inn at the Tides (www.innatthe tides.com, 707-875-2751, 800-541-7788, 800 Highway 1, P.O. Box 640, Bodega Bay, CA 94923; $$-$$$$). Six coastal acres with natural landscaping surround this inn—actually 12 separate lodges scattered over a hillside. The 86 guest rooms are agreeably designed, and each has a bay or ocean view, with a refrigerator, coffeemaker, and room service for dinner, if desired. The inn is home to Sonoma County's leading winemaker dinner; if interested, inquire when making your reservations.

Raford Inn (www.rafordinn.com, 707-887-9573, 800-887-9503, 10630 Wohler Road, Healdsburg, CA 95448; $$-$$$). In the heart of rural Sonoma County, this inn is ideally located for touring the wineries of Russian River and Dry Creek valleys. An 1880 Victorian, it sits like a jewel on a gentle slope overlooking vineyards and tall redwoods. Stately palm trees stand as sentinels on the front lawn, and at the end of a tall staircase is a wide porch, an ideal place to kick off your shoes and watch the hummingbirds flutter by.

Santa Nella House (www.santanella house.com, 707-869-9488, 877-869-9488, 12130 Highway 116, Guerneville, CA 95446; $$-$$$). Nestled in a quiet redwood forest, this inn is an 1870 Victorian

with a grand wraparound veranda. There are five guest rooms and a cottage in the woods, all with private baths and furnished with functional antiques and queen-sized beds. All have wood-burning fireplaces. A full breakfast—artichoke soufflé with basil-chive roasted potatoes is just one of many specialties—is served in the kitchen by the wood-burning stove. The parlor/music room is a favorite gathering place.

✪ **Sea Ranch Lodge** (www.searanch lodge.com, 707-785-2371, 800-732-7262, 60 Sea Walk Drive, Sea Ranch, CA 95497; $$$-$$$$). On bluffs above the Pacific Ocean, this lodge has one of the best vistas in Wine Country. The 19 rooms face the sea—cozy window seats offer front-row viewing for spectacular sunsets—and some of the rooms have fireplaces, and one room has a private garden with spa tub. The location is remote, but if you're in need of a peaceful getaway, this is it. Outside, the weathered wood recalls New England, and the interior feels like a rustic cabin, with knotty pine, cathedral ceilings, and quilted bedspreads. Three caveats: the lodge is historic, so the walls are a bit thin; locate your room's flashlight immediately because lighting is poor outside at night; and bring a sweater because fog keeps the locale cool even in summer. The restaurant is adequate but pricey— but, oh, that view! Hiking trails are well marked along the bluffs, and the inn is dog friendly.

Sonoma Coast Villa & Spa (www .scvilla.com, 888-404-2255, 16702 Highway 1, Bodega, CA 94922; $$$-$$$$). This Mediterranean-style resort on 60 acres is great for roaming. The pastoral hillsides are lovely, and there are plenty of meandering gardens. The inn's 18 rooms are furnished with modern Mediterranean decor, including Italian slate floors; all the rooms have fireplaces, and many have whirlpool tubs and private patios. There's also a 3,600-square-foot Grand Residence for large groups. A full breakfast is served in the dining room.

Sonoma Orchid Inn (www.sonoma orchidinn.com, 707-869-4466, 888-877-4466, 12850 River Road, Guerneville, CA 95446; $$–$$$). Within walking distance of Korbel Champagne Cellars and the Russian River, this circa-1906 inn is built of redwood and has 10 guest rooms, each with a private bath. Hawthorn Cottage has a king-sized bed, a fireplace, and a cozy window seat. Madrone has a king-sized bed, a sitting area with a sofa, and a private brick patio. The inn serves decadent "skip-lunch breakfasts," replete with caloric dishes such as stuffed French toast soufflé.

Timber Cove Resort (707-847-3231, 800-987-8319, www.timbercoveresort.com, 21780 N. Coast Highway 1, Jenner, CA 95450; $$–$$$). This inn is charming and has been completely renovated, with a breathtaking location perched on a rocky cliff overlooking the ocean. Many of the 46 rooms (including eight suites) have ocean views; some have fireplaces and private hot tubs. Included on the property are a restaurant and lounge.

✳ Where to Eat

Applewood Restaurant (www.applewood inn.com, 707-869-9093, 800-555-8509, 13555 Highway 116, Guerneville, CA 95446; $$$; cuisine: California). If you can't spend the night—Applewood is one of the best inns in Wine Country (see listing under *Lodging*)—then dinner is the next best thing. The main house, built in 1922, is an architectural gem done in the Mediterranean style. The restaurant is styled to be the estate's barn. Long and narrow with cathedral ceilings and a stone fireplace, it's handsome and masculine. The food is excellent, with Mediterranean cuisine its specialty. Desserts often include fruit from the inn's own orchard. The wine list is impressive, highlighting Russian River Valley selections, and is generally well priced. The service is sharp and

intelligent, well-paced, courteous, and professional.

Bay View Restaurant at the Inn at the Tides (www.innatthetides.com, 707-875-2751, 800-541-7788, 800 Highway 1, Bodega Bay, CA 94923; $$$; cuisine: seafood, California). If the hectic hum of The Tides or Lucas Wharf is too much, and if you seek something more than basic fish, the Bay View might be an alternative. Although the food is simply on par with those two popular restaurants—good, but not great—the presentation has more flair, and the view is more impressive. If these factors are important, you might not mind the added cost. The menu is dominated by local seafood, and two interesting entrées are the pan-fried sea bass and the cioppino. If you prefer meat, the filet mignon Hitchcock is a tasty pick. The wine list is superbly selected, with a credible list by the glass. The decor is elegant if a bit generic, with a beamed cathedral ceiling and Scandinavian furnishings. Servers are polite and efficient.

❍ Drakes Sonoma Coast Kitchen (www.drakesbodegabay.com, 707-875-3525, 103 Highway 1, Bodega Bay, CA 94923, at Bodega Bay Lodge; $$–$$$$; cuisine: seafood, California). This out-of-the-way restaurant—hidden amid the lush landscaping of Bodega Bay Lodge—is worth a search. It offers the best food on the Sonoma coast. The decor is strictly country club, but the views over the harbor and wetlands are gorgeous, and a blazing fire warms the room. The

WILDLIFE WATCHING IN SONOMA COUNTY

The Bodega Headlands stretch like a curved arm out to sea. Dramatic cliffs provide a spectacular vista of the Pacific coast. This is the best area to watch for whales in winter and early spring.

Goat Rock Beach extends from the sandbars along the mouth of the Russian River, where sea lions and their young can be seen at certain times of the year.

menu may be too broad, with the kitchen seemingly stretched at times. Offerings range from seafood to pork chops to steaks and chicken. Good picks include the Dungeness crab cakes, pan-roasted wild king salmon with a Grand Marnier demi-glaze, and the seafood fettucine. Service is solid, and the restaurant now has a full bar.

✪ **Farmhouse Inn & Restaurant** (www.farmhouseinn.com, 707-887-3300, 800-464-6642, 7871 River Road, Forestville, CA 95436; $$$$). With a kitchen that delivers one of the best food and wine experiences in Sonoma, this is one country inn that offers more than just charm. The setting is a 140-year-old farmhouse painted a pale yellow and trimmed in black and white and situated in the heart of Russian River Valley vineyards. Guests feel as though they're at a chic dinner party, not a restaurant. The food blends modern French with vibrant California cuisine. Specialties include something called Rabbit, Rabbit, Rabbit—rabbit done three ways: confit, bacon-wrapped loin, and roasted rack. It's delightful, as are fascinating creations such as farmhouse cassoulet with house-made rabbit sausage and duck confit. The impressive wine list takes a worldly view, with excellent selections from France, Germany, and, of course, California. Wine service is superb, thanks to the restaurant's smart lineup of sommeliers.

K & L Bistro (www.klbistro.com, 707-823-6614, 119 S. Main Street, Sebastopol, CA 95472; $$$; cuisine: French, California). A small space with exposed brick walls, this casual bistro draws a crowd of locals every night. It's hard to deny the appeal of the place—the food is decent in a hearty, comforting way, with a menu that includes crab cakes, mussels in white wine, a tasty hamburger, and steak frites. The wine list has some good finds and the price is right.

✪ **Lowell's** (lowellssebastopol.com, 707-829-1077, 7385 Healdsburg Avenue, Sebastopol, CA 95472; $$$; cuisine: California). Formerly known as Peter Lowell's, this hip café puts new meaning into the word "local." Owner Lowell Sheldon calls his work "hyper-local," as he sources most everything from his surrounding Sebastopol and West County, including his partner Natalie Goble's Two Belly Acres farm. The tiny restaurant is warm with large windows overlooking the bustling downtown neighborhood and a dine-in counter at the miniscule open kitchen. The rustic-chic decor translates to the health-centric food, too, starting with a breakfast of soupy-savory beans and greens with two baked eggs, breadcrumbs, and Parmigiano. At lunch, you can choose a Reuben with house-crafted pastrami or tempeh topped in Russian River dressing, Gruyere, and sauerkraut on MH rye. For dinner, piping hot wood-fired, Neapolitan-style pizza makes a great starter, followed by homemade ravioli stuffed with roast pork and ricotta under rich pork leg ragu and pecorino Romano. Any time is perfect for the signature macro bowl, meanwhile, in a tumble of red rice, heirloom beans, braised greens, marinated root vegetables, kimchi, miso ginger sauce, and choice of organic egg, tempeh, pork sausage, rockfish, or braised short rib. For refreshment, small-production beers and ciders share the menu with hand-made teas, plus boutique-label international wines.

✪ **Korbel Delicatessan** (www.korbel .com, 707-824-7313, 13250 River Road, Guerneville, CA 95446; $$). Under a cathedral ceiling on an acid-washed floor, five or six tables offer shady views through tall windows. Outside are plenty of additional tables. Here you can get muffins, salads, sandwiches, beer on tap, champagne and wine by the glass, and ales of all kinds (amber, pale, port, golden wheat). There are breads, jams and jellies, and vinegars, too.

Lucas Wharf (www.lucaswharf restaurant.com, 707-875-3522, 595 Highway 1, Bodega Bay, CA 94923; $$–$$$; cuisine: seafood). Built on piers overlooking Bodega Bay harbor, Lucas Wharf is cozy and romantic, with a fireplace and cathedral ceiling. From your table, you'll see great sunsets and fishing boats unloading the catch of the day. Choose what's fresh off the boat, and you won't go wrong—particularly salmon when it's in season (May through September) and Dungeness crab in season (from November to May). There's also a hearty fisherman's stew in a tomato broth. The wine list is weighted to local wines, with savvy picks in the lineup. Lucas Wharf is popular with locals and tourists alike, so be prepared to wait for a table on weekends.

✪ **Mom's Apple Pie** (www.momsapple pieusa.com, 707-823-8330, 4550 Gravenstein Highway N., Sebastopol, CA 95472; $$). This roadhouse makes fat pies better than most moms, served in tin pans or by the slice. The coconut cream and the fresh Gravenstein apple are to die for. There are two secret ingredients: the Gravenstein apples and the pampering. Mom (a.k.a. Betty Carr) says it's all about keeping a focused eye on the oven. "You must baby-sit this pie," she jokes. Not just pies are made here; Mom's also serves lunch, offering sandwiches and salads.

Screamin Mimi's (www.screamin mimisicecream.com, 707-823-5902, 6902 Sebastopol Avenue, Sebastopol, CA 95472; $$). They make their own ice cream and sorbets here, and it's all wonderful. Put your diet on hold to free yourself up for these delectable treats.

Spud Point Crab Company (707-875-9472, 1910 Westshore Road, Bodega Bay, CA 94923; $$). One of the joys of living on the Pacific Ocean is fresh seafood. Most prized locally are Dungeness crab and salmon. Crab season runs from mid-November to May, and the local salmon season runs from mid-May to September. People come from as far away as Europe to taste Carol Anello's clam chowder and crab cakes. She makes only 80 crab cakes on Saturdays and another batch of 80 on Sundays. They're ready at around noon each day, first come, first serve, and it's a mad dash. Spud's is open until 5 p.m.

✪ **Tides Wharf and Restaurant** (www .innatthetides.com, 707-875-3652, 800-541-7788, 835 Highway 1, Bodega Bay, CA 94923; $$$; cuisine: seafood). The Tides was immortalized by Alfred Hitchcock in *The Birds,* but you wouldn't recognize it now. The current dining room has a high-raftered ceiling and stunning views of the harbor from every seat. The food is competent at best, but the catch of the day is usually a good bet: a voluminous list including red snapper, swordfish, lingcod, and Pacific oysters. Local specialties include salmon, in season May through September, and Dungeness crab, in season from November to May. A delicious local classic is the crab cioppino: crab, prawns, scallops, mussels, and clams swimming in a shallow pool of zesty Italian sauce. The lunch menu is almost identical to dinner, but it's a few dollars cheaper. The wine list is sound; ditto the service.

✪ **Underwood Bar & Bistro** (www .underwoodgraton.com, 707-823-7023, 9113 Graton Road, Graton, CA 95444; $$–$$$; cuisine: eclectic). If you like to eat where the winemakers hang out, this restaurant is practically a private club for the West County wine industry. The interior is a masculine blend of urban and country, and there's a long bar that's always hopping. Service is a little

PORK FRESH FROM THE FARM IS THE STAR OF ZAZU TIM FISH

too laid back at times, but the food is appealing and hearty. The kitchen takes influences from all over the globe, with a menu that ranges from an eclectic selection of small plates such as crab cakes and roasted beets to hamburgers and Catalan fish stew. The wine list is modest but offers lots of value; it's devoted largely to California but with a handful of selections from around the world.

⚙ **Zazu Kitchen & Farm** (www .zazukitchen.com, 707-523-4814, 6770 McKinley #150, Sebastopol, CA 95472; $$–$$$; cuisine: northern Italian, California). Zazu blends delicious American classics such as buttermilk mashed potatoes and grilled sweet corn with creative variations on lamb, seafood, pork, and duck. Be sure to try the flat-iron steak with blue cheese ravioli and sautéed chard. Chef-owners John Stewart (a pork fanatic who once made a pig's heart concoction with a mustard sauce that was both indescribably delicious and creepy at the same time) and Duskie Estes are passionate about their digs at The Barlow, a hip food and wine village of sorts that has become the pulse of Sebastopol.

In 2010, chef Estes was a contestant on the Food Network's *Next Iron Chef*. Estes found the competition to be brutal, even though she'd been preparing for it since she was five, cooking with her Easy-Bake Oven. The restaurant is modern, with tall ceilings and roll-up garage doors in the warehouse-like space. This place offers hearty, good eats, great cocktails, and a savvy wine list. There are 100-plus wines on the list, and local producers are featured extensively.

✳ Entertainment

Dempsey's Ale House (www.dempseys .com, 707-765-9694, 50 E. Washington Street, Petaluma, CA 94952). This is Wine Country's best brewpub—period. From the outside, Dempsey's doesn't look like much—it's in a generic shopping center—but it offers a handsome interior plus outdoor seating right along the Petaluma River.

Main Stage West (www.mainstage west.com, 707-823-0177, 104 N. Main Street, Sebastopol, CA 95472). Since its inception in 1995, this company has quickly become the area's leading theater, staging a mix of classics and cutting-edge dramas, comedies, and occasionally a musical. Performances are in a small Sebastopol theater. Top productions have included Shakespeare's *The Tempest* and *Hamlet* as well as *Daddy Long Legs, Grace,* and Sam Shepard's *Buried Child.*

❂ Rialto Cinemas (707-525-4840, McKinley Street & Petaluma Avenue, Sebastopol, CA 95472). This five-theater cinema is inside a refurbished brandy distillery. It shows first-run films.

✳ Selective Shopping

Antique Society (707-829-1733, 2661 Gravenstein Highway S., Sebastopol, CA 95472). Sonoma County's largest antiques collective, with more than 125 dealers.

Global Village (707-829-4765, 172 N. Main Street, Sebastopol, CA 95472). Truly an international affair, featuring women's clothes from Bali, Peru, and India—to name just a few countries—and there's also jewelry and some men's and unisex clothing, too.

Ray's Trading Co. (707-829-9726, 3570 Gravenstein Highway S., Sebastopol, CA 95472). A salvage company recognized as an important resource for Bay Area people restoring Victorian homes, Ray's has bins full of antique doorknobs and drawer pulls, and the company is even a source for windows and doors. Call first; the business has limited hours.

Rosemary's Garden (707-829-2539, 132 N. Main Street, Sebastopol, CA 95472). This establishment is an herbal apothecary and gift store that's well stocked with products to soothe the soul, including Chinese herbs, tea blends, and massage oils.

❂ Sophie's Cellars (www.sophies cellars.com, 707-865-1122, 25179 Highway 116, Duncans Mills, CA 95430). This shop is a real find, a place where you can

score the best of the boutiques, and the cheeses are an adventure as well. Expect the top names in wine; while there are offerings from all over the world, the bottlings are weighted to California. A cadre of America's wealthiest movers and shakers gather each summer at the Bohemian Grove, and a Grove member once shocked the owners of Sophie's Cellars by purchasing $20,000 worth of wine in one day.

Toyworks (707-829-2003, 6940 Sebastopol Avenue, Sebastopol, CA 95472) has globes, kites, puzzles, and even kits for building your own volcano. Copperfield's Books (707-823-2618, 138 N. Main Street, Sebastopol, CA 95472) is a bookstore that seems to have a new age state of mind, with shelves lined with second-hand volumes and entire walls filled with art and fiction.

Wild Things (707-829-3371, 130 S. Main Street, Suite 102, Sebastopol, CA 95472). One of the hippest nature shops you'll ever come across, Wild Things has finger puppets, screen-painted T-shirts, and beautiful cards.

✳ Special Events

Bodega Bay Fisherman's Festival (www.bbfishfest.org, 707-875-3866, Bodega Bay, CA 94923). This is a decades-old tradition for this coastal town made famous by Alfred Hitchcock's *The Birds*. This spring (typically April, early May) celebration includes bathtub races, harbor tours, kite flying, a golf tournament, and a boat parade. The high point of the weekend is the annual blessing of the fleet.

☞ ✿ **Gravenstein Apple Fair** (www .gravensteinapplefair.com, 707-837-8896, Ragle Ranch Park, Sebastopol, CA 95472). Sebastopol, once the apple capital of the world, today specializes in the distinctive Gravenstein variety. There's a potpourri at this mid-August event: arts and crafts, music, hay rides, storytelling, and, of course, apple treats of all kinds.

Russian River Jazz and Blues Festival (www.russianriverfestivals.com, 707-869-1595, Johnson's Beach, Guerneville, CA 95446). For two days in mid-September, music lovers sun on the beach or listen from floating inner tubes. Saturday features jazz, while Sunday focuses on blues. The lineup in the past has included

GRAPE ALTERNATIVES

Not that you're tired of wine, but you won't want to miss these other great places to visit:

Sonoma Cheese Factory (www.sonoma cheesefactory.com). This deli, owned by a cheesemaking family, offers great sandwiches, cheeses, fudge, coffee, and a gelato bar.

BR Cohn Winery (www.brcohn.com). Producing fine olive oil and handcrafted vinegars is a hallmark of this winery.

Stephanie Mills, Tower of Power, and the Kenny Wayne Shepherd Band.

Sebastopol Apple Blossom Festival (www.sebastopol.org, 707-823-3032, downtown Sebastopol, CA 95472). When the apple trees are in striking form in April, you won't find a more beautiful place than Sebastopol. Apples rule, of course. Partake of the apple fritters, cobbler, and pies, plus enjoy music, games, a parade, and arts and crafts.

OPPOSITE: THE BEER BARON SPECIALIZES IN BREWS BUT HAS A VAST RANGE OF DRINKS TO OFFER

SANTA ROSA

anta Rosa is the "chosen spot of all this earth as far as nature is concerned"—that's according to the late Luther Burbank, the town's favorite son. The genteel plant genius courted Mother Nature as he developed more than 800 strains and varieties of plants over his 55-year career.

Burbank's "chosen spot" has grown to be the largest city in California Wine Country and the fifth-largest city in the San Francisco Bay Area. It's 50 miles north of the Golden Gate Bridge and 30 miles east of the Pacific Ocean, with Mediterranean weather.

Others who have left their indelible mark on the city are the late Charles Schulz, creator of the comic strip *Peanuts*, and John Ash, the celebrity chef who has been called the father of Wine Country cuisine. As you roam throughout the city, you'll spy small-framed sculptures of the *Peanuts* characters, a tribute to Schulz. You'll also hear good things about the John Ash & Co. Restaurant; the raves are well deserved, even though Ash no longer has ownership ties to it.

Santa Rosa may be the largest city in Sonoma County, but when it comes to tourists, it's often trumped by Healdsburg and Sonoma, which are even more immersed in wine culture. That said, Santa Rosa still manages to be the chosen spot for many tourists, because it has its share of boutique wineries. It offers a wealth of tasting opportunities, from giant Kendall-Jackson to boutique Siduri, with many in between.

Many of Santa Rosa's great buildings were lost in the 1906 earthquake, although many historic structures on McDonald Avenue on the northeast edge of downtown survived. Alfred Hitchcock filmed *Shadow of a Doubt* in Santa Rosa. Downtown has

A PEEK AT BENOVIA'S PRIZED COHN VINEYARD

changed considerably since then, but the McDonald Avenue residential area, shown extensively in the film, remains the city's architectural prize. Just east of downtown is a lovely neighborhood of large homes, wide streets, and tall trees. The centerpiece is Mableton, at 1015 McDonald. Built in 1878, it was inspired by the plantation homes of Mississippi.

THE CHARLES M. SCHULZ MUSEUM PAYS HOMAGE TO THE CREATOR OF *PEANUTS*, A SANTA ROSA NATIVE PHOTO BY STEPHANIE SHEA COURTESY OF THE CHARLES M. SCHULZ MUSEUM AND RESEARCH CENTER

✳ To See

MUSEUMS AND GALLERIES ✿ **California Indian Museum & Cultural Center** (www.cimcc.org, 707-579-3004, Santa Rosa Junior College, 5250 Aero Drive, Santa Rosa, CA 95403). Holdings here include artifacts and current works by Native American artisans.

✿ ✪ **Charles M. Schulz Museum** (www.schulzmuseum.org, 707-579-4452, 2301 Hardies Lane, Santa Rosa, CA 95403). This museum gives you a peek at how the late Charles Schulz actually created the *Peanuts* cast of characters. It also has galleries of comic strips and even a small auditorium to watch the *Peanuts* television specials. If you're a comic strip buff, you won't want to miss it. Schulz witnessed the heated debate over *Running Fence,* a 24-mile-long installation in west Sonoma County by the environmental artist Christo, and ultimately created a comic strip in 1978 with the final panel showing Snoopy's house wrapped in the white nylon fabric used in the Christo project. Here's the upshot: framed copies of a Christo-wrapped Snoopy house are for sale in the gift shop.

✪ ✿ **Luther Burbank Home & Gardens** (www.lutherburbank.org, 707-524-5445, 204 Santa Rosa Avenue, Santa Rosa, CA 95404). Plant genius Luther Burbank remains Santa Rosa's favorite son. More than 90 years after his death, buildings and businesses bear his name. At the turn of the twentieth century his fame was international. Burbank arrived from his native Massachusetts in 1877. In a letter home, he wrote—and Santa Rosans love to quote this—"I firmly believe this is the chosen spot of all this earth as far as nature is concerned."

Sonoma County Museum (www.museumsc.org, 707-579-1500, 425 Seventh Street, Santa Rosa, CA 95401). On the National Register of Historic Places, the structure is a mix of Spanish and Roman influences, and it's considered one of the few remaining examples of classic Federal-style architecture in California. Lobby displays detail the history of the building and its laborious move two blocks north. The main exhibition room offers rotating displays keyed to Sonoma history.

✪ **Santa Rosa Junior College Art Gallery** (www.art-gallery.santarosa.edu, 707-527-4298, 1501 Mendocino Avenue, Santa Rosa, CA 94503). Here you'll find group shows by faculty and students. Open limited days and hours; call ahead.

✳ To Do

BALLOONING **Up & Away Hot Air Ballooning** (www.up-away.com, 707-836-0171, 800-711-2998) offers daily flights for small groups. Balloons typically fly through the

Russian River Valley. Soaring silently above the vineyards and rolling hills of Wine Country in a hot-air balloon is an experience you won't quickly forget.

BIKING **Trione-Annadel State Park** (707-539-3911) at times has more mountain bikers than runners on its trails. Many local parks have extensive bike trails, including Spring Lake Regional Park in Santa Rosa (707-539-8092). Two excellent guides for specific trails are *Sonoma County Bike Trails* and *Rides In and Around the Napa Valley*.

Getaway Adventures (www.getawayadventures.com, 707-568-3040, 800-499-2453, 2228 Northpoint Parkway, Santa Rosa, CA 95407) organizes tours through Napa and Sonoma counties, suggests routes, and includes helmets and the like. It offers wine tours called "Sip and Cycle," and hiking, kayaking, and other themed tours. Many inns also offer bikes for casual day trips, and most bike shops rent two-wheelers for the day.

GOLF Golf courses cover the rich valleys and rolling hills of Wine Country as eagerly as vineyards. One of the region's favorite recreational activities, golf can be played year-round in this mild climate.

Bennett Valley Golf Course (www.bennettvalleygolf.com, 707-528-3673, 3330 Yulupa Avenue, Santa Rosa, CA 95405). This municipal course offers 18 holes, par 72; three pros; a shop; a driving range; a putting green; and a restaurant and lounge. Reserve one week ahead.

Oakmont Golf Club (www.oakmontgc.com, 707-539-0415, 7025 Oakmont Drive, Santa Rosa, CA 95409). This club comprises two private and public 18-hole championship courses, par 72, designed by Ted Robinson; four pros; two shops; a driving range; and lessons. Reservations are suggested.

HORSERIDING Sonoma County adamantly maintains its rural flavor, despite its growing population and worldwide tourist appeal. There is plenty of interest in horse breeding, competition, and riding.

Horse-racing fans converge each summer at the **Sonoma County Fair** (707-545-4200, www.sonomacountyfair.com, 1350 Bennett Valley Road, Santa Rosa, CA 95404) to watch California's fastest horses vying for a purse of nearly $2 million. During the rest of the year, the fairgrounds offer **The Jockey Club** (707-524-6340), with simultaneous broadcasting of races at Hollywood Park, Golden Gate Fields, and Santa Anita.

SKATING The late famed cartoonist and ice-skating buff Charles Schulz built the **Redwood Empire Ice Arena** (707-546-7147, www.snoopyshomeice.com, 1667 W. Steele Lane, Santa Rosa, CA 95403) in 1969, and it's one of Sonoma County's most popular spots. The rink, surrounded by walls painted with Alpine scenes, is the site for recreational and would-be Olympic skaters and birthday parties. Next door is **Snoopy's Gallery & Gift Shop** (707-546-3385), filled with every conceivable item relating to Snoopy and the Peanuts gang as well as skating gear, including high-tech, in-line skates.

TENNIS **La Cantera Racquet and Swim Club** (www.lacanteraraquetandswimclub .com, 707-544-9494, 3737 Montgomery Drive, Santa Rosa, CA 95405). Courts are open to members and guests. Altogether, there are 12 courts, four of them lit. There's an on-site pro, leagues, and tournaments.

Montecito Heights Health and Racquet Club (www.montecitoheights.com, 707-526-0529, 2777 Fourth Street, Santa Rosa, CA 95405). Courts are open to members and guests. There are five unlit courts, an on-site pro, leagues, and tournaments.

Santa Rosa Public Courts (707-543-3282) are available at Howarth, Finley, and Galvin parks, Santa Rosa Junior College, and Santa Rosa and Montgomery high schools.

GRAB THE KIDS AND GO

Kids and kids at heart can find all sorts of fun, from pony rides and water slides to a planetarium show guaranteed to stretch the imagination.

Howarth Park (707-543-3282, Montgomery and Summerfield roads, Santa Rosa, CA 95409). This popular, city-run park offers a merry-go-round; pony rides; a petting zoo; a small railroad; play and picnic areas; paddleboats, canoes, and rowboats to rent; and ducks to feed on Lake Ralphine. Some activities are open on the weekends in the winter.

⭐ Planetarium (707-521-6914, Santa Rosa Junior College, Room 2001 Lark Hall, 1501 Mendocino Avenue, Santa Rosa, CA 95401). This excellent planetarium is open to the public on weekends during the school year. Shows are offered at 7 p.m. Friday and Saturday, and 1:30 p.m. Sunday during the fall and spring academic year. There are no reservations, so arrive early to park. Admission: $8 general, $5 students, seniors, and children 13 and under.

Safari West (www.safariwest.com, 707-579-2551, 3115 Porter Creek Road, Santa Rosa, CA 95404). This 400-plus-acre park features 150 species, including 400 rare and endangered animals. Not a drive-through animal park, this is a 2.5-hour tour that's comparable to a real African safari.

Scandia Family Fun Center (www.scandiafunland.com, 707-584-1398, 5301 Redwood Drive, Rohnert Park, CA 94928). Here you'll find little Indy racers, miniature golf, baseball batting cages, bumper boats, spin bumper cars, and a game arcade. This is a favorite recreation center for kids and families and is packed on summer weekends. There's even a Viking Pizza vendor inside. Separate fees for each activity; hours vary.

GIRAFFES ARE AMONG THE WILD THINGS AT SAFARI WEST COURTESY OF SAFARI WEST

WATERSPORTS **Lake Ralphine** (707-543-3424, Howarth Park, 630 Summerfield Road, Santa Rosa, CA 95405). This is a popular spot for water activities, from boating to feeding ducks. Stocked with fish, this small man-made lake has a city-run boat rental where rowboats, canoes, and paddleboats are available for a minimal fee. Powerboats are not permitted.

Spring Lake (707-539-8092, off Montgomery Drive at 391 Violetti Road, Santa Rosa, CA 95409). This lovely 72-acre lake is open only to canoes, rowboats, and kayaks—all of which can be rented during the summer. Windsurfing and rafting are also allowed. There's a separate three-acre lagoon for swimming. For boat rentals, call 707-543-3424.

✳ Wineries

✪ **Benovia** (www.benoviawinery.com, 707-526-4441, 3339 Hartman Road, Santa Rosa, CA 95401; tastings by appointment). The wines here are top-rate, with striking pinot noir, chardonnay, zinfandel, and now sparklers. Pinot lovers will especially appreciate this winery. Vintners Joe Anderson and Mary Dewane named the winery after their fathers, Ben Dewane and Novian Anderson. Joe and Mary partnered with Mike Sullivan, a very well-respected winemaker in Northern California, so it's no surprise the wines are very tasty.

✪ **Carol Shelton Wines** (www.carolshelton.com, 707-575-3441, 3354-B Coffey Lane, Santa Rosa, CA 95403; tastings and tours daily 11–4 by appointment). Carol Shelton was assistant winemaker of Healdsburg's Rodney Strong when she decided she wanted to be her own boss. In 2000, Carol and her husband, Mitch Mackenzie, a former software engineer, launched the brand Carol Shelton Wines, specializing in powerhouse zinfandel. Their bottlings have whimsical names like Wild Thing, which is produced using only wild yeasts found on organic grapes. Another bottling, Karma Zin, refers to the good luck Shelton had in finding a 100-plus-year-old vineyard in the Russian River Valley. Shelton produces roughly 5,000 cases a year, making her operation decidedly boutique. Call for same-day appointments. You won't be disappointed.

✪ **De Loach Vineyards** (www.deloachvineyards.com, 707-526-9111, 800-441-9298, 1791 Olivet Road, Santa Rosa, CA 95401; tastings Friday–Sunday 10–5, Monday–Thursday by appointment). After the French wine company Boisset bought this winery from Cecil De Loach, we didn't know what to expect. The De Loach family had been making wines since the mid-1970s but fell on hard financial times and the wines began to suffer. In just a few years, Boisset turned things around dramatically. The chardonnays and pinot noirs are classic Russian River: supple, rich, and elegant. All of the De Loach wines are available in the tasting room located in the handsome and grand redwood building at the end of a long drive embraced by vineyards.

Kendall-Jackson Wine Center (www.kj.com, 707-571-7500, 5007 Fulton Road, Fulton, CA 95439; tastings daily 10–5). Kendall-Jackson is a major force in California wine, particularly in its home base of Sonoma County. K-J, as it's known, operates several wineries in the area and uses this faux chateau as a visitor center. It's rather Disney-like in its notion of grandeur, but the garden is lovely. Inside, you can taste a wide range of K-J wines. Be sure to try the fleshy yet crisp sauvignon blanc.

Matanzas Creek (www.matanzascreek.com, 707-528-6464, 6097 Bennett Valley Road, Santa Rosa, CA 95404; tastings daily 10–4:30). The winery, now owned by Jackson Family Wines, is best known for its sprawling field of lavender and its pricey red blend—the Journey brand—at $100 a bottle. The lavender makes the winery a favorite picnic spot, replete with a bocce court, and the wines continue to have appeal, although the merlot no longer has the stature it once had. The winery, founded in 1977, set the stage for others to follow suit and develop the Bennett Valley as a wine-growing region.

⚙ **Paradise Ridge Winery** (www.prwinery.com, 707-528-9463, 4545 Thomas Lake Harris Drive, Santa Rosa, CA 95403; tastings by appointment). This winery is, in a word, resilient. It rebuilt after burning to the ground in the 2017 wildfires and today it has a memorial chronicling the worst firestorm in California history, with charred artifacts, videos, and timelines. Rebirth has graced the winery and its striking, panoramic view of the Russian River Valley, a backdrop for many winery weddings. It continues to be a wine-centric hub of the arts with a seasonal lineup of live music, food trucks, theatre events, poetry readings, and world-class art exhibitions. The 156-acre estate is also a great place to roam because of its outdoor sculpture exhibition and historical exhibition. It's not surprising the winery was voted Best Tasting Room in California by *USA Today* in 2016.

⚙ **Siduri** (www.siduri.com, 707-578-3882, 981 Airway Court, Suite E, Santa Rosa, CA 95403; tastings and tours Thursday–Monday by appointment). The name *Siduri* comes from the Babylonian goddess of wine. Adam and Dianna Lee, two wine lovers, thought it was a fitting name for their house of pinot noir. They began modestly, with a small quantity of pinot from the 1994 vintage, and now produce pinot from vineyards as far north as Oregon's Willamette Valley and as far south as Santa Barbara County. These lush pinots are pricey but well worth the *dinero*. Siduri is a gravity-flow winery that operates out of a no-frills warehouse, and it's interesting to tour. A footnote: Siduri also produces a label called Novy, a non-pinot venture. Varietals include syrahs, zins, and grenache.

St. Francis Winery (www.stfranciswinery.com, 707-538-9463, 888-675-9463, 100 Pythian Road at Highway 12, Santa Rosa, CA 95409; tastings daily 10–5). The mission-style winery has as its centerpiece the crown jewel, the iconic 1,000-pound bronze bell tower that hails from Italy. Not a bad way to honor the patron saint. It's a great backdrop for events, especially the fun movie nights it hosts in the summertime. Aside from being picturesque, the winery is also ecofriendly, with solar panels providing up to 40 percent of the winery's daily needs. The building is also built from reclaimed materials and stones sourced from the area. As for the wines, the focus here is on Sonoma County grapes and on attention to detail with handpicking. When it comes to chardonnay, harvest is in the middle of the night because cool picking best preserves the flavors. While the winery makes a full slate of wines, these days there's a nod to red. The red blends here are rich, with a gentle note of vanilla.

✳ Lodging

⚙ **The Astro** (www.theastro.com, 707-200-4655, 323 Santa Rosa Avenue, Santa Rosa, CA 95404; $$). Located in the heart of the up-and-coming Burbank Gardens neighborhood of Santa Rosa, The Astro is a former 1963 motor lodge turned 2018 urban motel, where mid-century modern design meets today's urban, hip sensibilities. The 34-room property offers a variety of room sizes, perfect for everyone from solo travelers to couples, friends and families. Each room is unique, with vintage furnishings and linens, bathroom accessories, and headboards designed and made in Sonoma County. Organic fruit trees dot the property, which includes a guest lounge, serving local coffee, beer, and wine. There is also a working bike shop on-site that rents Shinola bikes to guests and repairs bicycles of cycling enthusiasts who flock to the region to ride the roads. The Astro is located next to hip boutiques, art galleries, and the acclaimed restaurant the Spinster Sisters, the sister-business to The Astro.

SHOP WHILE YOU SLEEP? IF YOU LIKE THE FURNISHINGS AT THE ASTRO MOTEL, YOU CAN BUY THEM COURTESY OF THE ASTRO MOTEL

✪ **Flamingo Resort Hotel** (www
.flamingoresort.com, 707-545-8530,
800-848-8300, 2777 Fourth Street, Santa
Rosa, CA 95405; $–$$$$). Contemporary
furnishings and mature landscaping
make this 170-room resort hotel friendly
and comfortable in an unfussy way.
Sonoma Valley's premium wineries are
just minutes east on Highway 12. Guests
have access to an adjacent fitness center,
and the 25-meter outdoor pool is heated
year-round. Specialty shops and excel-
lent restaurants are just blocks away
on Farmers Lane. It's popular with both
business travelers and tourists.

The Gables (www.thegablesinn.com,
707-585-7777, 800-422-576, 4257 Peta-
luma Hill Road, Santa Rosa, CA 95404;
$$$). The 15 gables over keyhole-shaped
windows lend the name to this 1877
high-Victorian Gothic Revival inn. Other
features include ceilings that soar to 25
feet, a mahogany staircase, and three
Italian marble fireplaces. The seven
spacious guest rooms at The Gables (all
with private bath, featuring a clawfoot
tub) include four suites. A separate cottage offers additional privacy. The inn is
air-conditioned throughout. A full gourmet breakfast and afternoon snacks are
included.

✪ **Hotel La Rose** (www.hotellarose
.com, 707-579-3200, 800-527-6738, 308
Wilson Street, Santa Rosa, CA 95401;

$$–$$$$). This historic hotel—built in
1907 from stone extracted from the
mountain ridges east of Santa Rosa—is
in Railroad Square, once the hub of
commerce in Sonoma County. Now the
square is an eclectic urban area busy
with bohemian coffeehouses, nightclubs,
and a few street folks. Reconstructed
in 1985, the hotel and adjacent carriage
house have a total of 49 rooms.

✪ **Hyatt Regency Sonoma Wine
Country** (www.sonomawinecountry
.regency.hyatt.com, 707-284-1234, 170
Railroad Street, Santa Rosa, CA 95401;
$$–$$$). A recent addition to downtown
Santa Rosa, this hotel appeals to conven-
tioneers more than tourists. Still, it's a
pleasing if somewhat generic hotel, with
155 rooms on three floors. The decor
is standard, but many rooms overlook
courtyards and the pool area, which is
situated along a bucolic creek. Highway
101 is nearby, making it easily accessible
to Wine Country touring, but traffic can
be noisy, even at night. Many of Santa
Rosa's best restaurants are within walk-
ing distance.

✪ **Safari West Wildlife Preserve
and Tent Camp** (www.safariwest.com,
707-579-2551, 800-616-2695, 3115 Por-
ter Creek Road, Santa Rosa, CA 95404;
$$$–$$$$). Billed as "The spirit of
Africa in the heart of Wine Country," at
Safari West you can stay overnight in

authentic, canvas African safari tents with hardwood floors, in close proximity to but separated from exotic wildlife. Each tent has a king-sized bed or two doubles and a bathroom with a shower. A three-hour tour, scheduled separately, will take you through the 400 acres of wilderness, revealing some of the 300 exotic mammals and birds. (The tour is not included in the price for an overnight stay.)

Sandman Hotel (www.sandmansanta rosa.com, 707-293-2100, 3421 Cleveland Avenue, Santa Rosa, CA 95403; $$). A modern twist on the classic roadside motel, the Sandman Hotel is located just off US 101, making it a prime place to call home to those seeking to explore Santa Rosa and surrounding Wine Country. A cool California vibe resonates through the property, in which rooms and communal areas are decorated with local art, handcrafted furnishings, vintage collectibles, and quirky art from surfer-turned-artist Ty Williams. The Sandman offers clean and simple rooms with

WINOS AND RHINOS

"**W**ild Nights in Wine Country" (also known as Winos and Rhinos) is an adventure package that features a tour and overnight at Safari West coupled with a complimentary tasting for two at the **Francis Ford Coppola Winery in Geyserville**.

touches that will impress the Scandinavian design crowd. For groups, the property offers a family suite, which includes a king bed and a bunk with a twin over a double bed. Relax by the pool after a day of wine tasting, sipping on craft cocktails and nibbling on pizzas and salads offered at the poolside bar. Complimentary continental breakfast is offered with each stay and the Sandman is pet friendly.

⚙ **Vintners Inn** (www.vintnersinn .com, 707-575-7350, 800-421-2584, 4350 Barnes Road, Santa Rosa, CA 95403; $$$–$$$$). Surrounded by a 70-acre vineyard, Vintners Inn is one of Sonoma

THE SANDMAN IS AN AFFORDABLE HOTEL FOR THE ROAD TRIPPER, THE BUSINESS TRAVELER, OR THE ARDENT EXPLORER COURTESY OF THE SANDMAN

County's finest establishments. It's a European-style hotel with an Old World atmosphere, from its French country decor to the central plaza with a fountain. The 44 guest rooms are separated into three buildings that ring the courtyard. Climbing the staircase in each building is akin to going upstairs to bedrooms in an elegant farmhouse. The oversized rooms in this Provençal-influenced inn have beamed ceilings and pine furniture, some dating back to the turn of the previous century. Continental breakfast is included; room service is also available. The inn is convenient to both Sonoma and Napa Valley wineries. Next door is the superb John Ash & Co. restaurant.

✳ Where to Eat

A'roma Roasters (www.aromaroasters .com, 707-576-7765, 95 Fifth Street, Santa Rosa, CA 95401). Facing historic Railroad Square, A'Roma is a touch bohemian, with exposed rafters, a copper countertop, and a coffee-bean roaster as a centerpiece. There are lots of tables, and you'll find yourself ogling goodies such as the chocolate decadent torte.

Beer Baron Bar & Kitchen (www.beer baronbar.com, 707-757-9294, 614 Fourth Street, Santa Rosa, CA 95404). This house of brews is irreverent fun with a tap list that amuses with offerings like Big Bad Baptist Stout and Mango Daze Pale Ale. Do not step in the door if you're on a diet. This place will corrupt your good intentions with snacks that include Belgian Style Duck Fat Fries and Smoked Olive Oil Guacamole.

Chevys (www.chevys.com, 707-571-1082, 24 Fourth Street, Santa Rosa, CA 95401). In Sonoma County, chains dominate, and the results are less than impressive. A better chain experience is at Chevy's. The food isn't authentic, but it's fresh and nicely done, especially the fajitas.

✪ **City Garden Doughnuts & Coffee** (707-595-1932, 1200 Fourth Street, Santa Rosa, CA, 95404; $). This is a trendy place for foodies who seek glazed

FOODIES WILL LOVE THE ARTISAN DOUGHNUTS AND THE AVOCADO TOAST AT CITY GARDEN

adventure. In Wine Country, you would expect nothing less than chic pastries, but these donut inventors over-deliver in every way. Some of their most popular items that get snapped up quickly include Pumpkin Spice with Pecans, Wild Huckleberry Glaze with Honey Donut, and Pumpkin Ginger Spice. The subtle approach works in their favor; we're particularly fond of their fruit-flavored lemon glaze, for example. But we also can't resist a decadent donut and their version is impressive—a splash of chocolate over a brioche donut. But sometimes you want to take a pass on sugar and opt for the truly amazing avocado toast. It's genius.

Flying Goat Coffee (www.flyinggoat coffee.com, 707-575-1202, 10 Fourth Street, Santa Rosa, CA 95401). This cozy coffee shop in Santa Rosa's historic Railroad Square has great lattes and impressive French-pressed coffee. It's a good place to meet up with friends or go solo to get some work done.

Jack & Tony's Restaurant & Whisky Bar (www.jackandtonys.com, 707-526-4347, 115-B Fourth Street, Santa Rosa, CA 95401; $$–$$$; cuisine: modern American regional cooking). Whisky lovers congregate here for good eats and serious drinking. There are more than 170 different expressions of scotch, bourbon, and Irish, American, and Japanese whiskies, ranging from $5 to $100. But there's also plenty of regional bottlings for wine lovers. The cuisine here is hearty, classic comfort food. Dishes include braised beef short ribs rigatoni, black tiger prawn spaghetti, and homemade soup.

✪ **Jackson's Bar and Oven** (www .jacksonsbarandoven.com, 707-545-6900, 135 Fourth Street, Railroad Square, Santa Rosa, CA 95401; $$–$$$; cuisine: California comfort). This savvy restaurant plays to the sophisticated family in Wine Country with great eats and smart prices. The decor is warm and inviting and the comfort food is irresistible. Popular entrées include wood-fired pizza, the grilled babyback ribs, and the wood-oven-roasted

THE INGENIOUS CHEF JOSH SILVERS OF JACKSONS BAR & OVEN

mac & cheese. Chef Josh Silvers and wife Regina are ingenious business partners who named this bistro after their son. It's not surprising it's a hit in Wine Country.

✪ **John Ash & Co.** (www.vintnersinn .com, 707-527-7687, 4330 Barnes Road, Santa Rosa, CA 95403; $$$$). Chef John Ash continues to pioneer Wine Country cuisine, but today, he has nothing to do with the daily operation of the restaurant. Executive chef Thomas Schmidt emphasizes local ingredients and strives to make each entrée visually beautiful. The menu is ever changing but offers imaginative salads and pastas, lighter seafood dishes, and hearty steak and pork chops. The wine list is one of the best in Wine Country, and the by-the-glass selection is excellent. The service is attentive and pampering. The setting is a bucolic site next to Vintners Inn,

EATING WELL AT LOCAL MARKETS

⊙ **Oliver's Markets** (www.oliversmarket.com, 707-537-7123, 560 Montecito Center, Santa Rosa, CA 95409; other locations include 707-284-3530, 461 Stony Point Road, Santa Rosa, CA 95401; 707-795-9501, 546 E. Cotati Avenue, Cotati, CA 95431; and 707-687-2050, 9230 Old Redwood Highway, Windsor, CA 95492). These upscale grocery stores may be bigger than others listed, but they're just as food and wine savvy. They carry high-quality food and well-chosen wines. The Cotati store has an ever-popular wine bar where people taste wines, with winemakers often there to provide running commentary. Winemaker Gina Gallo of Gallo of Sonoma is a frequent guest. The newest Oliver's in Windsor has a family-friendly tap room called Tavern Off the Green, because it's near Windsor's Town Green, a favorite gathering spot. This store also has a poké bar for excellent and healthy fast food.

Pacific Market (www.pacificmkt.com, 707-546-3663, 1465 Town & Country Drive, Santa Rosa, CA 95404; and 707-823-4916, 550 Gravenstein Highway N., Sebastopol, CA 95472). These stores are meccas for those who crave sophisticated cuisine. There's fresh produce, fish, meat, and a great assortment of pastas, sushi, and baked goods, with wine sections touting regional wines. Just order dinner—chicken Marsala, scalloped and baked veggies—warm it up, and impress your family and friends.

Santa Rosa Community Farmers Market (Wednesday and Saturday 8:30 a.m.–1 p.m., year-round, rain or shine; Veterans Building East Parking Lot, 1351 Maple Avenue, Santa Rosa, CA 95401). Shop like a local at this Saturday- and Wednesday-morning market, where you'll find fresh everything: coffee, fruit, vegetables, fish, and baked goods.

with vineyard views through French windows and plenty of outdoor dining when weather permits.

La Vera (www.laverapizza.com, 707-575-1113, 629 Fourth Street, Santa Rosa, CA 95404). For those who demand New York–style pizza, there's La Vera. The cheese stretches for a city block, and the meats are explosions of pepperoni and sausage. The crust is that perfect unison of crunchy and chewy. The atmosphere is more formal than most pizzerias, with polished brass and wood.

Mombo's Pizza (707-528-3278, 1880 Mendocino Avenue, Santa Rosa, CA 95401; and 707-823-7492, 560 Gravenstein Highway N., Sebastopol, CA 95472; $; cuisine: Italian). Great pizza here. Thin crust. Divine. If you're worried about calories, there's even an offer to "lighten up" your pizza and tone down your pie with less cheese and fewer toppings at a 20 percent discount. Mombo's also has tasty sandwiches, including hot meatball and hot Italian sausage. This pizzeria recently won a contest of local bests, which means something because the locals bring to the table discerning pizza palates.

⊙ **Monti's** (www.starksrestaurants .com, 707-568-4404, 714 Village Court, Santa Rosa, CA 95405; $$–$$$; cuisine: California). This restaurant, tucked in Montgomery Village shopping center, manages to have a hopping nightlife, with people elbowing for a spot at the bar. The food is also great, which is a draw. Specialties revolve around a rotisserie and include prime rib for two, sweet-and-sour roasted duck, and pomegranate-glazed baby-back ribs.

⊙ **Rosso** (www.rossopizzeria.com, 707-544-3221, Creekside Center, 53 Montgomery Drive, Santa Rosa, CA 95404; $$–$$$; cuisine: Italian). If you want to travel to Italy without a passport, this is the place to be. The food here has more than an Italian accent. It's fluent. The pizza is true Neapolitan style, crisp and yeasty. And other dishes are equally impressive, like the fried chicken and the Dungeness crab pasta. The brick oven is productive and a great visual. The wine list has a good supply of imports and local favorites offering over 100 wines at reasonable prices.

۞ Osake (www.osake.garychus.com, 707-542-8282, 2446 Patio Court, Santa Rosa, CA 95405). This amazing Japanese restaurant, owned by Gary Chu, is just off busy Farmers Lane. It has a sleek, upscale decor and innovative cuisine.

۞ Spinster Sisters (www.thespinstersisters.com, 707-528-7100, 401 South A Street, Santa Rosa, CA 95401; $$$$; cuisine: new American). Chef Liza Hinman captivates with her salute to Cal-Mediterranean featuring broad strokes of Asian, Latin American, and Italian cuisine. Hipsters in particular flock to the big, boxy building in the emerging SOFA arts district, coveting seats at the centerpiece redwood bar or communal table anchoring the always busy, always loud dining room. Extra stylish guests might even get their photos snapped by a local artist, to be displayed on the wall galleries. And it's drinks all around, from local boutique wines on tap, to European wines and cult craft beers and ciders. As for the food, the constantly changing menu offers some of Wine Country's most mouthwatering breakfast, lunch, dinner, and brunch dishes, be that rustic tostadas topped in puréed Rancho Gordo Midnight beans, cabbage, radish, queso fresco, avocado, salsa verde, and poached egg, or elegant pan-roasted local cod atop Forbidden rice, nettle fumé, Meyer lemon, and Tokyo turnips. Always, Sonoma County ingredients star, in complex recipes like the ricotta and nettle gnocchi with hedgehog and black trumpet mushrooms, prosciutto, green garlic, pine nuts, and Parmigiano.

۞ Stark's Steakhouse (www.starksrestaurants.com, 707-546-5100, 521 Adams Street, Santa Rosa, CA 95401; $$–$$$; cuisine: steakhouse). Stark's is playing to the millennials, the offspring of the baby boomers, a young urban population that loves the classics and cocktails in equal measure. Here prime and dry-aged steaks are the rage. The owners—Mark and Terri Stark—have a restaurant empire in Sonoma County. There's a page on their website devoted to it. They include Monti's Rotisserie & Bar in Santa Rosa and Willi's Seafood & Raw Bar in Healdsburg. These entrepreneurs have it figured out, pairing clever entrées with top-rate service.

Taqueria Santa Rosa (www.taqueriassantarosa.com, 707-538-2642, 791 Montecito Center, Santa Rosa, CA 95409; 707-528-7956, 1950 Mendocino Avenue, Santa Rosa, CA 95401) uses whole beans, not canned refried beans, and grilled meat.

THE TUDOR ROSE MAKES TEATIME A MUST

✪ **Tudor Rose English Tea Room** (www.tudorrosetearoom.com, 707-535-2045, 733 Fourth Street, Santa Rosa, CA 95404). Here you'll taste a proper crumpet while enjoying the whims of the waitstaff in long dresses with bustles and lace-up corsets. Other enticing items on the menu include bread pudding, mushroom and onion tart, and a house-made sausage roll. It's so delightful you'll want to linger here for hours.

Village Bakery (www.villagebakery winecountry.com, 707-527-7654, 1445 Town & Country Drive, Santa Rosa, CA 95404). Tasty quiches and savory pastries, pear and ginger muffins, and Swedish cardamom rolls. Caloric, but good.

Michelle Marie's Patisserie (www .michellemaries.com, 707-575-1214, 2404 Magowan Drive, Santa Rosa, CA 95405). This upscale café serves tasty sandwiches, salads, and soups, and offers inventive desserts and highbrow wedding cakes.

✳ Nightlife

There's plenty to do after 10 p.m. in Santa Rosa. The Friday edition of the *Santa Rosa Press Democrat* is a good source for what's happening.

Santa Rosa is the center of Sonoma County's nightlife, although the outlying areas have a number of fine night spots. Santa Rosa's hotels are another good source for late-night fun. Try the **Flamingo Lounge** (www.flamingoresort .com, 707-545-8530, 2777 Fourth Street, Santa Rosa, CA 95405).

✪ **Russian River Brewing Company** (www.russianriverbrewing.com, 707-545-BEER, 725 Fourth Street, Santa Rosa, CA 95404). The Russian River Brewing Company has 10 specialty brews on tap, ranging from Damnation, a Belgian-style ale, to Pliny the Elder, a double IPA. Brewmaster Vinnie Cilurzo is passionate about what he does. Cilurzo is experimenting with aging beer in wine barrels to make his brews more complex. Eats include thin-crusted pizza, calzones, and salads, and the atmosphere of the pub is big, roomy, and energetic.

Third Street Aleworks (www.third streetaleworks.com, 707-523-3060, 610 Third Street, Santa Rosa, CA 95404). A popular downtown hangout, this brewpub has a stylish, almost industrial atmosphere, with polished-metal highlights and an open balcony. Third Street makes some great beer, including the Annadel pale ale. The food is better than most pubs, particularly the pizza and the spicy Cajun selections. If the weather is good, there's plenty of room on the patio, and in the balcony there are two pool tables and large communal tables.

✳ Entertainment

6th Street Playhouse (www.6thstreet playhouse.com, 707-523-4185, 52 W. Sixth Street, Santa Rosa, CA 95401). This is a relatively new addition to the Sonoma theater scene but many of the players involved are veterans. Recent productions include *Death of a Salesman* and *Steel Magnolias.*

Airport Stadium 12 Cinemas (www .sregmovies.com, 707-525-8909, 409 Aviation Boulevard, Santa Rosa, CA 95403). This 12-screen complex has stadium seating and is one of the best in Wine Country. It even has a café.

THE LUTHER BURBANK HOME AND GARDENS IS A SANTA ROSA STANDOUT

✪ **Luther Burbank Center for the Arts** (www.lutherburbankcenter.org, 707-546-3600, 50 Mark West Springs Road, Santa Rosa, CA 95403). This is Sonoma County's premier stage. Once a sprawling church complex, the center's main stage is the largest hall in the area, seating about 1,500 people. Recent headliners have included k.d. lang, Tony Bennett, Jerry Seinfeld, John Hiatt, and Bonnie Raitt.

Santa Rosa Symphony (www.santarosasymphony.com, 866-955-6040, Green Music Center, 1801 E. Cotati Avenue, Rohnert Park, CA 94928). Francesco Lecce-Chong was chosen to succeed Bruno Ferrandis as the fifth music director of the Santa Rosa Symphony's 90-year history. The symphony's home is now at the Green Music Center and famed soloists are featured in each concert. Soloists have included guitarist David Tanenbaum, pianists Andre Watts and Anna Fedorova, and famed cellist Yo-Yo Ma.

Summerfield Cinemas (www.summerfieldcinemas.com, 707-525-8909, 551 Summerfield Road, Santa Rosa, CA 95405). It's a venue for independent, foreign, classic, and popular movies.

✪ **Summer Repertory Theatre** (www.summerrep.com, 707-527-4307, 1501 Mendocino Avenue, Santa Rosa, CA 95401). No one has a bigger local following than SRT. Every summer, the Santa Rosa Junior College organizes this three-ring circus of theater, bringing in talented student actors and technical staff from around the country. Opening several major productions in four weeks and performing them in a repertory format packs a year's experience into two months.

Roxy Stadium 14 (www.sregmovies.com, 707-525-8909, 85 Santa Rosa Avenue, Santa Rosa, CA 95404). This state-of-the art cinema has it all: great sound and projection plus stadium seating with rocking chairs. The place to see the latest action blockbuster, and it has a café to boot.

✷ Selective Shopping

Santa Rosa's downtown is on the cusp of a revival, with the action revolving around the Barnes & Noble bookstore in the old Rosenberg's department store. What was once just a cozy mix of bookstores and coffeehouses is now filling in with interesting gift shops and clothing stores—stores that appear to have staying power.

Barnes & Noble (www.barnesandnoble.com, 707-576-7494, 700 Fourth Street, Santa Rosa, CA 95404) appeals to the tourist, with expanded sections on local authors, local travel, and local wineries.

Bottle Barn (www.bottlebarn.com, 707-528-1161, 3331-A Industrial Drive, Santa Rosa, CA 95403). This warehouse in Santa Rosa has a huge selection, with a few hard-to-find wines and generally bargain prices.

California Luggage Co. (www.califluggage.com, 707-528-8600, 609 Fourth Street, Santa Rosa, CA 95404) carries a broad range of luggage plus convenient travel necessities. It also does repairs for travelers passing through.

Corrick's (www.corricks.com, 707-546-2424, 637 Fourth Street, Santa Rosa, CA 95404) features upscale gift items and office supplies in one shop.

✪ **Disguise the Limit** (www.disguisethelimitsr.com, 707-575-1477, 129 Fourth Street, Santa Rosa, CA 95401) carries theatrical goods, gag gifts, and clothing for the avant garde.

E. R. Sawyer (www.ersawyer.com, 707-546-0372, 638 Fourth Street, Santa Rosa, CA 95404) sells fine jewelry and watches—even waterproof watches.

Hampton Court Essential Luxuries (707-578-9416, 631 Fourth Street, Santa Rosa, CA 95404) carries obscure European fragrances, bath and body lotions, and even romantic clothing.

Hot Couture (www.hotcouturevintage.com, 707-528-7247, 101 W. Third Street, Santa Rosa, CA 95401) has vintage clothing that dates back to the early 1900s up through the 1960s.

✪ **Montgomery Village** (www.mv shops.com, 707-545-3844, 911 Village Court, Santa Rosa, CA 95405). While few tourists find their way there, Montgomery Village in Santa Rosa has become a popular place for locals to shop for clothing, home and garden accessories, and gifts. The outdoor shopping center encompasses about four blocks, so the best way to shop it is to stroll through it. Upbeat shops include Ireko, an upscale home and garden shop; clothing stores such as J. Jill and Chico's for the hip yet professional woman; and Sonoma Outfitters for outdoor and adventure wear.

✪ **Snoopy's Gallery & Gift Shop** (www .snoopygift.com, 707-546-3385,1665 W. Steele Lane, Santa Rosa, CA 95403) offers a wide selection of *Peanuts* memorabilia, attire, comforters, prints, and novelty items. If you're a fan of Charles M. Schulz and the *Peanuts* strip, you won't want to miss this shop.

The Last Record Store (www.thelast recordstore.com, 707-525-1963, 1899-A Mendocino Avenue, Santa Rosa, CA 95401) sells CDs, cassettes, and records, and its eclectic inventory includes rock, jazz, classical, world music, blues, and Celtic music.

The Pottery Studio (www.thepottery studio.net, 707-576-7102, 632 Fourth Street, Santa Rosa, CA 95404) allows you to play artist: select a ceramic piece, paint it, and fire it in the kiln.

Whistle Stop Antiques (www.whistle stop-antiques.com, 707-542-9474, 130 Fourth Street, Santa Rosa, CA 95401) is a collective with some 36 dealers offering collectibles and a general line of furniture.

✳ Special Events

Harvest Fair of Sonoma County (www .harvestfair.org, 707-545-4200, Sonoma County Fairgrounds, 1350 Bennett Valley Road, Santa Rosa, CA 95404). The fair brings in top wine experts from around the country. Then local wine buffs gather to compare their taste buds to those of the judges. This is great fun in October. There's also plenty of food, and the annual grape stomping contest is a crazy attraction.

Sonoma County Fair (www.sonoma countyfair.com, 707-545-4200, Sonoma County Fairgrounds, 1350 Bennett Valley Road, Santa Rosa, CA 95404). Sonoma County practically shuts down for 10 days every August as thousands pour in from the countryside for food, music, rides, blue-ribbon animals, and produce. You can even bet on horse races.

INDEX